Agile Productivity Unleashed

Proven approaches for achieving real productivity gains in *any* organization

Second edition

DEDICATION

To my parents and grandparents for giving me the love of words, the power of analytical thought, and the self-confidence to achieve anything.

Agile Productivity Unleashed

Proven approaches for achieving real productivity gains in *any* organization

Second edition

JAMIE LYNN COOKE

IT Governance Publishing

IT Governance Publishing
IT Governance Limited
Unit 3, Clive Court
Bartholomew's Walk
Cambridgeshire Business Park
Ely
Cambridgeshire
CB7 4EA
United Kingdom

www.itgovernance.co.uk

First published in the United Kingdom in 2010 as *Agile Principles Unleashed* (ISBN 978-1-84928-057-0).

This US edition first published in the United Kingdom in 2010
by IT Governance Publishing (ISBN 978-1-84928-071-6).

Second edition published in the United Kingdom in 2014
by IT Governance Publishing.

ISBN: 978-1-84928-563-6

FOREWORD

Every organization faces the challenge of how to sustain operations in the face of constraints. Are plans adequate? Do they address the right problems? Both horns of the dilemma are dangerous: over-elaborate planning risks "locking out" emerging evidence that does not fit with the plan; and the rejection of planning altogether risks trapping the organization in the unguided pursuit of short-term results. This problem is particularly acute for smaller organizations where there is little margin for error in work specification, cost management, client tolerance or staff capacity.

Rather than deploying elaborate methods, the key for these organizations seems to lie in *practical*, *common-sense* approaches that support the empirical development of new initiatives *without* risking time, money or support beyond what the organization can tolerate. Importantly, where our knowledge is bounded, these approaches also need to allow for adjustment or adaptation as new facts and experiences emerge. With that in mind, ***agility*** stands out as an important word in any organizational lexicon.

Agile approaches are common-sense methods for applying the finite resources of an organization to meet changing market or stakeholder demand. Agile techniques, such as responsive planning, direct stakeholder engagement and immediate status tracking, continually focus staff on high business-value activities by adjusting (and re-adjusting) their work to confront change.

These approaches enable organizations to avoid the trappings of extensive upfront planning by challenging staff and managers to be deeply engaged in short, but intense, planning and feedback cycles to produce tangible, high-quality benefits. There is a safety net in Agile approaches that protects the organization from large-scale loss by basing subsequent financial and resource commitments on the utility of work produced by earlier cycles. These approaches encourage market relevance, quality assurance and continuous improvement to become ingrained in the corporate culture.

Importantly, Agile approaches have champions in many large firms and big industries where they have operated as sustainable, proven methods for over two decades. But for any organization constrained by limits on knowledge, funding and resources, Agile approaches offer the compelling prospect of bringing on vital projects faster and more effectively.

Dr James Galloway

Chief Executive

Joint Accreditation System of Australia and New Zealand

PREFACE

Companies are constantly in search of better ways to run their businesses, maintain customer loyalty, and increase their competitive advantage. For over twenty years, Agile practices and techniques have addressed this demand by providing companies such as Yahoo!, Google, Nokia Siemens Networks and Microsoft with more efficient processes, higher quality outputs and greater customer satisfaction. It appears, however, that companies outside of the information technology and manufacturing sectors are generally unfamiliar with Agile approaches – and those that are familiar with Agile tend to see it as restricted to only these sectors. (This is largely due to the fact that proponents of Agile approaches tend to come from more technical backgrounds – and information regarding these approaches has generally been presented only in a technical context.)

Agile Productivity Unleashed: Proven approaches for achieving real productivity gains in any organization introduces the general business community to the Agile practices and techniques that have dramatically improved the information technology, product development and manufacturing sectors over the past three decades – and demonstrates how the key principles that underpin Agile approaches can be used to significantly increase productivity, quality and customer satisfaction in *every* industry sector.

Agile Productivity Unleashed helps businesses to understand why upfront detailed planning is destined to fail, why teams are significantly more productive when they control their own outcomes, and why market testing provides a false sense of security. It introduces the general business community to powerful Agile techniques, such as responsive planning, direct stakeholder engagement, management by self-motivation, "just-in-time communication" and immediate status tracking. *Agile Productivity Unleashed* challenges the reader to reconsider their "business as usual" activities in favor of more responsive, collaborative and customer-driven approaches.

Most importantly, *Agile Productivity Unleashed* describes Agile principles and approaches in terms that really make sense to business professionals.

We are at the forefront of the evolution of Agile approaches, from technology- and sector-specific practices to general business applicability. *Agile Productivity Unleashed* is designed to show the business community the latent potential in Agile approaches, and inspire readers to take the first step in introducing Agile benefits in their organizations.

ABOUT THE AUTHOR

Jamie Lynn Cooke has 24 years of experience as a senior business analyst and solutions consultant, working with more than 130 public and private sector organizations throughout Australia, Canada and the United States.

Her background includes business case development; strategic and operational reviews; business process modeling, mapping and optimization; product and project management on small to multi-million dollar initiatives; quality management; risk analysis and mitigation; developing/conducting training courses; workshop delivery; and refining e-business strategies.

She is the author of *Agile: An Executive Guide: Real results from IT budgets*, which gives IT executives the tools and strategies needed for bottom-line-driven business decisions on using Agile methodologies; *Everything you want to know about Agile: How to get Agile results in a less-than-Agile organization*, which gives readers strategies for aligning Agile work within the reporting, budgeting, staffing, and governance constraints of their organization; and *The Power of the Agile Business Analyst: 30 surprising ways a business analyst can add value to your Agile development team*, which details practical, achievable ways in which Agile business analysts can increase the relevance, quality and overall business value of Agile projects.

She is a well-regarded speaker on both business and technology topics, most recently presenting on issues such as *Getting Management and Business User Support for Using Agile* and *When is Agile Not the Answer?* at the

Business Process Modeling world conference in Brisbane, Australia and at the AgileCanberra professional forums.

Jamie has been working hands on with Agile methods and practices since 2003, and has researched hundreds of books and articles on Agile topics. She is a signatory on the Agile Manifesto, has attended numerous Agile seminars, and has worked with prominent consultants to promote Agile practices to large organizations.

Jamie has a Bachelor of Science in Engineering Psychology (Human Factors Engineering) from Tufts University in Medford, Massachusetts, and a Graduate Certificate in E-Business/Business Informatics from the University of Canberra in Australia.

ACKNOWLEDGEMENTS

My sincerest thanks to the pioneers and thought leaders of the Agile world, most notably Kent Beck, Martin Fowler, Alistair Cockburn, Jeff Sutherland, Mike Cohn, Ken Schwaber and Jim Highsmith, for their passionate work in developing and refining Agile practices over the past three decades. Particular thanks to Alistair Cockburn,[1] Petri Haapio,[2] Gabrielle Benefield,[3] 1105 Media[4] and BT[5] for kindly allowing me to share their wisdom in this book; to Dale Kleeman at the University of Canberra[6] for his guidance in my business process modeling research; and to Artem Marchenko of AgileSoftwareDevelopment.com™[7] for generously making his tracking tools available for everyone in the Agile community to use.

Thanks also to the small and large organizations worldwide that have allowed their experiences in using Agile approaches to be shared with others, including Nokia Siemens Networks, Yahoo!, Google, Microsoft and BT.Special thanks to Neil Salkind of the Salkind Literary Agency, and Vicki Utting of IT Governance Publishing for their incredible support and sage advice throughout the development of this book. Thanks also to Colin Bentley, Ex-Chief Examiner of PRINCE2, and Liz Gill, Copy Editor, for their helpful comments during the review

[1] Alistair Cockburn's website: *http://alistair.cockburn.us*.
[2] Reaktor: *www.reaktor.fi*.
[3] Scrum Foundation: *http://scrumfoundation.com/*.
[4] 1105 Media: *www.1105media.com/*.
[5] BT: *www.BT.com*.
[6] University of Canberra: *www.canberra.edu.au*.
[7] AgileSoftwareDevelopment.com: *www.agilesoftwaredevelopment.com*.

process, and to Jesica Lindgren for her invaluable assistance and advice.

Many thanks, as well, to the people who taught me the most about the strategies of the business world over the past 24 years, especially Roland Scornavacca, Tony Robey and Peter Walsh; to James Galloway for his insights and collaborative management style; to Rowan Bunning for being an unending source of Agile knowledge; and to the writers and teachers who inspired me, particularly Richard Leonard[8] for his amazing ability to encourage writers with his humor and enthusiasm.

Finally, my eternal gratitude to my parents, my US family, my Australian family, and my friends, most especially Susan, Michele, Linda, Janice and Elissa, for being my ongoing sanity check in this world. Most of all, thank you to my husband, David, for 22 years of love and laughter.

---

[8] Richard Leonard's website: *richardleonard.net*.

CONTENTS

INTRODUCTION

In the past three decades, service delivery has moved from the "bricks-and-mortar" shop front to the home telephone, to the Internet, to the cell phone. Consumers have come to expect convenience, rapid response times and ubiquitous 24/7 access to the services that they need – and there does not appear to be any slowdown in the number of delivery channels and services that are – and will be – available to these consumers in the future.

The challenges of *ubiquitous service delivery* are compounded by the availability of technologies (most notably, the Internet) which move consumers to a *global marketplace.* Organizations realize that they are no longer competing against two other local providers, or even ten other national providers – they are delivering products and services to well-educated consumers who, from the convenience of their kitchen table, can choose to acquire equivalent products and services from anywhere around the world. Although global delivery channels like the Internet will have much more of a competitive impact on a commercial product supplier than a government agency, *every* organization needs to, at a minimum, maintain public awareness through these channels. This is *on top of* the organization's other commitments, and often within the same overall budgetary and staffing constraints.

So, where does this leave your organization? If your business processes are already struggling to sustain the current level of customer demand, how will you address increases in service delivery without substantially cutting into your profits (or significantly increasing your overheads)? How are you going to reduce time to market, so that you can retain a competitive advantage and a positive public image? How are you going to ensure that the products and services that your organization supplies do not become obsolete because the excessive costs, time or resources required for effective delivery become unsustainable?

Even the most steadfast traditional organizations realize that the business processes and practices that they have relied upon in the past will have to be made more effective to carry the organization into the future. To stay in front of the competition – and to meet ever-increasing consumer expectations – organizations need to focus on *continuously improving* the work that they do to make it more cost-, time- and resource-efficient. It is a critical part of surviving in a global 24/7 service delivery marketplace. However, knowing that efficiencies are needed – and finding proven ways to implement these efficiencies in your organization – are two very different things entirely.

One of the most intriguing things about the corporate world is that most organizations share the same core challenges and inefficiencies, including:

- missed (or rushed) deadlines
- budget blow-outs
- overworked and stressed employees, and
- knowledge silos.

In fact, these inefficiencies have become so commonplace that many organizations now factor them into their upfront corporate planning. ("We have 15 full-time staff assigned to this work. So, at 80% productivity levels, we can expect 12 full-time staff worth of outputs.")

It does not matter whether your organization is a 40-person consulting firm or a large multinational; whether you work in the private, not-for-profit or public sector; whether you are a recent start-up or an established company which has been in the industry for over 50 years. No organization is immune to these issues. This is why it is so remarkable when organizations in *any* industry are able to find ways to genuinely overcome their inefficiencies and establish substantially more productive working environments.

During the same three decades in which technology innovations have created the platform for global market service delivery, selected organizations in two industries (information technology and manufacturing) have implemented a set of business practices and techniques (known as *Agile approaches*) that have enabled them to genuinely create more efficient work environments, to consistently manage their work within allocated budgets, and to regularly deliver high business-value (and high-quality) outputs on time.

The success of Agile approaches is based on the *12 core principles* that underpin Agile work:

- responsive planning
- business-value-driven work
- hands-on business outputs
- direct stakeholder engagement
- immovable deadlines
- management by self-motivation
- "just-in-time" communication
- immediate status tracking
- waste management
- constantly measurable quality

- rearview mirror checking
- continuous improvement.

Combined, these principles are able to create a work environment that produces high business-value outputs, motivates employees, encourages innovation and delivers tangible results. That is why Agile approaches have been (and continue to be) used successfully by numerous organizations worldwide, including Nokia Siemens Networks,[9] Yahoo!,[10] Google,[11] Microsoft[12], BT[13], , Bankwest[14], SunCorp[15] and Wells Fargo[16]. They have been equally successful in private and public sector organizations of all sizes, particularly throughout the United States and Europe.[17]

Agile approaches are ideally suited for situations where the outcomes are dependent on variable factors, such as resource availability, customer preferences and market

---

[9] *NokiaSiemens and Agile Development*, Haapio P, JAOO (2008): *http://jaoo.dk/file?path=/jaoo-aarhus-2008/slides//PetriHaapio_CanAGLobalCompany.pdf.*

[10] *Lessons from a Yahoo! Scrum Rollout*, Mackie K (2008): *http://campustechnology.com/articles/2008/02/lessons-from-a-yahoo-scrum-rollout.aspx*.

[11] *Scrum Tuning: Lessons Learned at Google*, Sutherland J (2006): www.youtube.com/watch?v=9y10Jvruc_Q.

[12] *Microsoft Lauds Scrum Method for Software Projects*, Taft D K (2005): *http://www.eweek.com/c/a/IT-Management/Microsoft-Lauds-Scrum-Method-for-Software-Projects/*.

[13] *Agile Coaching in British Telecom*, Meadows L and Hanly S (2006): *http://www.agilejournal.com/articles/columns/column-articles/144-agile-coaching-in-british-telecom*.

[14] The Bankwest Agile Journey, Weir A (2010): http://www.zdnet.com/bankwest-goes-agile-project-time-slashed-1339306091/

[15] Suncorp goes Agile for 19k desktop integration project (2008): www.itnews.com.au/News/130927,suncorp-goes-agile-for-19k-desktop-integration-project.aspx

[16] Ready, Fire, Aim! An Agile Approach to Architecture & Software Development (2009): www.milwaukeeagile.com/events/11787272/?eventId=11787272&action=detail

[17] See the *Who uses Agile* section of *Chapter 1: Agile in a Nutshell* for a more detailed listing of the organizations who use these approaches.

fluctuation. These approaches allow organizations to manage unforeseen circumstances by expecting – and embracing – changes in requirements. Conversely, Agile approaches can also be used to make the highly predictable and replicable business processes within these environments more efficient.

The surprising thing is that Agile approaches have been almost exclusively used only in the information technology and manufacturing sectors to date – even though organizations in *every* industry can benefit significantly from these approaches.

So, why have other industries not adopted these Agile approaches within their organizations? Most likely because the most vocal advocates of Agile approaches have tended to come from more technical backgrounds and, therefore, the information regarding these practices and techniques has predominantly been presented only in a technical context. In order for *every* industry to be able to fully appreciate the benefits of these approaches, Agile concepts need to be presented in *clear business language*, starting with an overview of what 'Agile' really means.

Agile: an executive summary

Agile is a collective term used to describe a range of business practices and techniques that have emerged over the past three decades to increase productivity, quality, efficiency and customer satisfaction in the workplace. These Agile practices and techniques (known as *Agile approaches*) range from high-level approaches for improving project management, through to more detailed approaches for improving industry-specific activities, such as software development and product manufacturing.

Each Agile approach works both independently and in unison to deliver successful business outcomes:

- ***Responsive planning***: involves breaking down long-term objectives into shorter delivery cycles; and then *adapting* ongoing work (and funding) based on the outcomes of each delivery cycle.
- ***Business-value-driven work***: involves prioritizing work in accordance with the amount of primary and secondary business value that each activity is likely to bring to the organization.
- ***Hands-on business outputs***: involves regularly inspecting outputs firsthand in order to determine whether business requirements are being met – and whether business value is being delivered for the organization.
- ***Direct stakeholder engagement***: involves actively engaging internal and external customers throughout a process to ensure that the resulting deliverables meet their expectations.
- ***Immovable deadlines***: are fixed time commitments that encourage staff members to deliver regular ongoing value to the organization.
- ***Management by self-motivation***: involves using the power of self-organized teams to deliver outcomes under the guidance and oversight of the customer.
- ***"Just-in-time" communication***: replaces traditional corporate meetings with techniques for more effective communication and knowledge transfer.

- ***Immediate status tracking***: provides tools that enable staff to keep others in the organization continuously aware of the status of the work that they are doing.
- ***Waste management***: involves maximizing the value of the organization's resources by reducing and, where possible, eliminating low business-value activities.
- ***Constantly measurable quality***: involves creating *active checkpoints* where organizations can assess outputs against both qualitative and quantitative measurements.
- ***Rearview mirror checking***: provides staff with tools for regularly monitoring and self-correcting their work.
- ***Continuous improvement***: involves regularly reviewing and adjusting business activities to ensure that the organization is continuing to meet market and stakeholder demand.

Combined, these Agile approaches create an organizational environment that is focused on real productivity gains[18], high business-value outcomes and responsiveness to changing market conditions.

Agile Productivity Unleashed provides detailed descriptions of each approach, case study examples, and a range of tools to assist you in implementing the most relevant approaches in your organization. It also presents these Agile concepts in *clear business language* to inspire organizations to see the significant potential in the use of Agile approaches beyond the information technology and manufacturing industries. The goal of this book is to make readers aware of the incredible efficiencies and real productivity gains that Agile approaches continue to deliver to organizations

---

[18] See *www.realproductivitygains.com* for further details on identifying and quantifying real productivity gains.

worldwide – and to see the potential for achieving equivalent advantages within their own organizations.

The path forward

The next section of the book, *Section 1: What You Need to Know About Agile*, provides background information on Agile principles and practices, to help you decide whether Agile approaches are suited to the needs of your organization, including:

- identifying the underlying business value of each Agile principle
- describing the business drivers that created the original need for Agile approaches in the IT and manufacturing sectors
- explaining why these approaches have been so effective in these industry sectors over the past three decades
- listing organizations that are successfully using Agile approaches today
- providing insight into why people in other industry sectors are relatively unfamiliar with Agile practices and techniques – or the extensive benefits that these approaches can bring to their organization.

The final chapter in this section, *Chapter 4: Agile Sounds Good, But ...* addresses the most common concerns that readers are likely to have about adopting Agile approaches in their organizations, so that you can determine whether or not it is worthwhile progressing to the other sections in this book.

If you are already able to see the benefits that Agile approaches can bring to your organization – and you want to begin using them today – you may want to go directly to

Section 2: 12 Agile Principles that Will Revolutionize Your Organization. This section walks you step-by-step through each of the 12 underlying principles that make Agile approaches so effective; guides you in applying each principle in real life business settings; and demonstrates how these principles are able to benefit business activities in every industry.

To further illustrate the practical application of Agile approaches, *Section 3: A Case Study* compares two competing companies that are trying to build a product website, make consumers aware of the website and fulfill customer orders using the *same budget allocation* and the *same number of employees* in the *same timeframe.* One company uses traditional business approaches to achieve these objectives, the other uses Agile approaches; and the two companies achieve vastly different results.

Once your head is swimming with all of the potential value that Agile approaches can bring to your organization, the final section of the book, *Section 4: Making Agile Work in Your Organization*, guides you through assessing which Agile approaches best meet your organization's needs and how to introduce Agile principles into even the most traditional organizations.

SECTION 1: WHAT YOU NEED TO KNOW ABOUT AGILE

CHAPTER 1: AGILE IN A NUTSHELL

This chapter explains each of the core Agile principles in clear business language, demonstrates how they have revolutionized one market sector (the information technology industry); introduces popular Agile practices and techniques that put these principles into action; and profiles some of the prominent organizations which have successfully adopted these Agile approaches, including Nokia Siemens Networks, Yahoo! and BT.

Understanding Agile principles

Embracing change

At the core of Agile principles is the understanding that change is an inevitable – and essential – part of any business. Market needs evolve, project funding gets re-allocated and staff move on. An organization which *expects and embraces change* in customer requirements, market demand, supply chain provision and internal resource availability has a significant competitive advantage over less responsive organizations.

Responsive planning

Responsive planning to accommodate inevitable internal and external changes is at the heart of Agile approaches. Because change is an inevitable part of business, Agile approaches avoid creating extensive upfront documents that endeavor to predict business requirements, costs and timeframes over the long term. Instead, Agile approaches are based around the iterative delivery of business value in short timeframes (usually every two to four weeks), with ongoing planning based on the feedback received from key stakeholders at each iteration.

This drive for responsive planning is most succinctly described in the Agile philosophy: "Apply, Inspect, Adapt." Responsive planning allows for changes in the business environment (e.g. a change in market demand) to be almost immediately reflected in the iterative activities undertaken by staff members – instead of waiting several weeks (and sometimes months) for an updated plan to be agreed, released and implemented.

Frequent and continuous business value

The goal of each Agile iteration is to provide stakeholders with *frequent and continuous business value*, so that the organization can benefit more quickly from their investment in money, people and time. Agile approaches are designed so that each iterative delivery contains the *highest-priority* items identified by the business to the greatest extent that can be provided in the time allocated. This results in each deliverable having immediate value for the business, thus maximizing the effort of each resource to focus on high-priority activities, and minimizing the likelihood of unnecessary work being done.

Importantly, Agile approaches also provide the organization with the opportunity to review *tangible outputs* at each delivery point, to redirect efforts (where required), and to determine whether further budget expenditure should be focused on additional work in this area – or reallocated to higher priority business activities across the organization.

Direct stakeholder engagement

So, how do Agile delivery teams ensure that their deliverables continuously meet the needs of the organization? The most effective way to ensure ongoing business value is to *directly involve* key internal and external stakeholders in the process. (When was the last time you included customer service representatives in the review of proposed products? Or invited prospective investors to comment on the draft annual plan?)

Representative stakeholders participate as *active members* of the Agile team during the process, providing the team with real-time input and hands-on feedback at two key points in the process:

- at the start of each iteration to describe and prioritize their business requirements
- at the end of each iteration to review and assess outputs against their stated requirements.

Ideally, these stakeholders are also able to make themselves available to the team *during* each iteration, to respond to questions and review work while it is being completed. The more available stakeholders are to the Agile team throughout the process, the closer that each deliverable will be to meeting the true needs of the organization. However, Agile approaches are also realistic in understanding that the full-time allocation of a key internal resource – or ongoing availability of an external customer – is not always possible. The objective for an Agile organization is to create this opportunity wherever possible, but no less than at the start and end of each iteration.

Regular face-to-face communication

Agile approaches strongly advocate that the most effective way to actively involve stakeholders in the process is through *face-to-face communication* (which can include online meetings where required). The underlying premise is that business requirements are most clearly stated (and clarified) in a forum where people can

- respond to each other in real-time
- draw diagrams on a whiteboard that others can immediately provide feedback on
- get a firsthand perspective on each stakeholder's reaction.

Conference calls and e-mails can be used (where required) to clarify ongoing questions during the iteration; but the description of the business requirements at the start of each iteration – and review of outputs at the end of each iteration – require physical (or virtual) face-to-face communication in order for these sessions to be effective. In the Agile world, there is no point where a pile of documentation is an acceptable substitute for active face-to-face communication.

Minimizing waste

The Agile imperative to deliver the highest business value possible in a short timeframe results in the added benefit of *minimizing waste* in work undertaken. Effort is not expended on low priority items that are less likely to be needed by the business, resulting in a reduced likelihood of over-production by the team. Regular feedback from stakeholders helps to ensure that ongoing efforts continue to be focused on the highest value activities.

Short timeframes also mean that, even if the team goes slightly off-track in one iteration, the cost to the organization is contained. Activities can be ended when the team has delivered every outcome that the organization considers essential – versus maintaining teams to meet pre-determined timeframes or budget allocations.

Agile approaches also minimize waste by encouraging employees to make business processes and deliverables as *efficient* as possible. This not only assists employees in delivering value within a short timeframe; it allows these processes and deliverables to be more readily reused and expanded upon in the future.

Tangible outputs

Agile methods work on the basis that the best way to measure the progress of work is not to create endless status reports, but to review the *tangible outputs* of the work as the primary measure of progress. Status reports are often time-consuming, generally sanitized for management review and can be designed to give the reader a false sense of security that things are progressing on track. Tangible outputs, on the other hand, are irrefutable indicators of the ongoing success or failure of each Agile team's activities.

Most important, however, is the effect that producing tangible outputs has on the way in which Agile teams undertake their work. The drive to deliver tangible outputs in short iterations forces the team to touch on every stage of the delivery process, from planning and design to quality control, packaging and presentation. It forces the team to avoid endless planning meetings and infinite rethinking of ideas before action is taken. It requires the team to go through every stage of the process upfront, providing an early identification of risks and hurdles that are likely to impact ongoing delivery. Arguably the most valuable outcome, it gives team members the satisfaction of regularly seeing tangible results from their efforts, providing them with inspiration and motivation for their ongoing work.

Empowering the team

Agile approaches rely on the mutual trust (and dependency) that emerges between stakeholders and delivery team members: delivery teams depend upon the expertise of stakeholders to accurately communicate and prioritize the business requirements; and stakeholders equally depend upon the expertise of the delivery team members to regularly produce outcomes that meet these requirements. If either group falters, the process fails.

It is this interdependency that makes Agile approaches so compelling for employees. Stakeholders are responsible for guiding the business priorities and for measuring the outcomes of each iteration, but they are *not* the people who determine the volume of work that can be achieved in that short timeframe. Instead, stakeholders defer to the multi-skilled delivery team to advise them on the actual work required to achieve their objectives, the estimated time for each task, and what the delivery team can realistically achieve in an iteration given their current workload and other commitments.

The structure of Agile approaches also means that stakeholders do not need to keep a close watch of every step that the delivery team makes, because they know that they are never more than a few weeks away from seeing the results of their work. Throughout each iteration, stakeholders also have the ability to both sit in on the delivery team's daily status reviews and to monitor the overall progress of the team through real-time status tracking tools. This means that stakeholders can be confident that work is progressing without having to constantly monitor the delivery team, and delivery team members are entrusted, empowered and left alone to do the work that they have committed to.

The interesting thing about this dynamic is that, as it progresses, it is able to feed off itself to create ongoing motivation for employees. Delivery team members know that their continued ability to self-manage their work depends on their regular delivery of high-value business outcomes. Additionally, because they are the ones who identify what work can (and cannot) be achieved in each iteration, they are motivated by their personal responsibility to achieve these outcomes. This combination of factors is heightened by the satisfaction and pride that delivery team members feel when they produce tangible outputs that truly meet the needs of the organization.

Quality by design

The requirement for Agile delivery teams to regularly deliver tangible outputs in each iteration makes quality control essential throughout the process. In order to be able to respond to stakeholders in short timeframes, deliverables must be designed to accommodate ongoing change. Agile teams learn early on that maintaining the quality, flexibility and extensibility of deliverables is critical in their ongoing ability to be responsive to change without impacting their levels of productivity. This knowledge drives Agile teams to build in quality by design in everything they deliver – not only to avoid the problems that can occur when faulty deliverables are handed over, but to reduce the impacts of low quality on their own work (and ongoing ability to self-manage) in the future.

Continuous improvement

The "Apply, Inspect, Adapt" philosophy, which underpins Agile approaches, provides the organization with a proven method for continuous improvement on an ongoing basis. Performance improvement is not reserved for annual employee reviews; it occurs as part of the review at the end of each iteration. Teams use Agile tools (such as the burndown charts described in *Chapter 12: Immediate Status Tracking*) to monitor their own progress during each iteration. Management is provided with real-time progress monitors (such as the executive dashboards described in *Chapter 12: Immediate Status Tracking*) to measure the advancement of work against the organization's objectives.

The very nature of Agile approaches is to continuously review and improve the work that is being undertaken, to ensure that the organization is focused on delivering the highest value outcomes at a regular and sustained pace. The active involvement of stakeholders throughout the process ensures that these deliverables genuinely meet the needs of the organization, and allows for real-time adjustment of the work if these objectives are not being met.

Agile in action

Although the core principles that underpin Agile approaches can deliver benefits in every market sector, there are currently two industries at the forefront in their use of Agile approaches: information technology (IT) and manufacturing. Several prominent organizations in these industries have publicly documented their success in using Agile approaches, including Google, Yahoo!, Nokia Siemens Networks and Microsoft.

The prominence of Agile approaches in these two industries can be attributed to a number of factors, most notably the fact that the most vocal proponents of Agile approaches have tended to come from more technical backgrounds – resulting in the information regarding these practices generally being presented only in a technical context. There is, however, another compelling issue which has driven the widespread adoption of Agile practices across the IT industry specifically – and understanding this issue is the key to understanding why Agile approaches are powerful strategies for *every* industry.

In the 1990s, the IT industry was plagued by the remarkably high failure rate of software development projects: projects that became notorious for their missed deadlines, substantially overrun budgets, faulty deliverables and dissatisfied customers. A handful of thought leaders in the industry believed that these IT project failures could be attributed to three key factors: over-planning, insufficient communication and "all-at-once" delivery.

Over-planning

IT software projects traditionally began with the production of extensive "upfront" documentation, including project plans, functional requirements, system design specifications and technical architectural designs. These documents, which often took months to produce (and even longer to get approved), were intended to ensure that the developed software would align with user requirements. In reality, however, these documents only served to provide corporate managers with a false sense of security in the expenditure of their IT budgets; and to ensure that delivered software would be substantially misaligned with the ongoing – and changing – needs of the business.

One of the biggest problems was that, by the time these big upfront documents were finalized, nearly everything about the proposed project was likely to have changed, including user requirements, market demand, internal resource availability and the capabilities of the underlying technologies. The time required to revisit and adapt these documents would have resulted in even further delays to the project. So, development work was undertaken against plans and designs that were clearly outdated on the first day, and significantly more outdated by the time that the software was delivered.

Another key problem in the industry's use of "big upfront documents" was the inevitable misalignment between text descriptions of the user's needs and the resulting software. Users who provided input into these documents often fell into two common traps:

- not clearly articulating their requirements
- wanting everything under the sun in an effort to guarantee that any requirement they could possibly have

in the future would be supported in the software. (Given the amount of time it took to deliver the software, who could blame them?)

Both of these factors ensured that the big upfront design documents were saddled with unclear requirements (which were left to the discretion of the technical team to interpret), or with highly critical business requirements lost in a sea of extraneous requirements. Most importantly, these documents ignored the simple fact that products which look good on paper may not always have the same appeal when presented on the screen. The bottom line is that software products delivered to meet these design documents were destined to fail – and businesses were losing millions in the process.

Insufficient communication

The second overwhelming driver in the ongoing failure of software development projects in the 1990s was the traditional – and often deliberate – separation of the business areas that required the software and the technical staff responsible for delivering the solution (i.e. development in a vacuum).

Once the big upfront design documents for an IT project were finalized, they were generally handed over to the technical team for development. The technical team was then sent back to their desks (often located in a separate section, floor or even building from the business areas), with a pile of paper and an immutable deadline. The next time that the technical team interacted with the business area was when they installed the resulting software on the users' machines for acceptance testing.

This isolation between the users with the business knowledge and the technical team tasked with delivering the software, created inevitable issues with the resulting software, including:

- user requirements left to the interpretation of the technical team members, without the benefit of understanding the business context
- the inevitable disconnect between the two-dimensional concept proposed in the documentation and the manifestation of that concept into tangible screens that the user could interact with
- not allowing for changes to business requirements that may have occurred between the time that the user was last consulted and the months (and sometimes years) that followed before the resulting software was installed on their system.

All of these factors resulted in the delivery of software that was frequently misaligned to the needs of the business users, including inadequate workflows, system errors, critical design flaws, and features that were rarely (or never) used by the business – with no remaining budget or resources available to address these issues.

"All-at-once" delivery

Software development projects in the 1990s depended heavily on "waterfall" project management techniques, where analysis, design, development, testing and delivery stages are undertaken serially, requiring the full completion of one activity before the next one can begin. The use of waterfall techniques on these projects meant that software design could not begin until all of the requirements analysis was complete; software testing could not begin until software development was complete; and software was not delivered to the users until all of the preceding stages had been completed.

This use of waterfall approaches in the IT industry was intended to reduce business risk in project delivery, requiring each step to be completed to management's satisfaction before further spending was incurred. In reality, waterfall approaches significantly *increased* the risk of IT project failure by:

- mandating big upfront documentation (with all of its related issues)
- discouraging responsiveness to changing requirements as the project evolved
- creating "silos" of ownership that reduced communication across project team members.

Perhaps the most risky impact of these waterfall approaches was delaying the delivery of tangible business outcomes until the very end of the project – when problems in the software are the most evident and changes to the software are the most costly.

Instead of enabling the organization to manage expenditures and risks throughout the software development project, executives were faced with an all-or-nothing proposition: keep pouring resources into a failing IT project, so that at least some value can be recovered from the previous investment, or end the project midstream and receive no tangible benefit to the organization. The "all-at-once" delivery approach often left these executives with no other options.

There were, of course, other factors that influenced the high failure rate of software development projects in the 1990s, including limitations in technology and the lack of availability of skilled technical resources. However, the three issues outlined above – over-planning, insufficient communication and "all-at-once" delivery – were factors that were within the control of the organization to change.

Thankfully, during this time, a group of innovative thought leaders[19] realized the power that Agile approaches could bring to the IT industry. Their insights revolutionized the way in which software is currently developed worldwide.

The core philosophies that these Agile thought leaders built upon are best described in the Agile Manifesto,[20] a doctrine which currently has thousands of signatories from Agile practitioners around the world:

Manifesto for Agile Software Development[21]

We are uncovering better ways of developing software by doing it and helping others do it.

Through this work wc havc come to value:

Individuals and interactions over processes and tools

Working software over comprehensive documentation

Customer collaboration over contract negotiation

Responding to change over following a plan

---

[19] Including Kent Beck, Martin Fowler, Alistair Cockburn, Jeff Sutherland, and Ken Schwaber.

[20] Agile Manifesto: *www.agilemanifesto.org*.

[21] Reprinted courtesy of *www.agilemanifesto.org*.

That is, while there is value in the items on the right, we value the items on the left more.

The introduction of Agile approaches in the IT industry created an environment that was ideal for addressing each of the key factors that were driving IT project failures.

Over-planning

As documented in the Agile Manifesto, Agile practices prefer "working software over comprehensive documentation" as a way of maximizing the productivity and value of the team.

Adopting Agile approaches within the IT industry eliminated the traditional low-value approach of building big upfront documentation. Instead, Agile teams worked in collaboration with stakeholders to create high-level "user stories" and then worked again in collaboration with these stakeholders to ensure that their deliverables were continually meeting the needs of the organization. This enabled software development teams to start actively producing value for the organization from the first iteration; reduced the levels of documentation to only record the most essential information; enabled plans to be regularly adjusted to meet the ongoing needs of the organization; and provided tangible outputs that stakeholders could respond to (*versus* the limited two-dimensional descriptions available through design documents).

The responsive planning of software development work based on the highest business priorities – along with the regular opportunity for stakeholders to adjust work to meet ongoing priorities – eliminated the need for the "everything under the sun" approach to collecting user requirements.

Because stakeholders were given an opportunity to escalate the software features that were most important to them throughout the process, users knew that there would be ample opportunity to review and adjust these priorities as the software development progressed. They no longer felt the imperative to ask for everything they might need upfront for fear that they would never again have the opportunity to influence the outcome of the software being developed.

Similarly, the hands-on nature of stakeholder involvement, while the software was being developed, provided users with a level of control and input into the process that they had never experienced in the past. The false security of extensive documentation was replaced with the opportunity to review and influence tangible outputs. The misalignment problems that used to occur when software was finally released became a thing of the past. The use of Agile approaches in the IT industry meant that there were few to no surprises when software was delivered to the users.

Insufficient communication

Introducing Agile practices in the IT industry minimized the isolation between the users with the business knowledge and the technical team that was tasked with delivering the software. The most forward-thinking IT organizations put representative stakeholders on the technical team to work hand in hand with the developers on a daily basis. Other organizations arranged for the business areas to be available to the technical team on an "as needed" basis, minimally as active participants in iterative reviews of the deliverables. Technical teams were no longer working in a "black box" environment. They were no longer expected to interpret unclear business requirements on their own. They were empowered with the ability to deliver real business value for their efforts. Stakeholders were provided with working software that was significantly better aligned to their business needs.

Agile approaches did not only have a positive impact on communication between the technical and business teams; they provided significantly higher levels of communication *within* the teams. Agile approaches encouraged teams to: participate in daily status updates and problem identification; pair team members when undertaking work to deliver consistently higher quality results; and undertake cross-disciplinary problem solving in providing end-to-end deliverables at each iteration. Most importantly, technical team members received a level of support, quality control and motivation that was unavailable to them in their previously isolated environments.

"All-at-once" delivery

Agile practices replaced serial "waterfall" project management techniques with iterative delivery of tangible outputs, where all stages (analysis, design, development, testing and delivery) were undertaken for a selected subset of features in each iteration.

The iterative release of end-to-end deliverables allowed for parallel work to be undertaken by the team, enabled risks and hurdles to be identified early on in the process, and provided tangible outputs which were able to bring immediate value to the organization. This ongoing delivery of high business priority outputs provided management with an unprecedented level of value from their IT investments, and a control over ongoing budget expenditure that the "all-at-once" delivery model could never provide.

So, what does all of this have to do with using Agile for organizations in other industry sectors? The interesting thing is that the problems that beset the IT industry in the 1990s – over-planning, insufficient communication and "all-at-once" delivery – are problems faced by organizations in a much broader range of industry sectors today: project teams caught up in endless planning and re-planning cycles; marketing teams making decisions without sufficient input from the product delivery areas; managers relying on paper-based status reports as assurance that work is on track, only to find out at the end of the process that work is either incomplete or insufficient to meet the current needs of the business.

The introduction of Agile approaches in software development revolutionized the IT industry. It is why so many prominent IT organizations, including Yahoo!, BT and Google have not only adopted Agile approaches internally, they have actively promoted the use of Agile practices and techniques throughout the industry.

Popular Agile methods

The following section provides further detail on a few of the more prominent Agile approaches that IT organizations around the world have successfully implemented, including formal Agile methods, such as Scrum, Feature-Driven Development (FDD) and eXtreme Programming (XP). Although the work described in these approaches is quite specific to the IT industry, they align directly with core

Agile principles, such as responsive planning, that can be applied to every organization.

Scrum

Scrum is an iterative project management approach that is most commonly used for Agile software development projects, but is suitable for any project-based work. Scrum provides a framework for businesses to identify and prioritize work required, and for project teams to commit to the subset of priority items that they believe can be delivered in each two- to four-week iteration (or "sprint").

> **Scrum®** is an Agile methodology for project management that involves:
>
> - Delivering software in time-boxed iterations
> - Focusing on the highest business-value software features in each iteration
> - Interacting directly with business users to confirm ongoing software usability, quality, relevance and business value throughout the process.

Scrum requires the nomination of resources to provide key roles in the project delivery, including:

- **the Product Owner** who represents the needs of the business, and is responsible for documenting and prioritizing high-level business requirements as input into ongoing work

- **the Scrum Team**, a cross-disciplinary team that is charged with undertaking the agreed work in each sprint, and enlisting input from the Product Owner when requirements need to be clarified
- **the ScrumMaster** who facilitates the team's work, removing project impediments and ensuring that appropriate Scrum practices are being followed by the team.

Core to the success of Scrum are two activities that are undertaken at each iterative sprint:

- **the Sprint Planning Meeting**, held at the beginning of each sprint; this is where the Product Owner, ScrumMaster and Scrum Team review the highest-priority items identified by the Product Owner and agree on the subset of priority items that will be included in the forthcoming sprint
- **the Sprint Review** held at the end of each sprint; this includes a demonstration of work completed in that sprint and a retrospective review of the work undertaken to enable continuous improvement for subsequent iterations.

Scrum also encourages project teams to engage in daily stand-up meetings: short update sessions held each morning that enable the team to quickly review required work and address any hurdles.

The progress of the Scrum Team's work is communicated to stakeholders through monitoring and measurement tools, such as the:

- **Executive dashboard:** a report that summarizes the work within (and across) Agile teams for easy progress monitoring across the department
- **Product backlog:** a reporting tool that enables both stakeholders and project teams to monitor the progress of work against the agreed business requirements
- **Sprint backlog:** a reporting tool that enables project teams to monitor and manage their actual day-to-day work.

Scrum is used by hundreds of organizations worldwide, including Adobe, Barclays Global Investors, BBC's New Media Division, BellSouth, Bose, CapitalOne, Federal Reserve Bank, GE, Google, Microsoft, Motorola, Nokia Siemens Networks, SAP, State Farm and Yahoo![22]

Dynamic Systems Development Method

The Dynamic Systems Development Method (DSDM) framework is another iterative approach to managing Agile software development projects that has its roots in Rapid Application Development (RAD), resulting in a strong emphasis on building prototypes and confirming the feasibility of the solution prior to undertaking full development activities. This method includes the need for

---

[22] The use of Scrum by these organizations is documented in a number of sources, including corporate websites, industry publications (e.g. *Microsoft Lauds Scrum Method for Software Projects*, Taft DK (2005): *www.eweek.com/c/a/IT-Management/Microsoft-Lauds-Scrum-Method-for-Software-Projects/*), the work undertaken by industry experts such as Jeff Sutherland (*http://scrumtraininginstitute.com/classes/show/85*) and case studies at industry events, e.g. *The Growth of an Agile Coach Community at a Fortune 200 Company*, Silva K & Doss C, AGILE 2007 (13-17 Aug 2007), Washington DC: *ieeexplore.ieee.org/Xplore/login.jsp?url=http%3A%2F%2Fieeexplore.ieee.org%2Fiel5%2F4293562%2F4293563%2F04293600.pdf%3Farnumber%3D4293600&authDecision=-203*.

Stakeholder Workshops, a Feasibility Report, a Feasibility Prototype and a Business Study to be undertaken in the first stage of the DSDM project lifecycle.

The **Dynamic Systems Development Method (DSDM®)** is an Agile methodology for project delivery that involves:

- Delivering software in time-boxed iterations
- Prototyping and documenting the software solution prior to undertaking full development activities
- Collaborating with users, producing tangible outputs, and ensuring quality management throughout the process.

The practices that underpin DSDM are at the very heart of Agile methods, including active user involvement throughout the process, iterative and incremental development, frequent delivery of tangible outputs and empowering the delivery team. Ongoing testing and quality control throughout the process are also emphasized.

Unlike Scrum, the DSDM framework requires a range of artifacts (e.g. development plans, functional models) to be developed at each phase of the project to provide ongoing confirmation that planned work is aligned with the needs of the business.

Although the approaches differ, both Scrum and DSDM have the same core objective – the delivery of high business-value outcomes in controlled, iterative timeframes. Scrum provides a high-level framework for achieving this objective, and relies on communication between the participants to ensure that work undertaken meets ongoing business needs. DSDM provides a more structured framework to achieve this objective, requiring proposed work to be documented and confirmed prior to continuing to the next stage.

Feature-Driven Development

Feature-Driven Development (FDD) is an activity-specific Agile method for software development work. However, there are a number of elements of FDD which could provide valuable insights into the successful delivery of any business outcome.

The basic driver of FDD is to provide incremental value to the business by delivering complete, working product capabilities (i.e. software 'features' and "feature sets") in every iteration.

FDD™ requires close collaboration with the business areas to establish an upfront 'domain model' of the business problem that the proposed system is intended to address. Once this domain model has been identified, it is broken down (decomposed) into smaller tasks (features) which can be developed and delivered iteratively. Teams are then assigned to deliver nominated feature sets which, once successfully tested, are incorporated into the larger system.

Feature-Driven Development™ (FDD™) is an Agile methodology that combines iterative project delivery with software development practices by:

- Having teams model the business problem upfront
- Decomposing the model into smaller, more manageable features and feature sets
- Integrating selected feature sets into the overall software solution through iterative releases
- Keeping a strong focus on collaboration with users, production of tangible outputs, and quality management throughout the process.

FDD promotes quality control throughout the software development process by focusing multiple team members on the same feature set, undertaking peer reviews of software code, and encouraging regular software builds to ensure that a *demonstrable system* is always available for customer review.

Although FDD is specific to software development work, it also includes practices that are valuable for any business activity, including:

- encouraging teams to take on *manageable workloads* within *short, fixed timeframes*
- providing team members with *a dedicated set of peers* to provide multiple perspectives

- *providing context* for work undertaken, so that team members appreciate how the activities that they are doing impact the overall deliverables
- measuring the progress of the team by their achievement of *tangible milestones*.

In many respects, FDD™ works according to the same underlying principles as other Agile methodologies (e.g. Scrum), in that the project team works closely with the business areas to deliver regular, incremental value to the organization. However, FDD™ is far more prescriptive about defining the boundaries of the solution upfront, assigning specific roles and responsibilities to the project team members, and controlling the scope of each team member's work during the actual software development process.

eXtreme Programming

Like FDD, eXtreme Programming (XP) is an activity-specific Agile method for software development work. However, XP also provides techniques which could be applied more broadly to deliver business value across a greater range of business activities.

XP encourages software developers to produce and deliver the *simplest possible technical solution* required to meet the customer's objectives; *anticipates that requirements will change* once the customer has had an opportunity to work with the delivered software; and encourages the *ongoing improvement and optimization of the solution* based on customer feedback.

Unlike the "big upfront documentation" approaches that burdened the IT industry in the 1990s, XP documents business requirements at a high level – and then works *hands on* with the customer to deliver their desired outcomes using the simplest designs, delivered in the earliest possible timeframes.

> **eXtreme Programming™ (XP)** is an Agile methodology for software development work that is based on:
>
> - Delivering the simplest possible technical solution required to meet the customer's objectives
> - Anticipating that requirements will change once the customer has had an opportunity to work with the delivered software
> - Encouraging the ongoing improvement and optimization of the software based on customer feedback.

XP incorporates the use of a distinctive Agile practice called *Test-Driven Development* (TDD), which encourages software developers to create the tests that will be used to validate the code that they are building *prior to* undertaking development work. TDD is an innovative quality management approach for delivering any business outcome, requiring employees to define and document their *measures of success* prior to undertaking the work required.

Another distinctive characteristic of XP is a concept known as *refactoring*, which allows the team to regularly review the existing system and modify it, where required, so that future changes can be implemented more easily. Amazingly, this includes full authority for the team to *throw away* existing software in favor of a replacement solution that will provide the organization with greater flexibility to address future requirements. XP advocates that the short-term loss of work undertaken is worth the long-term opportunity for deliverables to grow with the organization.

It is the simplicity of design, the focus on quality, the expectation of change and the freedom provided to the team to rethink and optimize solutions that enable selected elements of XP to be applied as a unique approach to resolving any business problem.

Kanban

Kanban is an Agile workload and change management methodology that can be used in conjunction with or independently from other Agile methodologies. Currently, it is being used most extensively to manage IT support and maintenance activities, where priority work can change on a weekly, daily or even hourly basis.

At the heart of Kanban is a drive to empower the project team to regularly deliver business value by managing their work in progress (WIP) at any point in time. This means that the team only commits to work that they can genuinely deliver: no more and no less. If the business requires a higher-priority task to be addressed, stakeholders must determine what current work should be postponed in order to free up sufficient resources to address the requirement. Equally, if the team has an opening in the WIP queue, stakeholders can determine the highest-priority work that the team should focus on next.

> **Kanban** is an Agile methodology for workload and change management that is used to allow project teams (particularly support and maintenance teams) to manage their workload in order to:
>
> - Ensure regular outputs
> - Accommodate changing requirements
> - Make ongoing work transparent to all stakeholders to encourage communication, collaboration and problem solving.
>
> Kanban can be used in conjunction with other Agile methodologies (e.g. Scrum) to allow the project team to work closely with stakeholders and to deliver outputs in time-boxed intervals.

Kanban visualizes the flow of work through the use of centralized *Kanban boards* to make the following information evident to all stakeholders at any time:

- The status of all of the project team's planned, current and completed work
- The team's availability to take on additional work
- Any hurdles that are preventing work from progressing.

Not only does this practice create an environment of open communication, transparency and collaboration – it also promotes a culture of continuous improvement by encouraging teams to address bottlenecks, overcome hurdles and maximize their productivity throughout the process.

While Scrum prescribes managing work in time-boxed iterations, and FDD™ prescribes committing to work by deliverable features, Kanban is far less prescriptive on *how* a body of work is defined and *when* it can be delivered. Instead, Kanban allows the team to manage ongoing work by establishing review cycles and release timeframes based on the changing requirements of the organization.

The lack of defined work in Kanban is why some organizations have begun using hybrid methodologies, such as Scrum-ban (a combination of Scrum and Kanban) to achieve the benefits of Kanban within a project delivery framework. In Scrum-ban, the responsiveness of Kanban is aligned with the most effective Scrum practices – such as iterative releases and daily stand-up meetings.

Most often, however organizations use Kanban to more efficiently manage teams that have a constant flow of ongoing work (e.g., maintenance teams), rather than teams with project-based deliverables or predetermined schedules.

The Agile approaches described thus far have had a heavy focus on the application of Agile practices and techniques in the IT industry. However, Agile approaches were being successfully used in the manufacturing sector decades before they were used in the IT industry, with indications that Henry Ford had been using elements of an Agile approach, known as *lean manufacturing*, as early as 1922.[23]

Lean manufacturing focuses on eliminating the wastes that add little or no value to business processes, including:

- ***Overproduction***: producing more than is needed to satisfy the organization's (or the customers') requirements.

---

[23] *My Life and Work*, Ford H with Crowther S, Garden City Publishing Company, Inc. (1922), ISBN 9781406500189.

- ***Waiting***: where work cannot progress due to the unavailability of required resources, materials, management decisions or management approvals.
- ***Non-value-added processing***: this includes over-inspection, reworking and other added tasks to compensate for a lack of effective quality control in the overall process.
- ***Under-utilized people***: where staff cannot work to their full mental and physical potential due to ineffective workflows, restrictive organizational cultures and inadequate training.

To address these areas of waste, the manufacturing sector has implemented a number of techniques, including Total Quality Management (TQM)[24], KAIZEN[25], Just-in-Time (JIT) logistics and Batch Size Reduction – each designed to optimize work to align with customer demand and team capacity, to provide materials to employees on an "as required" basis, and to facilitate collaboration through cross-disciplinary teams.

---

[24] Total Quality Management (TQM) – An Integrated Approach to Quality and Continuous Improvement, Kotelnikov V (last updated January 27th, 2011) www.1000ventures.com/business_guide/im_tqm_main.html

[25] KAIZEN – The Japanese Strategy for Continuous Improvement, Kotelnikov V (last updated November 9th, 2010)

> Lean Manufacturing (Lean) is an Agile methodology that focuses on eliminating the wastes in business processes, including:
>
> - overproduction
> - waiting
> - non-value-added processing
> - under-utilized people.
>
> The core objectives of Lean are to
>
> - use the most efficient processes to deliver the highest business-value outputs
> - deliver results as quickly as possible
> - enforce stringent quality management through integrity checking and continuous improvement
> - empower and enable skilled cross-functional teams to achieve the required outcomes

The wastes identified in the manufacturing sector clearly align to wastes that can occur in any sector:

- delivered work that is misaligned with the needs of the business;
- work that is on hold awaiting materials, staff availability or management approval;
- talented staff who are frustrated because their capabilities are not fully utilized – or because they feel powerless to address inefficiencies in their work.

Other industry sectors have taken the lead from lean manufacturing, adopting quality improvement methodologies, such as SixSigma, in an effort to better measure, improve and control their business processes. These quality improvement methodologies focus on identifying corporate goals, measuring current processes for benchmarking, identifying areas of potential improvement, and then piloting and measuring the effect of the proposed improvements. Although the approach differs, these methodologies have the same primary goal as Agile methods: to more efficiently meet customer needs by *maximizing resource efforts*, *minimizing waste* and *maintaining high quality* throughout the process.

Who uses Agile?

Agile approaches have been successfully used by hundreds of organizations worldwide, most notably in the United States and Europe. Although the list of companies which are currently using Agile approaches covers a range of industry sectors, the vast majority of these organizations have only adopted Agile approaches in their software development activities to date. Therefore, market research related to Agile approaches has been generally undertaken only in this context.

One of the first formal studies of Agile approaches, Forrester's September 2006 survey of technology decision makers[26], identified that 17% of North American and European businesses were using Agile practices at the time, while another 29% were aware of them. This quantified the level of Agile adoption, but not the benefits that were being achieved.

---

[26] "The state of application development in enterprises and SMBs: business data services North America and Europe", Stone J, *Database & Network Journal* (1 Apr 2007): *http://www.thefreelibrary.com/_/print/PrintArticle.aspx?id=162832944*.

A more recent survey undertaken by VersionOne[27] in 2011 indicates that organizations that use Agile approaches are achieving increased productivity (75% of respondents), improved team morale (72% of respondents) faster time to market (71% of respondents) improved ability to manage changes in priorities (84% of respondents), and greater project visibility (77%).

Over the past decade, a number of prominent IT organizations have actively promoted their use of Agile throughout the industry by publishing case studies and experience reports. Selected examples of these are provided in the following sections:

Yahoo![28]

Gabrielle Benefield has been a highly prominent figure in the Agile arena, having championed the use of Agile practices within Yahoo! since 2005. Ms Benefield, who was the Senior Director of Agile Development at Yahoo!, advises that Yahoo! has "more than 200 teams using Agile development processes to create software for the highly volatile general-public Web application market" where they "can easily get 200 to 300 percent productivity improvements."

Yahoo! is an avid user of the Scrum method of Agile project delivery, including the use of user stories to confirm their customers' requirements. In Yahoo!'s approach to Agile, "active stakeholder involvement" is getting feedback

[27] *6th Annual State of Agile Development Survey 2011*: http://www.versionone.com/pdf/2011_State_of_Agile_Development_Survey_Results.pdf.
[28] Reprinted with permission from 1105 Media: *www.1105media.com*.

on proposed features from their millions of customers, and refining their products based on customer input prior to full release.

One of the co-founders at Yahoo! said that "Agile has been one of the most positive things to happen to the company."[29]

Nokia Siemens Networks[30]

Petri Haapio has lead Lean and Agile transformation in some of the world's largest organizations, including Nokia Siemens Networks.

Petri advised that over 40 products at Nokia Siemens Networks have used Agile software development practices with projects undertaken in one- to four-week time-boxed iterations. These products employed a range of Agile practices, including Scrum, continuous integration, test-driven development, pair programming, refactoring and multi-skilled teams.

Petri further advised that Nokia Siemens Networks' primary drivers for moving to Agile practices were:

- to be more responsive to changes in the business environment
- to increase productivity and quality
- to increase customer satisfaction by focusing on the most value added features first

---

[29] The full interview with Ms Benefield is available from 1105 Media at: *http://campustechnology.com/articles/2008/02/lessons-from-a-yahoo-scrum-rollout.aspx*.
[30] Printed with permission from Petri Haapio: *www.reaktor.fi*.

- to establish a culture that is focused on continuous improvement.

In Petri's work with Nokia Siemens Networks, Agile product development has involved teams with 10 people working in a single location, to teams with 500 people working from multiple locations and across multiple time zones.

BT[31]

Agile practices have become a central part of BT's transformed ways of working. The move away from traditional waterfall methods in BT Innovate & Design – which designs and develops all BT's technology – has come as telecommunications networks have become more software driven. Agile became the logical approach to take.

At the start, five years ago, a comprehensive training and education regime was put in place. BT developed "The BT Agile Cookbook, an online guide to Agile delivery as applied to BT" which recognized five core Agile practices:

- customer involvement
- user stories
- iterative development
- automated testing
- continuous integration.

In addition, BT instituted a program for pairing Agile coaches within the organization to exponentially increase their training activities, and established learning events

---

[31] Printed with permission from BT: *www.bt.com*.

such as The Agile Road Show, Agile Program Days and Agile Learning Projects.

The five core practices and the Agile approach are now completely embedded in the operating model that BT uses to design and develop its networks, and the products and services it offers to its customers.

CHAPTER 2: WHY IS AGILE SO EFFECTIVE?

The previous chapter gave you background information on the business drivers that lead to the establishment of Agile approaches, described how each of these approaches delivers business value, and identified a number of organizations that are active users (and proponents) of Agile. The most compelling argument for considering Agile approaches may, however, be the following three bottom-line factors:

- Agile approaches *protect your organization* from *controllable risk* on a number of levels
- Agile approaches *cost relatively little* for your organization *to start (or to stop) using*
- Agile approaches are able to *deliver both initial returns* and *ongoing benefits* to your organization.

The following sections identify how each of these factors is impacted by Agile approaches.

Management of *controllable* risk

One of the key business benefits to Agile approaches is their ability to protect the organization from *controllable risk.* Market fluctuations, employee turnover and variable resource levels are all factors that, to a large extent, organizations cannot control. However, an organization *can* control the way in which it plans for – and responds to – these risk factors.

Each Agile principle works in a different way to protect organizations from *controllable risk*, but these principles also complement each other.

Responsive planning

Every time an organization commits financial, human or physical resources to a business activity, it is taking a calculated risk that the cost of supplying these resources will provide a significant enough return to justify the initial expenditure. The more that these resources are committed *upfront*, the greater the risk to the organization that the intended outcomes will not yield the level of return that was anticipated if circumstances change. The ideal position for an organization is to undertake a moderate upfront investment in time, money and resources, and then monitor the ongoing return on that investment before additional resources are committed.

Responsive planning is designed to enable organizations to commit small amounts of resources towards their objectives, monitor the progress of these resources against both internal and external influencing factors, and adjust the ongoing commitment based on the most current information available. This does not eliminate the potential for unforeseen issues to affect the work that is being done, but it minimizes the impact of these issues when they arise.

Frequent and continuous business value

Even when Agile work is stopped due to unforeseen risks, the initial commitment that the organization made can be partially (or fully) recoverable. Agile approaches require delivery teams to produce high business value outcomes in every iteration, such as:

- sales reports that include real customer data
- working (and releasable) website functionality
- efficiencies to business processes that have been applied (and measured) in live conditions.

These are not thought papers or conceptual discussions, they are *tangible outputs* that the organization can continue to utilize, even if the Agile work is postponed or stopped altogether. (If you stopped the year-long projects in your organization after three months, how many of them would be able to deliver more than a pile of project plans and status reports?)

Agile approaches enable the upfront investment that the organization has made to deliver at least a portion of the intended returns. Moreover, because that portion represents the highest-priority work for the organization, there are times when receiving only these initial outcomes is sufficient for the organization to have achieved its intended objectives.

Direct stakeholder engagement

One of the biggest risks that organizations take is the assumption that the work that they are doing will meet the needs of the intended audiences. The further removed work is from the people that require these outputs, the greater the likelihood that these outputs will be misaligned. At a minimum, this means that the organization is risking absorbing the cost of rework (or discarded work); in more critical circumstances, it means that the organization is risking market share, customer loyalty, staff productivity and employee retention.

In any competitive marketplace, there is always the risk that other organizations will deliver a product or service that is more appealing to audiences. Equally, there is always the risk that customer needs will change over time. The differentiator here is *controllable* risk.

Agile approaches encourage the direct involvement of internal and external stakeholders so that, to the largest extent possible, their input will reflect their most current requirements, including:

- the most up-to-date information that staff members have about the organization (e.g. resource availability, changes in corporate direction)
- hands-on feedback on whether (or not) interim deliverables are meeting the needs of internal staff
- input from external customers on their projected short- and long-term future needs
- the most current information that both internal and external stakeholders have about competing products and services.

Although this does not guarantee that every possible requirement will be known in advance, it significantly shortens the window of time between when the organization *identifies a need*, and when it *delivers the outcomes* that are intended to address that need.

Regular face-to-face communication

In the same way that direct stakeholder engagement reduces the risk of business requirements not being known, face-to-face communication reduces the risk of business requirements not being *understood.*

As mentioned in the *Agile in action* section of *Chapter 1: Agile in a Nutshell*, one of the biggest factors in the failure of IT projects in the 1990s was insufficient communication. This was particularly evident in both the reliance upon upfront documentation to articulate business requirements, and the isolation of the staff members who were doing the work from the business areas that required the outcomes.

Even when organizations involve internal and external stakeholders in the identification of requirements, the value of their involvement is directly correlated to how well the people who are doing the work clearly understand what is needed. This is particularly true when the people who are doing the work do not have the same level of specialist business knowledge as the stakeholders. The more that the business requirements are misinterpreted, the greater the risk to the organization of rework and discarded work.

Regular face-to-face communication not only ensures that work will not be done in isolation of the people who best understand the business requirement. It also minimizes the potential for employees to act on the assumptions or misinformation that can arise from the one-way communication channel of documentation. Combining regular face-to-face communication with tangible outputs in fixed iteration timeframes can remove this ambiguity (and the corresponding risk) altogether.

Minimizing waste

Until now, the focus of risk management through the use of Agile approaches has been on risk mitigation by minimizing upfront commitments in planned business activities. Included in this, is waste management by reducing the risk of resources over-producing (or going too far off-track) before their work is contained. There is also an equivalent *ongoing risk* when organizations allocate resources for business processes that are inefficient.

Maximizing resource utilization involves giving staff the tools, skills, resource levels, and corporate environment that they need to get the work done. In the same way that faulty equipment can stop a production line from moving forward, ineffective communication channels, low-quality outputs and excess movement can bring work to a virtual standstill. Organizations not only risk productivity leakages in these inefficient processes, they also risk delays in deliverables and employee frustration.

Tangible outputs

The requirement for delivery teams to produce *tangible outputs* in each iteration provides significant risk mitigation beyond the ongoing business value that these outputs provide; it also reduces the potential for theoretical concepts (or prototypes) to *oversimplify* the work that is required for production-level deliverables to be generated. This can include everything from a physical product that takes more money to produce than the prototype indicated, through to mock-ups of corporate reports that cannot actually be produced because the information required is unavailable (or too costly to acquire). The more information that an organization has about the *real costs* involved in producing a required output, the better positioned the organization is to determine whether ongoing investment is justified.

Empowering the team

The very nature of Agile work provides employees with levels of satisfaction and self-motivation that go far beyond what they can get from traditional approaches to work. With Agile approaches, teams have input into the estimation and planning process. They can see tangible outputs of their work on a regular basis. They can interact directly with the stakeholders to avoid wasted effort and rework. They can produce business value instead of writing up status reports. Furthermore, because management is able to see the outputs of their work in short timeframes, these teams often get a level of independence and trust that is generally not available to them in the traditional workplace. Self-motivated and empowered teams are a critical part of the success of Agile approaches, and the rewarding nature of Agile work creates an ongoing source of motivation for employees, which reduces the risk of staff turnover.

Quality by design

The direct (and indirect) costs of low-quality outputs can put an organization in a greater position of risk than even the most inefficient business process. Internally, organizations risk lost resource time as defects are addressed and outputs reproduced. Externally, organizations risk their reputation in the marketplace and ongoing customer loyalty.

Agile approaches mitigate this risk by putting *active checkpoints* in place throughout the process to confirm (to the largest extent possible) that ongoing work is delivering high-quality results for stakeholders. These approaches further mitigate the risk of low-quality outputs by encouraging continuous improvement throughout the process, including simplified (and more sustainable) business processes. This positions the organization to not only identify risk, but to be able to respond more quickly, and cost-effectively, to any unexpected issues that arise.

Individually, each of these Agile principles has the ability to protect organizations from some degree of risk. When they are *combined* in Agile approaches, however, the level of risk mitigation for the organization increases significantly – and, when they are used systematically across the organization, the level of protection from risk can increase exponentially.

Minimal start-up costs

In the same way that Agile approaches protect the organization from the risk of large upfront commitments, they also do not require a large upfront commitment from the organization in order to be used.

Agile approaches are not highly regimented management structures that require hundreds of staff to attend workshops (and receive doorstops of documentation) before they can be used in the organization. You can immediately apply many of the core Agile approaches (and principles) described in this book to your current business activities, without attending week-long training courses, acquiring mounds of manuals, or enlisting the services of high-end consulting firms.

That is not to say that organizations cannot benefit from more formal guidance on adopting and applying Agile approaches. The IT industry, for example, has benefited greatly by having formal training and certification courses to teach people how to more effectively apply Agile methods (such as Scrum) in their software development projects. As the adoption of Agile approaches grows and matures in your organization, you can refine your use of Agile by enlisting qualified consultants, attending training courses and reading industry-specific resources, such as those listed in *More Information on Agile*.

Equally, Agile approaches do not require a significant upfront commitment from internal and external stakeholders. For Agile approaches to succeed, stakeholders minimally need to be available to guide and review the outputs of each iteration. Generally, this is no more than eight hours of their time each iteration (i.e. every two to four weeks). Their active involvement throughout the delivery process can substantially reduce the time that is normally required of them at the end of the process to address problems in the deliverables that they received.

All of this can make trialing Agile approaches in an organization a cost-contained activity, which the organization can opt to extend (or reduce) without having jeopardized a significant upfront investment. The downside, of course, is that employees will not have the opportunity to bury their "certificates of completion" for the latest cure-all management trend in the mounds of paperwork on their desks, but that is a risk that most organizations will happily absorb.

Initial and ongoing returns

Agile approaches are designed to provide organizations with a combination of the immediate benefits of having fit-for-purpose outputs, as well as a number of long-term benefits for the organization overall, including:

- more efficient business processes
- reduced overheads in ongoing service and product delivery
- greater customer satisfaction
- stronger competitive advantage
- higher employee retention rates.

The success of Agile approaches creates a dynamic in the organization that feeds off itself. Departments are encouraged to interact and communicate with each other more often, which means that an iteration planning session which was intended to identify upcoming work can also become a forum where staff exchange organizational information and share ideas. Employees feel more empowered to influence and improve the organization, which motivates them to proactively think about other ways in which their work can be done more efficiently. Everyone involved in the process gets the satisfaction of seeing real outcomes from their work, which can create an environment that is focused on *outcomes delivery* instead of paperwork generation.

All of these factors mean that Agile approaches can create a climate of productivity, delivery and possibility that will better position the organization to respond to inevitable internal and external changes. This can create a more sustainable environment to move the organization forward in a service-driven (and ever-changing) global marketplace.

CHAPTER 3: WHY DON'T MORE ORGANIZATIONS USE AGILE?

The Agile community is a tightly knit and extremely supportive group of professionals who are passionate about using – and refining – Agile practices and techniques to provide the greatest benefit to their organizations. The only problem is that the work that they do – and the language that they use – has been so heavily focused on two specific sectors (IT and manufacturing) that other industries have had minimal exposure to the benefits of these approaches.

For example, books on Agile project management techniques have focused, almost exclusively, on how these approaches can improve *software development* projects, even though much of the content could be equally applied to any time-, cost- or resource-constrained project work in other industry sectors.[32]

This focus on industry-specific activities is, arguably, a primary reason why these exceptionally dedicated Agile practitioners have often had a difficult time convincing senior management within their own organizations to support these approaches – let alone convincing customers in other organizations. This lack of management support has often meant that the adoption of Agile approaches within an organization has needed to come from a series of smaller successes in "grass-roots" work (i.e. "Agile-by-

[32] One very notable exception is the DSDM consortium whose guidebooks on the use of DSDM Atern have provided examples of the application of this Agile method to business activities outside software development. In fact, these publications were what inspired me to first consider the potential of Agile approaches beyond technical projects.

stealth"), instead of a collaborative initiative between staff and management.

In addition to an overall lack of awareness about Agile approaches, there may be other factors that would make an organization initially hesitant to adopt these approaches, including:

- ***Technical terminology:*** much of the language that is currently used to describe Agile practices and techniques (e.g. Test-Driven Development) is quite specific to the IT and manufacturing industries, which makes it more difficult for people to see the potential beyond these two industries. Also, some of the terms used (e.g. eXtreme Programming) can create the impression that these are "rogue" practices instead of proven approaches.
- ***Agile myths:*** rumors about Agile approaches that have grown from misunderstanding. For example, the mistaken impression that using Agile approaches means no documentation when, in actuality, it means using more effective communication channels to work together (e.g. face-to-face communication) and using documentation where required to record the outcomes of this work.
- ***Misapplication:*** there are instances where an organization has endeavored to apply Agile approaches in the past, without fully understanding the underlying principles. For example, an organization that moves to an "Agile" iteration-based project management model, but still requires all of the work to be signed-off in an upfront specification. Truly Agile organizations understand that responsive planning is only valuable when the organization is in a position to *adapt* ongoing work as it progresses. Otherwise, iterative work just

becomes shorter delivery cycles that are limited by the same core constraint; and Agile approaches get an unjustified bad reputation when this pre-constrained process inevitably fails.

- ***Trusting employees:*** at the heart of Agile approaches is the firm belief that people can – and will – do the right thing by the organization if they are given the opportunity. If the senior management of an organization sees employees as unmotivated people who have to be supervised closely in order to get any work done, they will be far less willing to entrust delivery teams to self-manage. The irony is that these same managers rarely appreciate that a corporate culture of mistrust breeds unmotivated people.
- ***"Business as usual" mindset:*** there is no doubt that Agile approaches require organizations to act – and think – differently to the way that they have in the past. Those organizations which are self-aware (and humble) enough to recognize that their business practices of the past may not sustain them into the future, will be more amenable to considering Agile approaches, especially given their widespread support and long history of success. In contrast, executives who are committed to "the way we do things around here" are likely to see Agile approaches as too radical for their organization. The bottom line is that Agile approaches *are* a significant change in the way in which organizations operate – but change can be for the *better*.

The previously referenced statistics from Forrester and VersionOne identified that organizations are both aware of Agile approaches and are receiving benefits from their use of these approaches. To date, these statistics have predominantly been focused on the experience of organizations in the IT industry, but they are good indicators that Agile approaches really do result in positive outcomes for the organizations that are forward-thinking enough to apply them. So, the most likely reason for the limited uptake of Agile approaches outside the IT and manufacturing industries, is simply that organizations in other industries may not be aware that they, too, could achieve real productivity gains from these approaches.

CHAPTER 4: AGILE SOUNDS GOOD, BUT ...

The decision to shift to (or even trial) a new way of doing business can be daunting for any organization. There may be inefficiencies in your current business process – and times when you wish that staff were more productive – but is this enough of an argument to forego the "devil you know" in favor of unchartered territory? Moreover, even if you are convinced that your organization has room for improvement, that does not necessarily mean that moving to Agile approaches is the answer.

The most compelling argument in favor of trialing Agile approaches is the fact that it costs the organization very little to get started. All you need is one project that is small enough to influence, but important enough that its success will be meaningful to the organization. It could be a scheduled corporate event, a planned marketing campaign, a new product feature, a new customer service activity or an internal improvement initiative. Commit to trialing Agile approaches on this project for three months and monitor the progress:

- Is the delivery team producing high business value outputs?
- Is work being done more efficiently?
- Are the stakeholders getting the outcomes that they need?
- Are employees happier to be working in a high-communication environment, rather than in a documentation-centric one?
- Is the quality of their work better than before?

If the answer to most (if not all) of these questions is *yes*, then that can give you sufficient confidence to consider broadening the use of Agile approaches to other activities within the organization. If the answer to these questions is *no*, that equally tells you about the suitability of Agile approaches within your organization (or at least their suitability for the selected project) – without requiring the organization to walk away from a huge upfront investment.

Agile principles encourage organizations to work with *tangible outputs* instead of theoretical ideas, prototypes and analysis reports. Equally, the benefits of Agile approaches are best demonstrated by their *active use* and *measurement* within an organization, rather than by any argument that can be made in this book. None of the theoretical discussions in the world is going to convince an organization about how powerful these approaches are in the same way that their hands-on use will.

SECTION 2: 12 AGILE PRINCIPLES THAT WILL REVOLUTIONIZE YOUR ORGANIZATION

CHAPTER 5: RESPONSIVE PLANNING

Why every upfront plan fails

Reality is every plan's worst enemy. Plans represent a snapshot in time, an approximation of what *might occur* based on the information known at the time the plan was developed. At best, plans are reasonable estimates of required activities, resources, costs and time based on previous experience with similar work. At worst, they represent educated guesswork of what *may be* required in order to achieve the desired outcome.

Organizations develop business plans, project plans, financial plans, marketing plans – all designed to provide managers and executives with a sense of control over the future. The problem, of course, is that the corporate world is constantly in a state of change. People join and leave the organization, technology evolves, project funding gets cut and market demands shift. No upfront plan, no matter how well thought out, can predict *everything* that could possibly occur during the course of the plan's execution. So, all plans face the same challenge: they start to become obsolete the moment they reach the printer.

If you have ever been tasked with creating (or reviewing) a detailed project plan, then you have firsthand knowledge of the challenges and pitfalls of upfront planning. Let's consider, for example, that you are an events manager who is responsible for planning a launch event for your company's new product line in three months' time. You develop a project plan based on your past experience in organizing promotional events – this includes:

- assigning tasks to specific people on your team
- estimating the duration of work required for each task (i.e. "write up the press release" should take around six hours)
- identifying task dependencies ("we must measure the room size before we order the red carpet")
- organizing the tasks to fit within the predetermined deadline ("the shareholders and the press have already been notified that the product launch will take place on August 25th").

On paper, the work appears to be achievable within the specified timeframe. So, you present the plan to your executive, and the work is authorized to begin.

Week One: One member of the planning team calls in sick on the Wednesday; he will be out for the rest of the week. In addition, the Chief Financial Officer has just released a memo requesting urgent budget updates from each department by the end of the month. It will take at least two days for you to put these figures together.

Week Two: The task of acquiring promotional giveaways is proving to be more challenging than originally estimated. None of the usual suppliers has stock available, so the team will need time to find another supplier and get authorization from the finance department.

Week Three: The finance department advises that it will take two weeks to process the approval forms for the new supplier. Additionally, the only graphic designer on your team has been reassigned by your boss to urgently address a problem on another project.

Week Four: The event coordinator advises you that there are three more critical tasks that need to be done in order for the product launch to be successful. These tasks require two additional resources on a part-time basis at a cost of $8,000 against the event budget. Neither the tasks, nor the added costs for the resources, were included in the original plan. This additional work is expected to delay the launch by at least a week.

So, now the team is one month into a three-month project plan and, already, the original delivery timeframes are in jeopardy. As a project manager, you are faced with the dilemma of:

- admitting to your boss that the project is likely to miss the deadline (and risking the perception that you have failed to manage the work properly); or
- asking your team to put in extra hours and weekend days to do "whatever it takes" to meet the deadline; or
- hiding the fact that the project is off-course with "creative" status reports and behind-the-scenes negotiations for additional resources.

This is a classic "no win situation" for everyone involved in the process. Selecting any of the above options will either make the project manager feel like a failure, put undue stress on the team, or provide executives with a false sense of security that the project is on track – and reaffirm the myth that upfront project planning works.

Now, consider that this project is *one* activity that your organization is currently undertaking and multiply it by the *hundreds* of things that people are working on. This is the perfect recipe for missed deadlines, burnt-out staff members and exponential budget blowouts across the organization. Amazingly, this is how most organizations currently operate.

This chapter offers *an alternative approach* to upfront planning that has had proven success in the information technology and manufacturing sectors over the past two decades. This approach is known as *responsive planning* in the Agile world, and it is positioned to revolutionize the corporate world.

Apply, Inspect, Adapt

Responsive planning aligns closely with the "Ready, Fire, Aim" approach espoused by Thomas J. Peters in his classic business and management texts.[33] At the heart of this approach is the premise that the only way to see if something works is to *try it*, *review the results* and *adjust your ongoing activities* based on what you have found from your review. In the Agile world, this approach is known as "Apply, Inspect, Adapt" and it underpins everything that makes Agile approaches successful.

Responsive planning puts a structure around the "Ready, Fire, Aim" approach, which is based on breaking down long-term objectives into shorter delivery cycles with tasks that are achievable within the shortened timeframes.[34] Each delivery cycle (or iteration) is generally scheduled to take between two and four weeks. This provides organizations with the opportunity to receive valuable outcomes every month, instead of waiting until the end of a year-long initiative before any return on investment (ROI) is

---

[33] *In search of excellence: lessons from America's best-run companies*, Peters TJ, Harper & Row (1982) ISBN 978-0060451530.

[34] Responsive planning, like many of the Agile principles in the book, is derived from the Scrum method, with adaptations applied to make it more aligned to the needs of the corporate world.

achieved. Just as importantly, it allows key decision makers to regularly *review* and *adjust* the work undertaken to meet the changing needs of the organization.

There are two key groups of participants in the responsive planning and delivery process:

- ***Business owners***: Anyone in the organization who has a business requirement – or who represents the interests of external stakeholders (e.g. customers, partners) with a business requirement.[35]
- ***Delivery team members***: Anyone in the organization who is tasked with undertaking the work required to fulfill that business requirement.

Combined, these two groups of participants are referred to as the *Agile team.* The Agile team, as a whole, is *collectively* responsible for ensuring the successful outcome of any work assigned to them.

In the responsive planning process, business owners communicate their key strategic objectives to the delivery team (focusing on "what" needs to be achieved; not "how" to do it) as part of an *iteration planning session* at the beginning of each iteration. The delivery team is then empowered to meet these strategic objectives through realistic and achievable activities that they control.

The fulfillment of strategic objectives by the delivery team is achieved through six core ACTION plan steps, as shown in Figure 1, overleaf.

---

[35] External stakeholders can directly represent their own interests as business owners, however, this generally requires a strong existing working relationship (e.g. a long-term customer) and logistical planning to coordinate their availability to provide input and attend meetings throughout the iterative process.

Figure 1: ACTION plan steps

- **Actionable goals**: business owners break down their strategic objectives into smaller actionable business goals and communicate these goals to the delivery team as part of the iteration planning session.
- **Communicating priorities**: business owners identify their highest-priority business goals (i.e. those that require the most immediate action) in the iteration planning session.
- **Tell us what can be done**: the delivery team advises the business owners in the iteration planning session on how much high-priority work they can reasonably deliver in that iteration.
- **Iterative work**: the delivery team undertakes the agreed work for that iteration, ideally with the business owners available throughout the iteration to provide input and feedback.

- **Outcomes review**: at the end of each iteration, the delivery team presents the outcomes of their work to the business owners in an *outcomes review session.*
- **Next iteration**: based on the outcomes of that iteration (and ongoing review and adjustment of the business priorities), the business owners identify their highest-priority business goals for the next iteration.

In addition to regularly delivering business value to the organization, responsive planning provides a number of ancillary benefits, including:

- business owners are able to review and respond to *tangible outputs* on a regular basis
- risks and hurdles are able to be identified (and mitigated) earlier in the delivery process
- delivery team members work with *imminent deadlines* ("next week" *versus* "next quarter"), creating a greater sense of urgency to complete the required work
- delivery team members get greater satisfaction in seeing their efforts produce *genuine business value* for the organization
- most importantly, business owners have the opportunity to *adjust the priorities, activities and deliverables* of the team in near real time, to achieve greater ongoing business value for the organization.

This last point cannot be emphasized enough. Responsive planning is *not* just breaking down a big upfront plan into smaller delivery cycles to receive more frequent feedback. It is *evolving the plan* as you progress, based on that feedback, and regularly *reviewing* and *adjusting* the plan to reflect the most current information available.

With only a few weeks to complete required work, resources are encouraged to *take action* instead of over-planning. They become more focused on deliverables than status reports. They see the results of their efforts more quickly and are encouraged to continue producing valuable outcomes. They are truly positioned to respond to the changing needs of the organization.

Defining (and refining) your goals

The ACTION plan model identifies the achievement of key strategic objectives through ***A**ctionable goals* and ***C**ommunicating priorities*. Business owners drive the responsive planning process by establishing the overarching strategic objectives that the delivery team is expected to attain (e.g. *provide a better service to our customers*) and turning these objectives into achievable tactical goals (e.g. *increase our customer service hours of operation, establish customer surveys to gather feedback, do market research to identify the needs of current and prospective customers*). These achievable goals represent what the business owners believe are the most effective (and cost-efficient) ways to meet the stated objective. The first step of the ACTION plan (***A**ctionable goals*) is for business owners to convey these to the delivery team in the iteration planning session, respond to any questions, and ensure that everyone in the room understands each goal.

The next step of the ACTION plan (***C**ommunicating priorities*) provides the opportunity for business owners to order the actionable goals by priority, focusing the team on those goals that can deliver the highest business value to the organization. (*See Chapter 6: Business Value-Driven Work* for further detail on assessing and prioritizing business value.) The highest business value goals identified by the business owners then represent the most critical items for the delivery team to tackle in the upcoming iteration. This not only enables all of the delivery team's efforts to be focused on the work that will produce the greatest return for the organization; it also provides a "sanity check" on whether the goals that were initially thought to deliver the greatest cost-benefit return actually will.

In the above example, one of the stated goals for *providing a better service to our customers* was to increase the customer service hours of operation. Let's say that, in the iteration planning session, the business owners identified this goal as the highest priority for the upcoming iteration: the delivery team is then tasked with undertaking the work involved in delivering this outcome (or a reasonable subset of work towards the outcome) by the end of the iteration.

Four weeks later, the business owners and delivery team reconvene to review the outcomes of the team's work towards increasing the customer service hours of operation. The delivery team presents the following in the outcomes review session:

- The customer service hours have been extended to be from 8am to 6pm on weekdays. This has incurred additional salary costs of $22,000 per annum and has required two customer service representatives to shift their hours to accommodate the overflow work. However, all of this has been able to be achieved within normal work hours (i.e. without incurring overtime costs).
- Investigation by the delivery team has found that increasing the customer service hours beyond this

timeframe would incur significant additional costs to the organization, including:

- overtime payments for four customer service representatives and two supervisors ($56,000 per annum)
- "on-call" charges for the information technology team to be available out-of-hours if the customer service systems fail ($25,200 per annum)
- additional costs for building security and air-conditioning while staff is on-site ($48,000 per annum).

The business owners now have realistic information in hand to determine the priority goals for the team's next iteration. They may decide that the cost of extending the customer service hours beyond 8am to 6pm is worth the competitive advantage that having greater levels of support will bring to the organization. Alternatively, they may decide that the currently extended hours are sufficient and focus the team's energies for the next iteration on establishing the customer feedback survey. Or they may ask the team to investigate alternative approaches to after-hours customer service support, such as having staff work remotely to eliminate the building security and air-conditioning costs.

Whichever option is selected, the responsive planning approach has provided the business owners with *tangible outcomes* and *realistic information* on which to base their next steps. The delivery team has not incurred significant costs (or spent substantial amounts of time) to provide this feedback to the business owners, and the organization has had the opportunity to review and refine their tactics without sacrificing the original strategic objective.

Empowering the delivery team

The customer service example in the previous section focused on how an organization can position high-priority work to be done, and how the outcomes of this work can progressively refine the ongoing activities of the organization. The critical piece that was *not* addressed in this example was how the delivery team identified the work that would be required to achieve the stated goal – and how they kept themselves on track to deliver valuable outcomes at the end of the iteration.

One of the most critical elements of the ACTION plan is the ***T****ell us what can be done* step. It is the point in the responsive planning process where the delivery team translates the highest-priority actionable goals into the *specific activities* that will be required to achieve these goals. The thing that truly differentiates ACTION planning from standard "top-down" management approaches, is that the business owners defer to the multi-skilled delivery team to advise them on the work required, the estimated time for each task, and what can realistically be achieved in the iteration given their current workload and other commitments. The business owners determine what high-priority goals the organization needs to meet; the delivery team determines what high-priority work they are in a position to deliver.

The delivery team identifies the work, they set the bar for how much work can be done, and, because of their direct involvement in the decision-making process, they become personally responsible for the outcomes. (*See Chapter 10: Management by Self-motivation* for further detail on the benefits of empowering the delivery team.)

Any work that the delivery team *cannot* achieve in the upcoming iteration is retained in a *requirements backlog* (as described in *Chapter 12: Immediate Status Tracking*). The requirements backlog becomes a *living document* where ongoing and evolving business requirements are recorded – and prioritized – in preparation for subsequent iteration planning sessions. It ensures that critical goals and activities are never more than one iteration away from business owner review and reconsideration.

In order for the *Tell us what can be done* step to be effective, the delivery team must represent a sufficiently broad range of areas across the organization to realistically determine the work required. In the *providing a better service to our customers* example, having only customer service team members in the delivery team may not provide sufficient input regarding the impact of proposed initiatives on employees (human resources), computer systems (information technology) or building administration (facilities). The broader the delivery team, the more likely that impacts and risks will be identified early – and the more realistic the proposed actions will be.

It is also beneficial, where possible, to include delivery team members who have addressed similar issues in the past, as they can bring both their experience on what work needs to be done and more realistic estimates on how long it will take to do each task.

Once the work to be undertaken for the iteration has been determined by the delivery team, they are now responsible for making it happen. This is the *Iterative work* step of the ACTION plan. Although the actual work that is required will inevitably vary depending on the goals and the skills of the team, the Agile world provides a number of tracking tools to assist the team members in managing both their individual workload and the remaining work for that iteration (no matter what the work itself entails). These tools are described in *Chapter 12: Immediate Status Tracking* and templates are provided in *Section 4: Making Agile Work in Your Organization* for you and your team to use in your responsive planning work.

The critical decision points

The value of an iteration is measured by its outputs. Therefore, at the end of each iteration, the business owners and the delivery team come together to review the work that has been accomplished, the issues that have been encountered, and to determine the next steps for the organization to pursue. These are the final two steps of the ACTION plan: the ***O****utcomes review* and the ***N****ext iteration.*

This is an opportunity for the delivery team to "show off" what they have accomplished and get real-time feedback directly from the people in the organization who will benefit the most from their work. It is an opportunity for the business owners to see (and respond to) tangible outputs, give meaningful feedback to the delivery team, and use this input to confidently progress work in the organization. It is an opportunity for the organization to *immediately leverage* the outputs of the iteration work, instead of waiting until the end of a two-year project to gain business value. Most importantly, it is an opportunity for the original goals (and even the strategic objectives) to be *reviewed*, *refined* and *adapted* to meet the *changing needs* of the organization.

The outcomes review session at the end of each iteration is both the *inspect* and the *adapt* elements of the "Apply,

Inspect, Adapt" approach; it is the *aim* in the "Ready, Fire, Aim" strategy. It is both the culmination of the work undertaken to date and the launching pad for future work. It brings together everything that makes Agile approaches so effective, and is, arguably, the most satisfying part of the responsive planning process.

Techniques for conducting effective iteration planning and outcomes review sessions are provided in *Chapter 7: Hands-on Business Outputs* and *Chapter 8: Real-time Customer Feedback.* Methods for assessing outputs and planning future work are provided in *Chapter 6: Business-value-driven Work* and *Chapter 16: Continuous Improvement.*

Paving the pathway

Effective iteration planning, iterative work activities and outcome review sessions are critical to the success of Agile approaches. If the business requirements are not communicated effectively in the iteration planning session (e.g. too much or too little detail) – or if the delivery team feels pressured by the business owners to take on more work than they can handle in the forthcoming iteration – then the Agile team is not ideally positioned to deliver high business-value outcomes to the organization. Equally damaging is the potential for the delivery team to face issues in the ***I****terative work* step that stop their work from progressing (e.g. a lack of needed equipment, a non-responsive stakeholder). Iterations are such relatively short timeframes that even a slight delay or hurdle can significantly impact the delivery team's ability to achieve the agreed objectives in the remaining time.

This is why most of the steps in the ACTION plan are guided by a specially trained member of the Agile team known as an *Agile facilitator*. (In the Scrum method, the Agile facilitator is referred to as the *ScrumMaster*. It is such a crucial role to the success of Scrum that there are extensive courses in the IT industry solely dedicated to training and certifying ScrumMasters.)

The role of the Agile facilitator is to guide the Agile process:

- to ensure that communication between business users and delivery team members is clear
- to confirm that Agile approaches are being followed most effectively
- to take ownership of addressing any hurdles that the Agile team encounters throughout the process.

Further information about the critical role of the Agile facilitator is provided throughout this section, most notably in their guidance of iterative work (*Chapter 11: "Just-in-time" Communication*) and their removal of impediments in the Agile process (*Chapter 13: Waste Management*).

When to walk away

In the customer service ACTION planning example above, the iteration review session offered three options that the business owners could choose to undertake in the next iteration:

- extend the customer service hours beyond 8am to 6pm, for the competitive advantage that having greater levels of support will bring to the organization

- keep the currently extended hours and focus the team's energies on establishing the customer feedback survey
- ask the team to investigate alternative approaches to after-hours customer service support.

The one option that was not presented in this example was the option for the business owners to choose to *do nothing* in the next iteration. This is another critical differentiator in the responsive planning approach; there are times when doing nothing is actually more beneficial for the organization than taking action.

For this example, the hands-on review of the outputs from the iteration may result in the business owners deciding that:

- Sufficient work has been undertaken to meet the strategic objective and the delivery team resources would provide better value to the organization if they focused on other high-priority work.
- The original actionable goals are too risky, too costly or too time-consuming to pursue any further. In this case, the business owners may choose to put the work on hold to provide them with time to consider alternative options (or to speak with a senior executive to reconsider the original strategic objective).
- There is too little information available at the time to make an informed decision on the best way to move forward. The business owners may ask the team to pursue further investigation in the next iteration, or they may endeavor to take investigative action themselves, independently of the delivery team.

In all of these circumstances, the business owners have made the strategic decision that *no further iterations are required*, allowing the delivery team members to be allocated to other teams, or assigned to other work within the organization.

Ending a responsive planning process (even if it has not yet achieved its intended objectives) is, in reality, an extremely positive outcome for the organization. Either the process has ended because it has achieved its objectives, or it has been ended well before significant budget funds, time or resources were expended. Initiatives with huge budgets and long-term delivery timeframes often do not get stopped midway unless something catastrophic occurs. Moreover, if they are stopped midway, the work that they have undertaken up to that point is often valueless to the organization. In the Agile world, the team is tasked to deliver regular incremental value for the organization. So, no matter when (or why) the responsive planning process is completed, the organization is always in a position to leverage the value of the outcomes that have been delivered to date.

Publicizing your success

The interesting thing about Agile approaches is that they often generate so much short-term business value that participants forget to promote their successes within the organization. (This may be because incremental business value across 12 monthly iterations does not seem to have the same dramatic impact as the end of a year-long project.)

So, it is often up to the business owners and the delivery team to self-promote: announce outcomes to staff at the end of each iteration; update executives on how effective the Agile process is within your area; encourage other areas of the organization to try it. If needed, you can even put together the outcomes of several iterations into a product or service "launch" – notwithstanding the fact that the product or service is likely to have been actively in use by the business for several months prior to the actual launch.

Agile processes have historically had a slow emergence in traditional organizations. Because they present a decidedly different way of working, much of the adoption of Agile approaches has been due to participants publicizing the exceptional results that they experienced – and encouraging other areas of the organization to trial it. In some cases, members of successful Agile teams have also strategically volunteered to work with other departments on their Agile projects, to enable them to benefit from their experience.

Agile approaches may seem like a radical shift for some organizations, but they have also been proven to produce *radically improved outcomes* for those organizations that have applied them – which is exactly why the effectiveness of Agile approaches needs to be promoted by those who have benefited from their success.

CHAPTER 6: BUSINESS-VALUE-DRIVEN WORK

Real productivity

Is your organization *truly* productive? Real productivity has little to do with how hard the staff works, how many hours they put in, or even how much output they produce. Real productivity is measured by the *business value* that their work generates for the organization, which can be quantified through *primary* and *secondary* business-value outcomes.

Primary business-value outcomes

Primary business-value outcomes directly relate to the core function of the organization. For private sector organizations, where the core function is generally increasing the bottom line, primary business value can be measured by:

- increased revenue
- increased profits (or profit margins)
- reduced overheads.

For public sector and not-for-profit organizations, where the core function is generally service delivery, primary business value can be measured by:

- increased service delivery
- more effective service delivery
- greater funding allocations
- reduced overheads.

Secondary business-value outcomes

Organizations also benefit from *secondary* business-value outcomes that indirectly support their ability to deliver primary business-value outcomes. These secondary business-value outcomes are used to generate interest from prospective customers, employees and shareholders (which can lead to increased revenue or greater funding allocations), to retain the loyalty of current customers, employees and shareholders (which can increase profits), and to provide greater efficiency in the workplace (which can reduce overheads). Secondary business-value outcomes can include:

- better customer service
- increased employee satisfaction
- higher quality outputs
- reduced risk
- more efficient business processes
- greater market awareness
- more positive image in the marketplace.

It should be noted that, although each of these secondary business-value outcomes has the potential to positively impact the primary business-value outcomes, secondary business-value outcomes are generally harder to quantify and measure (as explained in *Chapter 19: Using Agile Tools*).

No matter how your organization defines (and measures) business value, it is often the ultimate determining factor for the ongoing success or failure of the organization.

The responsive planning approach described in *Chapter 5: Responsive Planning* focused on the delivery of business value, particularly in the *Communicating priorities* step of the ACTION plan. In the responsive planning approach, business owners are not only responsible for turning strategic objectives into actionable goals, they are equally responsible for *prioritizing* these goals in accordance with the amount of *business value* that they are likely to bring to the organization.

The challenge for business owners lies in determining the relative business value of competing activities, not only in what they can bring to the organization, but in how much their delivery *will cost* the organization. The *Measuring cost/benefit* and *Communicating actionable goals and priorities* areas of this chapter address how the highest-priority activities are determined (and communicated), including a methodology for undertaking a comparative cost/benefit analysis of each activity.

Dancing around the budget bonfire

Real productivity has a natural opposing force in the corporate world, a force upon which too many organizations rely to measure their success or failure. That opposing force is *paper productivity*.

Paper productivity is the use of status reports, budget reports and other paper-based measurement tools to give management the *appearance* of productivity in the workplace. It is, equally, the strategic use of "selective metrics" in these reports to present the team's work in the most favorable position. For example, focusing a status report on how many hours the team worked in the previous month, not on how much business value they produced in this timeframe.

Employees, managers and executives all use favorable reports (i.e. paper productivity) as a mechanism for securing their bonuses, increasing their pay rises and ensuring ongoing funding for their work. Publicly held corporations equally use paper productivity (in the form of annual reports) to encourage and retain shareholders. Public sector and not-for-profit organizations use performance reports to secure funding allocations. The more paper that is generated, the more the budget bonfire is fuelled. Amazingly, most organizations do little to discourage staff from dancing around the budget bonfire as it burns. That is, until all that is left is smoke and embers.

Agile approaches measure productivity almost exclusively through *tangible business-value outcomes*. At the end of each iteration, teams are encouraged to demonstrate what they have *actually achieved* in that timeframe. Depending on the nature of the work, these demonstrations can include:

- a presentation of newly-developed products or product features
- a "burndown chart" of actual work completed (*see Chapter 12: Immediate Status Tracking* for more information on burndown charts)
- testimonials from key audiences (e.g. employees, customers) regarding new or improved services.

Iteration review sessions are *not* the forum for 20-page status reports that include spreadsheets with colored bar graphs. Quantitative metrics, where appropriate, *can* help support the demonstration of business-value outputs (e.g. showing the increased number of calls handled by the call center), but the focus (and challenge) of the iteration review session is the team's ability to demonstrate that this increased number of calls has not resulted in a reduced level of customer service, and, where possible, to demonstrate that improvements in the call center service (a *secondary* business-value output) has actually resulted in add-on sales from existing customers (a *primary* business-value output).

Over-delivery is wasted money

Generating business value has as much to do with what the team delivers as what it *does not do* in the process. Anytime that the team works on low business-value activities (including extensive status reporting) is time that could have been better spent delivering *actual value* to the organization. Miscommunication, extensive delays in management approvals and a lack of quality control processes can create an atmosphere of misaligned deliverables and rework – which results in wasted resource time and costs for the organization. Equally wasteful, is having the team do *more work than is required* to satisfy an objective (commonly known as *over-production* or *over-delivery*).

In the ACTION planning example in *Chapter 5: Responsive Planning*, one of the potential outcomes of the iteration review session was the business owners deciding that sufficient work had been undertaken to meet the strategic objective; and that the delivery team resources would provide better value to the organization if they focused on other high-priority work. This is one example of effective waste management – combating over-production by choosing *not to* continue work on an initiative that has achieved its intended outcomes. It is yet another differentiator between Agile approaches and the predetermined timeframes and outputs of upfront planning.

There are a number of proven Agile approaches that focus on the concept of *waste management* by eliminating any activities which add little or no value to the business. The responsive planning process is specifically structured to minimize waste by:

- providing teams with only enough time and resources to achieve the identified highest business-value outcomes
- identifying risk areas and delivery issues as early as possible in the process to avoid pursuing a goal which may be unachievable within the stated budget
- providing checkpoints throughout the process where business owners can review, refine and even stop (or postpone) the work undertaken by the team, if it is no longer producing the highest business-value outcomes.

Specific details on Agile approaches to managing waste are provided in *Chapter 13: Waste Management*.

Measuring cost/benefit

One of the core activities in responsive planning is prioritization of actionable goals, based on the level of business value that each goal is likely to deliver. So, how do business owners differentiate between those goals that are able to generate high business value for the organization and those that are less positioned to generate the equivalent value? This is one area where Agile approaches generally defer to the expertise of the business owner and their current cost/benefit analysis methods. However, at the heart of the process is a simple *expected business-value* formula, as shown in Figure 2.

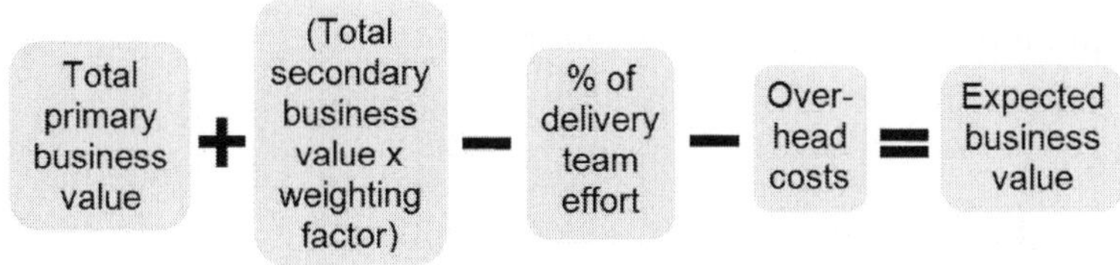

Figure 2: Expected business-value formula

This formula allows organizations to determine the expected business value of each actionable goal by identifying, quantifying and weighting its expected outcomes against the delivery cost of achieving that goal. Values are based on the primary and secondary business-value outcomes described earlier in this chapter, generally based on one of the following:

- the percentage of work that the actionable goal represents within the *value of an overall initiative* (e.g. the delivery of one of ten equally important functions in a website that the organization has valued at $630,000 overall, would deliver $63,000 of primary business value), or
- where the actionable goal is not part of an overall initiative, using an equivalent calculation based on the Key Performance Indicators (KPIs) established for the organization.

This approach to cost/benefit analysis provides business owners with a comparative expected business value for each actionable goal, allowing them to prioritize goals by their expected business-value return, with the highest return goals at the top of the list for each iteration.

It is important to note here that calculating the delivery cost of achieving each goal is generally not something that business owners are able to finalize before the iteration planning session. In fact, business owners often rely on input from the delivery team to determine:

- What work is required to deliver the required outcomes?
- How long is each task expected to take?
- Which resources/skills are needed to successfully undertake this work?
- What additional equipment and facilities are required?
- How complex/risky is the requirement (to determine if upfront investigation is required)?

This means that comparative expected business values may be adjusted (and the priorities of actionable goals reordered) as part of the iteration planning session. (*See When priorities change* at the end of this chapter for further information.)

An explanation of how the expected business-value formula is used is provided in *Chapter 19: Using Agile Tools*, which is in *Section 4: Making Agile Work in Your Organization.* Additional sources of information on cost/benefit analysis are provided in *More Information on Agile.*

Communicating actionable goals and priorities

Once an actionable goal has been identified and confirmed as a priority activity for the iteration planning session, the business owners are tasked with the challenge of *effectively communicating* that goal to the delivery team. In the Agile world, the communication of actionable goals is primarily achieved through *user stories.*

User stories follow three basic rules:

- each user story is a short description of a discrete business requirement (actionable goal)
- each user story is written on a 3x5 inch index card
- the focus of the language in the user story is on business needs (i.e. "what" the business is looking to achieve) not delivery methods (i.e. "how" it will be achieved).[36]

The discrete business requirement in a user story *must* be described at a low enough level of detail to be actionable by the delivery team within the timeframe of an iteration:

> Build a website that encourages customers to buy additional products.

The above requirement is too broad and all-encompassing to be actioned by the delivery team in a four-week iteration.

> Add a mailing list to the current website in order to encourage customers to buy additional products.

This is a more specific and achievable requirement for the delivery team to progress.

Even more valuable, however, would be the equivalent user story with a little more detail on the desired features of the mailing list:

---

[36] Adapted from www.agilesoftwaredevelopment.com and www.extremeprogramming.org.

Add a mailing list to the current website in order to encourage customers to buy additional products. The mailing list should allow customers to select the product categories that are most relevant, identify their preferred frequency for receiving these messages and remove themselves from the mailing list at any time.

This level of detail in a user story increases the potential for the delivery team to produce something that aligns with the expectations of the business owners.

In addition to describing the business requirement (actionable goal) on each 3x5 inch card, it can also be valuable for business owners to include, at the bottom of each card, the comparative expected business value (or equivalent weighting) for that goal, based on the cost/benefit analysis undertaken.

An example of a user story with an expected business value is presented below:

Estimated vs. actual quarterly sales

Management can run a report which shows actual sales for the previous quarter against sales estimates. Report must break down sales by product type and by region.

Expected value = $42,000

The use of one 3x5 inch index card to document each user story, forces business owners to keep their descriptions short and simple. It also has the added benefit of enabling multiple actionable goals to be pinned up to a wall in a conference room for the iteration review session. This is especially valuable when further discussion with the delivery team results in changes to expected delivery costs – and subsequent adjustments to the original expected business values. The simplicity of user stories means that reprioritizing actionable goals is as simple as reordering the index cards on the wall.

Drawing the line

The *Tell us what can be done* step of the ACTION plan empowers the delivery team to advise business owners on how much high-priority work the team believes that they will be able to achieve within the two- to four-week iteration timeframe. In a top-down prioritized list of actionable goals, the delivery team is literally "drawing the line" to indicate those goals and activities that are scheduled to be addressed in the upcoming iteration (those above the line), and those goals and activities that will need to be considered for future iterations (those below the line). Goals and actions below the line remain in the requirements backlog until business owners determine that they are of a sufficiently high business value to be considered in a future iteration, or of a sufficiently low business value to be removed from the requirements backlog altogether.

For the responsive planning process to succeed, it is critical that business owners defer to the expertise of the delivery team to determine what is realistically achievable in the allocated timeframe. Pressuring the delivery team to do more work than they reasonably can undertake in the specified timeframe inevitably results in unachieved (or lower quality) outcomes, burnt out delivery team members and strained relations between the business owners and the delivery team for subsequent iterations. *Chapter 10: Management by Self-motivation* provides further detail on the risks and drawbacks of overloading the delivery team.

If there are high-priority goals and activities that are not being addressed in the upcoming iteration, business owners have the option of:

- reordering the goals and activities in the current iteration, so that items beneath the line replace one or more items that are currently above the line
- breaking down goals into smaller parts, so that the highest business-value portion of that work may be achievable by the delivery team in the upcoming iteration
- increasing the resources of the delivery team (or employing a second concurrent delivery team) to accommodate the additional work required.

By employing these methods, business owners are likely to find a reasonable balance of business-value outcomes and achievable work that everyone can live with.

When priorities change

In *Chapter 5: Responsive Planning*, it was identified that one of the strongest benefits of Agile approaches was their ability to overcome the pitfalls of upfront planning, particularly when it involves responding to organizational change. Agile approaches provide a strategy for accommodating the inevitable changes in resources, market demands and business priorities that occur in the normal course of the corporate world. The responsive planning techniques described in the previous chapter directly address this inevitable change by dividing work into two- to four-week iterations, and by providing business owners with the opportunity to adjust and refine their priorities at the beginning and end of each iteration.

The planning session at the start of each iteration enables business owners to establish a priority order for actionable goals that reflects the most current information in the organization – and a further opportunity to adjust these priorities based on:

- delivery team feedback at the session
- corresponding changes to expected business values
- review/adjustment of the items "above the line" to reflect the work that the business owners feel will provide the organization with the greatest business value in the upcoming iteration.

The review session at the end of each iteration provides business owners with realistic feedback on what could (and could not) be achieved, what risks were encountered, and what cost, time and technology hurdles may jeopardize future work. This is valuable input for the business owners in their prioritization of work for subsequent iterations, as it will likely impact the original cost/benefit analysis of these goals and activities – and may result in a previously lower value actionable goal being promoted "above the line" if it is seen as a less costly or risky endeavor. As part of this exercise, business owners can also factor in any additional organizational information that they have gathered over the course of the iteration, to adjust and reprioritize the items in the requirements backlog to reflect the most current organizational priorities.

So, what happens when a major organizational or industry change occurs *during* the course of an iteration? Depending on the nature and potential impact of the change, business owners can opt to:

- meet with the delivery team to discuss the change and jointly determine the effect that it might have on their current work
- stop the current iteration altogether and reconvene with the delivery team to plan for a replacement iteration planning session with a revised priority list
- take no immediate action involving the delivery team; instead, business owners can opt to use the change as input into their iteration planning session and prioritization for the next iteration.

Iterations are not intended to be a closed period where the delivery team is "left alone" to work on the activities that they committed to in the iteration planning session. In fact, the exact opposite is true: business owners ideally should make themselves available to the delivery team throughout the iteration to provide clarification of business requirements and hands-on feedback. This not only provides the business owners with higher value outcomes at the end of the iteration, it creates a high-value communication environment where everyone on the team is best positioned to respond to corporate changes. *See Chapter 8: Real-time Customer Feedback* and *Chapter 11: "Just-in-time" Communication* for more detail on the benefits of business owners being available to the delivery team throughout the iterative process.

It's *more* than the baton

Changing the focus of an organization from tracking timesheets to tracking business value generated is at the heart of Agile approaches.

The *Lean Primer*[37] uses the following statement as a simple way to encourage organizations to focus on monitoring *outputs* not *people*:

Watch the baton, not the runners

Although this statement is elegant in its simplicity, it also understates the complexity of what organizations need to do to ensure high business-value outputs.

The baton is *not* the end goal for the organization; the end goal is reaching the finish line, ideally in a top position. Watching the baton is not going to tell you that there is an obstacle 300 meters down the track that will make any progress achieved meaningless once the runner stumbles. That is because the baton is a measurement of progress, not a factor in influencing the outcome of the race.

A truly effective organization will take measures to address *all of the factors* than can influence the outcome of the race (i.e. the ability of people to generate *real business value* in their work to move the organization ahead). This includes the pace and the form of the runners, the quality of the track, the design of their running shoes and the humidity in the air. An effective organization will also take measures to ensure that the process for exchanging responsibility and communicating between resources is done in the most effective way (i.e. to avoid having staff "drop the baton").

---

[37] *Lean Primer*, Larman C & Vodde B (2009): *www.leanprimer.com/downloads/lean_primer.pdf*.

Organizations need to create an environment that maximizes the factors that can be controlled (such as the design of the runner's shoes), and is responsive to the factors that cannot be controlled (such as a spectator who unexpectedly runs onto the track during the race). By doing these things, the organization has created an environment that is responsive, an employee base that is motivated and a process that is self-correcting. Thus, watching the baton in the race becomes just a formality.

The following chapter focuses on *hands-on business outputs* as a way for organizations to differentiate between the *appearance of progress* and the *delivery of tangible business value* to the organization.

CHAPTER 7: HANDS-ON BUSINESS OUTPUTS

The "try before you buy" power position

Would you buy your next house from a website profile alone? No matter how much information is provided about a house on a website (detailed descriptions of its features, three-dimensional views of each room), most people would prefer to *walk through the house themselves* before deciding whether or not to purchase it. They know that seeing the description of a house is no substitute for checking the quality of its construction firsthand, for speaking with the people in the neighborhood, for physically going through it to see if it will really meet the needs of your family.

Doing a hands-on check of a prospective house is a reasonable and practical way of determining whether such a large investment will suit you and your family before you make the purchase. You know that it would be too risky for you to invest your future in something that may not meet your requirements, no matter how appealing it looked on the website. Yet, in most organizations, budgets which are as large (or larger) than the cost of a house are often approved from their "website profile" alone.

In *Chapter 6: Business-value-driven Work*, the term *paper productivity* was used to describe status reports and other paper-based outputs which are designed to give the appearance of productivity. Similarly, the term *paper planning* can be used to describe the business plans, funding submissions and expert advisory reports which are used by management to "sell" a concept in order to receive budget allocation (i.e. so that the organization will "buy" the idea). Once approved, ongoing feedback about the progress of the concept is generally left to monthly status reports and, even less frequent, executive committee review sessions. Management is trusting that the outcomes of their investment will meet their expectations from the paper proposal alone.

The "Apply, Inspect, Adapt" approach in the Agile world includes the core concept of regularly *inspecting* outputs firsthand, in order to determine whether business requirements are being met – and whether business value is being delivered. Ongoing funding of work is contingent upon the outcomes of these inspections. Work that is not delivering the expected level of business value may be adjusted, scaled down or cancelled altogether. The delivery team controls the work that is undertaken for each iteration; the business owners control whether their hands-on review of the outputs of each iteration is sufficiently valuable to justify ongoing work.

The Agile approach puts business owners in a unique "try before you buy" power position. They are not forced to make a significant upfront investment. Every iteration presents the opportunity for them to review and reassess their expectations; and if they do decide to cancel the work, the time and budget expenditures have been minimized. It is the equivalent of commissioning a house to be built from a blueprint, doing a hands-on check of the construction every three weeks and having the option to stop your investment, *at any time*, if the house being built does not meet your expectations.

There is no substitute for reality

One of the most common misconceptions about Agile approaches is that they are the equivalent of prototyping. ("We show our customers mock-ups of products and they give us feedback all the time. Why are Agile approaches any different to what we have been doing for years?")

From a distance, the similarity between Agile approaches and prototyping is understandable:

- both involve showing customers deliverables before they are finalized
- both involve gathering feedback from the customer
- both involve adjusting and refining the deliverables based on that feedback.

The most critical difference between the two approaches is *what* is being presented to the customers for their feedback.

Prototyping generally involves creating a *mock-up* of a deliverable, in order for customers to get a feel for what it might look like (and how it might behave), prior to investing significant financial resources in creating a working (production) version of the deliverable. On the surface, prototyping appears to be a cost-effective way of getting feedback on a product (or any other business output) without investing significant time, resources or finances.

Agile approaches, on the other hand, present business owners (i.e. customers) with *functional deliverables* – actual products and services that include working capabilities, real corporate information, production-ready outputs (which also allows delivery teams to report on the *actual effort* that was involved to make them work). Delivery teams are responsible for doing all of the required work for a functional deliverable. Real information is gathered and analyzed, real risks and constraints are identified, and more realistic outputs are delivered to the business owners for their feedback. The downside is that work undertaken in a two- to four-week iteration tends to generate a smaller subset of deliverables than can be demonstrated in a prototype (as functional deliverables generally require more effort than mock-ups). However, when they are produced, business owners can be confident that the outputs delivered with an Agile approach are more realistic, more achievable, and that the estimates for ongoing work are more accurate.

Most importantly, functional deliverables can often be used *immediately* after the outcomes review session for real day-to-day work. It is a sales report with real production information, a live survey that can be released on the corporate website, a marketing brochure that is print-ready, a customer service initiative that can be announced to staff that afternoon. Unlike prototypes, functional deliverables are able to deliver real value to the organization in every iteration they are released.

In the information technology world, this distinction is reasonably straightforward. It is the difference between seeing screen shots of how a software product might look, *versus* using actual working software hands on.

How does this distinction translate to day-to-day business activities? Sales reporting provides one example of the difference between delivering mock-ups and delivering actual outputs.

Let's consider that you are asked by the sales department to provide a report that shows the geographic and demographic breakdown of prospective customers. You meet with representatives from the sales department to determine the information that they would like to include in this report. The result of this meeting is that the sales department would like to see the following breakdowns of prospective customer information:

- by country
- by sales region within each country
- by age bracket
- by number of children
- by household income.

They would also like comparisons to the equivalent profiles for current customers.

Next, you meet with the marketing department to determine what information is being collected about current and prospective customers. The Marketing Manager assures you that all of the details that the sales department has asked for are included in their market research statistics for prospective customers. A quick call to the Customer Service Manager confirms that they store the equivalent information about current customers in their customer relationship management (CRM) system.

Armed with this research, you put together a mock-up of a report containing all of the requested customer information in an easy-to-read layout. You even include calculations across multiple demographic dimensions to show how they correlate. The Vice President of Sales is impressed by the level of thought that you have put into the report and gives you the approval to go ahead. You now have three weeks to put together the report showing the data from the previous quarter before the annual sales meeting.

So, you return to the marketing department to get the prospective customer statistics from the previous quarter.

They tell you that they can have these numbers to you by this Friday. The customer service department has a backlog of customer issues to address, but will do everything that they can to have the details to you no later than Tuesday of next week. Not your preferred timeframe, but it still gives you two weeks to put the report together, which you are confident will be more than enough time. Confident, that is, until you see the actual statistics that they give you.

The statistics for current customers are reasonably comprehensive. The only issue is that the geographic details for each customer are recorded by city name, not by sales region. Some extra effort will be required to determine the sales region for each customer, but it is still an achievable task.

The statistics for prospective customers are not as straightforward. In most cases, the only details available for prospective customers are their names and their sales regions. There are a few prospective customers with full profiles that contain all of the required details, but these are generally people who are close to finalizing their purchase. Looking at these numbers, you realize that the only way that you can deliver the information that was presented in your report mock-up is to either:

- give the sales department skewed data by only including those prospective customers who have a full profile (i.e. those finalizing their purchases), or
- undertake further market research to gather the equivalent details for a broader sample of prospective customers (which would require significantly more time and resources than are available).

Either way, you have set an expectation level with the Vice President of Sales that you are not able to fulfill. What looked achievable on paper became insurmountable in reality. It does not matter how impressive a mock-up is if it cannot deliver the required outcome.

Agile approaches mitigate the risk of situations like these occurring by requiring the delivery team to do the *actual work* required before presenting outputs to business owners. Every interim deliverable represents a slice of the final deliverable, including *all of the work required* to make it a production-ready output. Knowing the hurdles upfront means that the risk of having insufficient information, resources, time or finances is substantially mitigated.

The following section explains how using an Agile approach to deliver the sales report could have significantly reduced the risk of non-delivery – and protected your reputation with the sales department.

Mitigating risk

In the previous section, you realized that presenting a mock-up of a sales report to the Vice President of Sales set an expectation level that could not be fulfilled once the actual work was undertaken: the sales department was not able to get the data it required before the annual sales meeting; the organization was not in a position to do the strategic work required for the next financial year; and, your personal reputation was jeopardized in the process. So, how are Agile approaches able to avoid these situations?

Let's again consider that you are asked by the sales department to provide a report that shows the geographic and demographic breakdown of prospective customers. This time, however, you decide to use an Agile approach to fulfill the requirement.

Using this approach, you (the *delivery team*) meet with representatives from the sales department (the *business owners*) to determine the most valuable information that they would like to include in this report (i.e. their *Actionable goals)*.

The result of this meeting is that the sales department would like to see the following breakdowns of prospective customer information:

- by country
- by sales region within each country
- by age bracket
- by number of children
- by household income.

They would also like comparisons to the equivalent profiles for current customers.

This time, instead of recording their requirements and saying that you will get back to them, you put each of their requested report features on a 3x5 inch index card (i.e. creating a *user story* for each requirement).

You then walk through each requirement with the business owners, asking questions such as:

- For each piece of information requested in the report (e.g. household income):
    - How critical is this information to your analysis?
    - Where would this information come from?
    - How much work would be required to gather this information?
    - What would you do if this information was not available in time for the annual sales meeting?
- For the overall report:

- What format would you like the information to be presented in (e.g. spreadsheet, paper printout)?
- How essential is it to include both prospective customer and current customer information in the report?
- Do you need features such as aggregated numbers, total counts, or calculations across multiple pieces of information (e.g. the average household income for each sales region) to be included in the report?
- What would you do if the full report was not available in time for the annual sales meeting?

Answering these questions will assist the sales department representatives in analyzing and prioritizing their most critical requirements (i.e. ***Communicating priorities***).

It is important to note that going through all of these questions with the sales department representatives may turn a 15-minute meeting into a one-hour meeting, but it is likely to be one of the most valuable hours that they have spent in the organization.

The meeting with the sales department representatives is likely to result in two key outcomes:

- identification of the most critical subset of information and features for the report (i.e. the prioritized list of actionable goals)
- realization that the people attending this meeting do not have enough information in hand regarding where the report details will come from (i.e. the delivery cost) in order to calculate the true business value of each requirement.

Having insufficient information on the delivery cost of each requirement means that it is difficult to finalize the priorities – or to progress the actual work – without exposing the organization to unnecessary risk. Therefore, your next step (as the *delivery team*) is to determine who in the organization has sufficient knowledge of what current/prospective customers' profile details have been collected and how they can be obtained. You realize that, without this information, it would be too risky for you (and the organization) to commit to the deliverables in the specified timeframe. That is why the ***T****ell us what can be done* step in the ACTION plan requires this input.

Two days later, you hold another meeting with the sales department representatives. However, this time, you include representatives from the marketing department and the customer service department in the meeting. As a group, you discuss what current/prospective customer information can be realistically provided in time for the annual sales meeting.

You work with the sales department representatives to determine how the available information could be presented to add the most value possible, in light of these constraints. The attendees agree on an achievable outcome, and commit to deliver their input within the next week. This may not be exactly what the sales department originally wanted, but they will be getting *something valuable* in time for their annual sales meeting (versus a mock-up with no real information behind it). Additionally, they have *firsthand knowledge* of the organizational constraints that limited the scope of the sales report (instead of pointing the finger at you).

In this scenario, using the Agile approach has mitigated the organizational risks of non-delivery and work stoppage, and the personal risk of tarnishing your reputation. Most importantly, all of the risk mitigation occurred *before* any actual work was begun. So, how does this relate to hands-on business outputs?

The value of Agile approaches often occurs well before the work itself is undertaken. The requirement for hands-on business outputs throughout the Agile delivery process influences all of the earlier work leading up to it. Delivery teams are not willing to commit to work that they cannot reasonably achieve. This also means that business owners are not working from false expectations, or dealing with non-delivery issues.

Prototyping allows delivery teams to get customer buy-in upfront (and worry about the actual work required once the customer has signed the bottom line). In some situations (such as product manufacturing), using prototypes and mock-ups may be the only viable option available, as it is not cost-effective to invest in machinery without customer confirmation of the proposed design. These are the exception cases, where the ACTION plan may not add the same level of value that it does for other business activities. In most other circumstances, however, prototyping can be a recipe for disappointment, frustration and budget blowouts.

Agile approaches, on the other hand, set the stage for the delivery process to be *reality-driven* from the very beginning.

Continuous delivery of valuable outputs

The distinction between Agile approaches and prototyping is not limited to getting initial approval from the business owners. The nature of Agile approaches means that *each iteration* is able to present business owners with hands-on deliverables that they can confidently commit to, adjust, or decide not to progress.

The ***Outcomes** review* step of the ACTION plan is the point during each iteration where delivery teams are able to present the work that they have done to the business owners. It is also the time when business owners can ask detailed questions about the work presented. If the deliverable is a product (or a component of that product), the business owners can trial it at the review session – or ask for the session to be rescheduled, so that they have time to test it in detail. If the deliverable is a service (such as the customer service example in *Chapter 5: Responsive Planning*), business owners may request additional statistical information from the delivery team – or a hands-on tour of the facilities – before committing to additional work. No matter what is being delivered in the ACTION plan, the business owners reserve the right to gather all of the information needed, in order to determine the most valuable next steps for the organization (i.e. the ***N**ext iteration* step of the ACTION plan).

When the end does *not* justify the means

Previously in this section, the concept of *paper planning* was introduced, along with the pitfalls of making a large investment based on a "web profile" alone. What was not discussed was the challenge of having hands-on business outputs that convince business owners to take a *different approach* to what was agreed in the original plan.

In traditional business environments, the paper plan is the gospel. All activities and outputs are measured by how well they meet (or fail to meet) the original plan. There is rarely accommodation for reallocating funding (or resources) when what the business requires is *different to* what was projected in the original plan.

The delivery of hands-on business outputs throughout the iterative process provides business owners with the benefit of having *tangible evidence* that can show whether the work undertaken is bringing business value to the organization. It also has the potential to present business owners with a dilemma: how to advise executives when the hands-on business outputs indicate that the original plan they signed off needs to change.

The *When to walk away* section of *Chapter 5: Responsive Planning* advised that business owners always reserve the right to decide when they believe that the work undertaken by the delivery team has sufficiently achieved its original objectives (i.e. when no further iterations are required). However, enforcing that right could contradict the timeframes, budget allocations or goals in the original plan. Therefore, business owners need to have the confidence to do what is best for the organization – even if it means going back to the executives to adjust their expectations.

When hands-on business outputs indicate that ongoing work should be *put on hold*, the "sell" to the executives needs to focus on the ability for delivery team members to be reallocated to other high-priority work within the organization. The trade-off is that some of the outcomes that they had originally anticipated (e.g. *establish customer surveys to gather feedback*) will not be delivered.

When hands-on business outputs indicate that ongoing work should be *altered* from the originally agreed approach, the "sell" to executives needs to focus on why the alternative approach proposed will deliver greater business value to the organization, than the agreed approach in the original paper plan. Note that this may include presenting comparative delivery costs for both approaches as part of the business value assessment.

Either way, business owners should expect to have any proposal that "goes against the plan" to be challenged by executives. Accordingly, they should be prepared to support their decision with the tangible outputs produced through the Agile process (e.g. evidence of better call center service, or actual *versus* estimated time for each activity). They should also be prepared for intangible factors (such as the egos of those who established the original plan) to be a factor in the final decision.

The ideal situation, of course, would be to work within an organization that supports Agile approaches by:

- providing funding based on *strategic objectives* being achieved (not pre-defined outcomes)
- encouraging employees to present alternative approaches that can bring greater business value to the organization.

However, until your organization has reached this point of enlightenment, you may be faced with the challenge of seeking prior approval for proposed changes before the *Next iteration* step of the ACTION plan can be undertaken.

CHAPTER 8: REAL-TIME CUSTOMER FEEDBACK

Every audience is a customer

Throughout this book, the terms "business owners" and "customers" have been used almost interchangeably. In the traditional business environment, there is a significant difference between these terms:

- A "customer" is an external client. Customers are the ones who use your products and services. They provide the funding that drives your work. In many organizations (particularly commercial ones), they are the only ones that matter.
- A "business owner" is usually an internal staff member. They are a part of the organization, but their needs may not be considered as important as those of external customers.

In the Agile world, the terms "customer" and "business owner" are essentially the same.

The Agile world considers a customer to be *anyone* who needs you to deliver an outcome, whether they are external to the organization or sitting in the office next to yours. This is because the products and services that are delivered to the external customer are often the end result of a number of intermediary outputs within your organization. The sales department depends upon the promotional materials delivered by the marketing department; the finance department depends upon the delivery of products and services that can be invoiced; executives depend upon everyone in the organization to accurately report on their work, so that they can get a realistic understanding of the corporate status. Any break in this internal supply chain can result in delays, budget blowouts, poor quality deliverables and disappointed external customers. So, it is essential that each step in the internal supply chain runs as smoothly as the organization's outwardly facing activities.

The critical importance of the internal supply chain means that every activity in the Agile world is focused on the people who are intended to receive the outputs, regardless of whether they are the top client in your portfolio, the senior manager, or the packaging department two floors down. Failure to deliver high-value business outputs to the people within your organization can be just as damaging to its long-term viability as failure to meet external customer demand. The problem is that most organizations are happy to undertake market research to meet the needs of their external customers, but very few understand that meeting the needs of internal customers is just as important.

As *every* audience is a customer, this can also include people who work with the organization in other capacities (e.g. shareholders, suppliers, partners). It can also include people in the organization who represent the interests of those external stakeholders (e.g. customers, partners) who have a business requirement.

Agile approaches are designed to ensure that the delivery team works directly with any audience (internal or external) intended to receive the work that they are undertaking, to ensure that deliverables will fulfill their requirements. The critical distinction is determining who the end recipient of the work is – and understanding what they genuinely need.

The false security of market testing

Market testing is traditionally an outwardly facing activity that occurs at the beginning of the product (or service) development process. Organizations put significant finances into market research, prototypes, focus groups – all designed to ensure that the outputs of the organization will meet the needs of external customers. On paper, market testing appears to be a cost-effective way to gather critical customer feedback without committing significant development funds. It looks particularly compelling on presentation slides (especially when accompanied by colored pie charts and statistical graphs), but it is inherently flawed.

The limitations in market testing go well beyond its underlying design flaw as a process that is primarily intended to confirm (or negate) *pre-determined outcomes* (e.g. by presenting audiences with fixed choices for selection). The two real weaknesses in external market testing are:

- the lack of corresponding *internal market testing*
- the lack of *ongoing consultation* with the customer during the development process.

Internal market testing is working with the employees who are actually tasked with doing the proposed work to ensure that it is achievable. (When was the last time your marketing department took its market testing materials to the internal production staff that are required to deliver the outcomes?) There is little value in the organization getting extensive market testing feedback on a deliverable that cannot realistically (or cost effectively) be achieved.

Agile approaches are designed to ensure that the internal work that is required to produce these outputs is confirmed before work begins and reconfirmed throughout the delivery process.

Ongoing consultation with the customer is a critical component in confirming whether their original market testing feedback *continues to be valid* as the product or service is being developed. This is particularly important in light of the circumstances that are likely to have changed since the original market testing feedback was provided, including:

- customer needs maturing and changing
- development constraints affecting the translation of the conceptual design into the functional deliverable
- customers responding differently to the functional deliverable than they did to the conceptual one.

Agile approaches do not negate the need for customer feedback at the beginning of the design process; they see it as the first step in an *ongoing relationship* with the customer to confirm that the work being undertaken *continues* to meet their needs.

Intrinsic customer satisfaction

The only way to ensure that deliverables at the end of a process meet the expectations from the beginning of the process is to involve the internal or external customer (i.e. the business owners) *throughout* the process. The business owners will be the first to tell the delivery team whether a proposed capability will (or will not) add value to their work. In addition, no one is better placed to provide the delivery team with feedback on the outputs than the people who will be working with what is delivered. The most valuable aspect of the Agile process, however, is not its ability to give customers what they *want* (or even what they *need*). It is the ability to give customers what they *expect*.

Setting (and meeting) customer expectations is the most important part of the customer engagement process. This is not unlike your expectations when you schedule a doctor's visit. Anyone who has visited a doctor's office (particularly a medical specialist) has come to expect delays in the process. You walk in for a 2 pm appointment knowing that you will be lucky if the doctor sees you before 3 pm. You bring a newspaper to occupy your time in the waiting room. You tell the people at work that you will not be returning to the office until 4 pm at the earliest. You are pleasantly surprised when the doctor is able to see you at 2:45 pm.

Now, imagine that the same scenario occurs at your local restaurant during your lunch break. What if it took the waiter 25 minutes to take your order, and another 20 minutes to bring your food to the table? You would inevitably be frustrated with the service, concerned about getting back to the office in time, and likely not to return to that restaurant anytime soon. The same 45-minute wait that was a positive result in the doctor's office becomes a criticism of the restaurant's service. Same elapsed time: wholly different expectations.

Agile approaches set (and maintain) customer expectations by involving the business owners in every step of the process. Business owners are involved in the iteration planning session, where the delivery team identifies what they can (and cannot) achieve in the upcoming iteration (the ***T****ell us what can be done* step of the ACTION plan). This session is a two-way exchange of information between the business owners and the delivery team, resulting in customer expectations that reflect what the business owners want, combined with what the delivery team can reasonably achieve. The outcome of this session is a mutually agreed set of deliverables for the forthcoming iteration that both sets of attendees have agreed to. This means that the business owners walk away with *realistic expectations* for what they will be receiving at the end of each iteration.

Business owners are ideally also involved in the work during each iteration, providing input to the delivery team and reviewing interim deliverables as they are developed. Most importantly, business owners review the hands-on business outputs at the end of the iteration to identify where deliverables have – or have not – met their expectations. Based on this review, the business owners are able to identify the highest priorities for the delivery team to work on next. These are the ***O**utcomes review* and the ***N**ext iteration* steps of the ACTION plan, and they provide continuous confirmation to customers that ongoing work is aligned to their needs.

This collaborative approach leads to intrinsic customer satisfaction by establishing achievable goals that empower the delivery team to continually meet the expectations of the business owners.

The "expert by proxy" myth

In order for Agile approaches to work most effectively, business representatives with *accurate knowledge* of the business requirements need to be actively involved as business owners in the collaborative process. It is important to note that this is *not* a full-time commitment for the business owners. At a minimum, it involves four to eight hours of their time during each iteration to identify, prioritize and communicate requirements, and to be subsequently involved in the hands-on review of business outputs. Ideally, it also includes a few more hours of their involvement, during the iteration, to work with the delivery team as needed. However, even in the more collaborative model, their involvement should not take up more than 10-20% of their time.

In some situations, the representative with the most relevant business knowledge is immediately obvious. (In which case, the challenge is often organizing their availability, as discussed in the *Hiring a customer* section that follows.)

In other situations, it can be difficult to identify any one person with sufficient knowledge to represent the interests of all of the business areas that require the deliverables; or to get a representative with a sufficient breadth and depth of knowledge to adequately reflect the full spectrum of the business requirements.

At this point, the organization needs to make a critical business decision before the Agile approach can begin:

- adjust priorities and workloads so that one (or more) knowledgeable staff members can jointly participate as business owners
- hire a highly qualified business analyst to represent the requirements of the business owners, with the expectation that the business areas will be available to work hands on with the business analyst for up to two hours a week
- postpone the work required until knowledgeable staff members (or highly qualified representatives) are

available to participate to the degree required for the Agile approach to be successful.

One approach that is strongly discouraged is using the delivery team members as representatives on behalf of the business areas (i.e. "experts by proxy"). This is detrimental to the process on two levels: (1) because the delivery team rarely has the level of in-depth knowledge about the business requirements that the business areas do (and having decisions made based on high-level business knowledge alone can be a risky and costly substitute for the organization); (2) because the delivery team's involvement in the work undertaken reduces their objectivity in reviewing the outputs and determining the next priorities.

Another approach that is strongly discouraged is using less qualified representatives from the business area (e.g. junior staff members) simply because they are more likely to be available than the more experienced staff. The same caveat about having high-level business knowledge alone also applies in this circumstance, as does knowing the procedures of the business area without fully understanding the business context of the work.

Finally, if the organization decides to pursue the option of using a business analyst as the representative for the business area, it is important to make the distinction between highly qualified business analysts and "requirements recycler" business analysts. A highly qualified business analyst takes the time to truly understand the needs of the business, questions and critiques the input from the business representatives, and critically reviews the hands-on outputs from each iteration on behalf of the business areas. A "requirements recycler" business analyst records the requirements from the business areas exactly as stated, repeats these requirements verbatim in the iteration planning sessions, and describes the hands-on outputs from each iteration to the business areas for their input (versus providing direct feedback to the delivery team at the review session). This not only adds little value to the Agile approach, it could actually add significant delays, resource overheads and miscommunication to the process. Therefore, unless the person tasked with representing the business areas is a highly qualified business analyst[38], it is recommended that the organization either adjusts priorities to free up the required resources or postpones the work.

The only way that the Agile approach can be truly effective is by directly involving business owners (or their highly qualified representatives) who truly understand the requirements, who are able to accurately communicate these requirements to the delivery team, and who are positioned (and authorized) to make priority decisions on behalf of the organization.

Hiring a customer

As mentioned in the previous section, finding sufficiently knowledgeable business representatives to act as the business owners can be a challenge; finding time in their schedules for them to participate in the process can take a miracle.

Not surprisingly, the people in the organization which are the most knowledgeable are often the ones who are the

---

[38] For more information on the benefits of working with a business analyst on Agile projects, refer to The Power of the Agile Business Analyst, http://www.itgovernanceusa.com/shop/p-1379-the-power-of-the-agile-business-analyst.aspx#.Uwpw2s4xgqY

most in demand. They are usually so busy with their current workloads that they are reluctant to commit to the added time that the Agile approach may require, even if it is only four to eight hours each month. (The irony is that the majority of work that is taking up their time is likely to be the result of inefficient traditional business practices, e.g. paper productivity work).

As difficult as it is to find internal representatives with available time to work on the Agile team, it is even more challenging finding *external* customers with the required levels of availability; especially where your organization's customers are physically distributed across the country – or around the world.

Note that business owner participation can be through face-to-face meetings or, where distance is a factor, by web meetings and videoconferencing. (*See Chapter 11: "Just-in-time" Communication* for the importance of Agile meetings involving real-time interaction, instead of endless e-mails and extensive documentation.)

In order for the Agile process to work, an alternative arrangement needs to be put into place that enables the most knowledgeable business representatives (internal or external) to participate in the process. One possible approach is to "hire" a business representative by either:

- "Selling" the value of their involvement as the benefits that they will receive by participating in the process, such as control over determining the highest-priority work and hands-on review of the outputs. (This is often an easier sell once the exceptional cost-benefit return of Agile approaches is better understood across the organization.)

- Negotiating with internal and external resources for their time. This can include resource sharing, so that the person volunteering their time gets the benefit of one or two members of the delivery team to do other work in their area.
- Making financial (or other arrangements) with external customers to compensate for their time. (This is similar in concept to the costs associated with market testing, and can return far more value to the organization.)

Once business areas begin to understand the benefits that they will receive by participating in the Agile process, getting the involvement of a qualified business owner becomes a much less arduous task. Initially, however, delivery teams (or their managers) may need to hone their negotiation and persuasion skills to convince the most qualified resources to participate.

Using the customer to manage your budget

One of the most difficult challenges in the traditional business environment is effective budget management, particularly as the amount budgeted for an initiative is often:

- identified at the beginning of the process (i.e. before the actual work is undertaken)
- fixed throughout the duration of the process
- based on a combination of previous budget allocations (e.g. adding 10% to last year's budget) and/or educated guesswork.

This means that the same issues that plague upfront planning (*see Chapter 5: Responsive Planning*) equally plague upfront budgeting. This is why organizations need to shift their expenditure model to *responsive budgeting*.

Responsive budgeting is not a new concept in the business world. It has been defined as everything from daily budget adjustments to annual budget reviews based on the actual expenditures in the previous financial year. However, the Agile world takes a different approach to responsive budgeting by empowering customers to control ongoing expenditures, based on the *business value* that they expect to receive.

In Agile approaches, the business owner "manages" the expenditures of the delivery team at each iteration by determining:

- How much work is to be undertaken in each subsequent iteration, including whether the delivery team needs to be supplemented, maintained or reduced based on the amount of work that they are able to commit to in the upcoming iteration. For example, if the delivery team advises that meeting the business owner's desired level of productivity in the forthcoming iteration requires additional resources, the business owner is able to determine whether the business value of the additional work justifies the cost of adding staff to the team.
- Whether work should continue in the next iteration altogether. At the end of each iteration, business owners reserve the right to determine that sufficient work has been undertaken by the delivery team (or that the level of expected business value is not being achieved) and to make the decision to end – or postpone – any ongoing Agile work for that initiative.

- Whether budgeted resources should be *reallocated* to other work (including other delivery teams) that would bring greater business value to the organization.

Using the Agile approach discourages people in the organization from fully expending a budgeted amount simply because it was allocated. (This is especially important where the efficiencies of Agile approaches result in significant under-utilization of the allocated budget.) Agile approaches encourage people to think beyond the work that has been assigned to them in favor of the work that can bring the greatest benefit to the organization. This can reduce "empire-building" mindsets where staff hoard their budgets for fear of losing them in the future. However, it requires an organizational climate that encourages and rewards effective budget utilization.

Making the decision to reduce a delivery team for a subsequent iteration is generally easier than supplementing the delivery team, especially where the additional resources required are in another area of the organization (or are absolutely overwhelmed with their current workload). It is for this reason that Agile approaches encourage a *moderate* amount of planning ahead to reduce the potential that required resources will not be available. This means that the outcomes review session should include a quick review of those goals and activities that are being considered for future iterations (i.e. those "below the line"), to predict where a particular resource or skill set may be required in the next two to three months. The ongoing work for each iteration will confirm (or negate) whether the predicted resources are actually required. However, if these predicted resources are needed, the staff members (and their managers) will have been given a reasonable amount of preparation time beforehand.

So, how does the Agile approach work in an organization that is based upon predetermined annual budget allocations and fixed funding models? Can responsive budgeting be applied where the amount budgeted will not change over the financial year? The answer is a qualified yes.

If the organizational environment mandates a fixed, immovable budget amount for each scheduled activity in the organization, then the aim of the business owner is to use Agile approaches to maximize the *business-value* return for the allocated funds. This may involve making upfront decisions on the number of iterations (and the quantity of delivery team resources) that can be supported by the allocated budget – and then maximizing the value-added work of these resources for each iteration. Tools for calculating the number of iterations and delivery team resources that are available within an allocated budget amount are provided in *Section 4: Making Agile Work in Your Organization.*

Working within a fixed budget amount may mean that there are insufficient funds to achieve everything that the organization would like (as is generally the case with budget allocations). Unlike traditional business environments, however, the very nature of Agile approaches can guarantee that the limited budget available will not be squandered on work that brings little value to the organization.

CHAPTER 9: IMMOVABLE DEADLINES

Why you should *never* move a deadline

New Year's Eve celebrations provide a fascinating study in human perseverance. Every year, cities prepare for these events months (sometimes years) in advance of the December 31st deadline. They know that it is a fixed, timeframe, a deadline that cannot change.

In most cases, the New Year's Eve event coordinators aim to present something even more spectacular than the year before – despite inevitable increases in the costs of materials, equipment and security. It is a daunting challenge for them to accomplish in a relatively limited timeframe. So, they hold planning sessions, allocate tasks to teams, acquire sub-contractors (e.g. fireworks technicians) and map out all of the activities that will be required for the New Year's Eve celebrations to be a success.

Inevitably, no matter how well they prepare, there are always last minute changes, mishaps and unforeseen delays. (No amount of planning can avoid the unexpected.) Yet, by the night of December 31st, the celebration commences with cheering crowds and news cameras rolling, despite all of the hurdles that were encountered. The coordinators know that there is no choice – the event must go ahead on the scheduled date – and somehow, it always does.

It is the immovable nature of New Year's Eve celebrations that forces the organizers to do *whatever they have to* in order to meet this timeframe. In some cases, this means scoping down the preparation work in order to make it achievable, especially as the deadline gets closer. In other cases, it means supplementing the staff with other resources who can assist when the work gets overwhelming. Everyone involved in the process knows that the timeframe cannot be changed, so they do whatever else is needed to ensure that they are ready to go on the scheduled date. That is the power of the immovable deadline.

Organizations regularly deal with immovable deadlines in the form of compliance due dates (e.g. tax returns), publicized product launch dates and staff departure dates. These deadlines represent commitments for the organization that, in many cases, are (or become) beyond the organization's control. This means that staff members must do everything within their power to ensure that the work required to meet these organizational commitments is completed by the deadline.

What about ongoing business activities that are not tied to a fixed date commitment, such as promotional activities, customer service initiatives and continuous improvement work? How do you prevent these activities from being postponed indefinitely in favor of work that staff members consider to be more urgent? You create accountability by replacing "flexible" work with fixed time commitments for *all* critical organizational activities, and you ensure that staff members *truly* see these fixed time commitments as immovable deadlines.

Immovable deadlines bring a sense of urgency to work that flexible deadlines lack. It is human nature for people to focus on work that has a committed timeframe over work that can be completed "when time allows." Staff members quickly learn to differentiate between truly urgent work (immovable deadlines) and somewhat urgent work (movable deadlines). This includes timeframes that were originally defined as immovable deadlines, but were able to be changed over time to accommodate other competing resource commitments. Once staff members realize that deadlines – even "immovable" deadlines – are flexible, these activities will be relegated to roughly the same category as "when time allows" work. This means that these deadlines become, in effect, "toothless tigers" in the corporate environment.

Project management literature would classify the immovable deadline as a fixed constraint in the classic "project management triangle" of scope, time and costs/resources. They would argue that immovable deadlines force the duration of work to be fixed, therefore, if a project is in jeopardy, the only options available to the team are:

- decreasing the project scope, or
- increasing the project budget/resources

in order to meet the required timeframe.[39]

What these project management texts generally fail to recognize is that immovable deadlines often have an incredibly powerful emotional impact on a delivery team, more than budget or scope constraints. Team members can disassociate themselves from a fixed budget by rationalizing it as a "management" issue. They can even disassociate themselves from a fixed scope by reasoning that, in a worst-case scenario, activities can be cut down or improvised. In contrast, fixed timeframes are non-negotiable; you cannot change the calendar.

---

[39] It should be noted that some project management texts recognize quality as a fourth constraint, i.e. teams can opt to keep the same scope and budget with the same deadline, but produce a lower quality result.

This is why immovable deadlines can have an extraordinarily unifying effect on a delivery team (not dissimilar to having a shared enemy). Passing time presents a constant reminder of what work has (and has not yet) been completed. Looming deadlines allow everyone on the team to be continually focused on a shared goal. Moreover, because of the team's unified focus, management can be reasonably assured that *something of value* will be delivered by the team in the agreed timeframe.

The power of immovable deadlines is why Agile approaches structure work to be undertaken and delivered in *fixed time iterations* with *immovable review sessions* at the end of each iteration. These immovable deadlines can ensure that activities *do not* get put on the back burner in favor of work that is perceived by staff to be more urgent. They are equally designed to ensure that the outcomes review session at the end of each iteration is *not* a movable feast that can be continually postponed in favor of other priorities. In the Agile world, immovable deadlines create a continuous reminder for the delivery team and a sense of urgency that flexible (i.e. movable) deadlines do not provide.

For the customer service example described in *Chapter 5: Responsive Planning* the immovable deadline of the four-week iteration meant that the delivery team could not – and did not – spend infinite amounts of time analyzing options for improving customer service. Knowing that they had a commitment to deliver results in four weeks forced the delivery team to organize themselves quickly. They understood that any new or changed initiatives proposed would need to be in a production setting for at least a week before the outcomes review session, in order for statistical information to be gathered. Having this fixed commitment prevented the organization from entering the endless spiral of meetings and discussions to weigh options. The "Apply, Inspect, Adapt" nature of Agile approaches also meant that other stakeholders in the organization (such as the customer service team) were more compelled to participate in this work, instead of continually rescheduling in favor of other activities.

It is important to note that the Agile approach of enforcing immovable deadlines in iterations does not mean that delivery teams perceive their work to take absolute precedence over other activities in the organization. In fact, Agile approaches are able to accommodate any higher priority requirements of the organization that may arise during an iteration – even if it means that the entire delivery team needs to be temporarily reallocated to other work. (See *When priorities change* in *Chapter 6: Business-value-driven Work* for further details on the options available for Agile teams to accommodate higher priority work in the organization.)

In those rare circumstances where some (or all) of the delivery team members have to be reallocated to more urgent work during the course of an iteration, the outcomes review session and next iteration planning work always take place as scheduled. No matter how much (or how little) work is achieved in an iteration, it is important to hold these sessions in order to maintain the ongoing momentum of the team.

From a distance, the enforcement of immovable deadlines in an organization may appear to create a rigid and unyielding environment for employees. Surprisingly, however, people generally appreciate the structure of delivering outcomes within fixed timeframes far more than managing endless "when time allows" commitments. Immovable deadlines create an environment where staff members are compelled to deliver valuable outputs regularly. This gives them an ongoing sense of satisfaction in seeing meaningful results from the work that they do. It also creates a sense of purpose that can motivate people to continue delivering results. *See Chapter 10: Management by Self-motivation* for further information on creating organizational environments that encourage employee productivity.

The power of imminent timeframes

Agile approaches not only enforce immovable deadlines, they deliberately structure these deadlines to be in *two- to four-week iterations*. This creates a working environment where the next deadline for required work is never more than a month away. Not only does this encourage staff members to deliver regular ongoing value to the organization, it creates a sense of urgency for the work that they do by establishing *imminent timeframes* for delivery.

Long-term deadlines are easy for people to ignore. They create a climate where work can be easily postponed, or rescheduled in favor of more urgent activities. Imminent timeframes, on the other hand, compel people to *take action*. It is the basic psychological principle that underlies "limited time offers" in marketing campaigns. It is why (most) people organize to send out their Christmas cards by December 21st – and continue shopping for presents until December 24th. Imminent timeframes create an urgency in people's minds that keeps commitments at the forefront of their thoughts. The imminent timeframes in Agile approaches are strategically designed to ensure that required work is either actively addressed – or deliberately delayed in favor of more critical priorities in the organization – but *never* ignored.

More important than staying prominent in people's minds, however, is the fact that imminent timeframes leave *no time to waste* in order to achieve the required outcomes. As explained in the customer service example, short-term deadlines mean that delivery team members do not have the luxury of endless weeks to contemplate what should (or should not) be done. Everything about the shortened timeframe encourages:

- business owners and delivery team members to propose *achievable solutions* at the iteration planning session
- delivery team members to meet *directly after* the iteration planning session to determine what *specific tasks* are needed in order for the required work to be achieved in the few weeks available for the iteration
- delivery team members to break down tasks that cannot reasonably be achieved in the iteration timeframe into smaller sub-tasks that can be achieved. For example, it may not be realistic for the delivery team to undertake comprehensive testing of the new sales report in the time available, but basic quality checks can be done
- delivery team members to hold *five-minute* "stand-up meetings" every day to *quickly* review required work and address any hurdles (*see Chapter 11: "Just-in-time" Communication* for further information on stand-up meetings).

The combination of imminent timeframes and immovable deadlines in Agile approaches means that delivery teams can prepare themselves for the workload; they can pace themselves to meet the agreed timeframe; they know what to expect when they come in to the office each day; and they are generally able to *self-manage* to ensure that work is achieved without requiring excessive overtime or weekend work.

Interestingly, it also means that delivery team members are somewhat insulated from the pressure of the "fire-fighting" activities and last-minute deadlines that plague most organizations. The same commitment that has delivery team members organizing themselves to deliver regular value to the organization each iteration, also binds the organization to avoid distracting these employees from their work unless it is absolutely necessary.

If imminent timeframes are so powerful, why not complete iterations and hold outcomes review sessions on a *weekly* basis? Agile approaches appreciate that delivery teams need sufficient time to accomplish required work before they can be in a position to bring valuable results to outcomes review sessions. For most activities in an organization, a week would not provide the delivery team with enough time to organize key stakeholders, take action on their input and measure their results.

Could your organization design a new sales report; gather, manipulate and populate the required information in the report; test the information in the report for accuracy; review the new report with key stakeholders (e.g. sales executives); and present the outcomes of this work in a five-day period? If so, your organization is either extraordinarily efficient or lucky enough to have exceptional corporate reporting systems. For most organizations, however, these activities would take at least two to three weeks – and more – even with the most dedicated and focused delivery team. That is why Agile approaches deliberately discourage meetings that are too frequent for attendees to be able to provide (or receive) valuable input (*see Chapter 11: "Just-in-time" Communication* for further differentiation between valuable meetings and time-wasting meetings).

It should be noted that some organizations prefer to structure their Agile work in *two-week iterations*. This preference could be due to:

- the nature of the industry (e.g. if quicker turnaround times are needed to retain a competitive advantage)
- the nature of the work (e.g. requiring more frequent approvals from business owners for work to progress)
- the organizational climate, particularly where Agile approaches are relatively new to the organization, and management wants to confirm whether or not they are effective.

Structuring Agile work in two-week iterations is a perfectly valid option for organizations, as long as they understand the limitations of what a delivery team can *reasonably* achieve in such a short timeframe. Expecting four weeks' worth of business value in a two-week timeframe is both unrealistic for the organization and unfair to employees. Imminent timeframes are intended to encourage employees to self-organize and work towards a shared goal; not to burn out from the pressure and resign.

Early delivery means early payback

In *Chapter 7: Hands-on Business Outputs*, the distinction was made between prototyping and functional deliverables. Prototypes are mock-ups of deliverables that are designed to give customers a feel for what they might look like (and how they might behave). Functional deliverables are *actual* products and services (such as a sales report with real production information) that can often be used by the organization *immediately* after the outcomes review session for real day-to-day work.

One significant benefit to having regular immovable deadlines is that organizations that use Agile approaches can often immediately utilize the functional deliverables that result from each fixed time iteration. This means that the organization is regularly in a position to realize the return on their investment sooner than business activities would normally deliver (e.g. business-value outputs every month *versus* every six months). Additionally, the imperative of meeting an immovable deadline means that this business value is not postponed indefinitely in favor of other competing activities.

The regular delivery of production-ready outputs through Agile approaches provides another significant benefit for the organization. Even if Agile work is postponed or cancelled after a few iterations, the organization can continue to get business value from the functional deliverables that were produced in the initial iterations.

Let's consider, for example, that an Agile team is put together to develop 12 new reports that will assist the executive office in analyzing corporate productivity. In the first four-week iteration, the team delivers two complete reports that contain actual statistics comparing the productivity levels of each department against agreed organizational KPIs. The executives immediately add these reports to their regular monthly updates.

In the next four-week iteration, the Agile team expands on their previous work by delivering three new reports that include comparative information against the productivity levels of like organizations in the industry. Again, the executives are in a position to immediately include these reports in their regular monthly updates.

The following week, however, the marketing department advises that they need the delivery team to undertake some urgent market analysis in time for a scheduled product launch. The executive office agrees to postpone the development of the seven remaining reports, so that the delivery team can focus on the more urgent requirement.

In a traditional business environment, stopping an initiative after two months generally means that the work undertaken up to that point is filed away until a future time when the work is resurrected (if ever). In many cases, this half-completed work sits indefinitely on a network drive (or in a filing cabinet) until it is moved into an archive. Worse still, by the time the initiative is resurrected, the amount of time that has passed may make the work obsolete.

In an Agile environment, stopping an initiative after two months means that the organization gets eight weeks' worth of valuable deliverables. This means that the executive office gets five fully functional reports that they can continue to use, even if the reporting initiative is never resumed. It may not be the full set of reports that the executives originally envisioned, but five fully functional reports are far better than twelve report mock-ups (or a scoping paper that analyzes how this work might be done, along with a detailed project plan).

The final benefit to having regular immovable deadlines is that business owners are in a position to stop work that is not delivering sufficient business value *before* significant revenue is expended. Frequent checkpoints enable Agile work to be regularly self-correcting, instead of allowing non-valuable work to continue indefinitely without accountability.

Setting the next deadline

As indicated, the iterations in an Agile approach can be scheduled in two-, three- or four-week cycles. It is up to each organization (and, in some cases, each Agile team) to determine the optimal duration for their iterative work.

To assist in the selection of optimal delivery timeframes, Agile teams need to consider two primary factors:

- the rate of productivity for the delivery team
- the complexity of the work being undertaken, including both the nature of the work itself and the availability of key stakeholders.

Determining the rate of productivity for a delivery team is based on a combination of two key measurements in the Agile world: *Yesterday's weather* and *velocity*.

Yesterday's weather is a record of the historical rate of productivity for the *same delivery team* doing work with an *equivalent level of complexity*. For example, a delivery team that was previously able to create a print-ready marketing brochure in three weeks can reasonably assume that it will take them approximately the same amount of time to create the next marketing brochure of an equivalent size.

It should be noted that the measurement of yesterday's weather is not a precise science; just an approximation of the degree of productivity that the organization can reasonably expect from this team in the equivalent circumstances. If external factors change, such as reducing the number of people on the delivery team – or even *replacing* someone who has been working on the team with a new resource – the yesterday's weather measurements need to be adjusted to include these changing circumstances in the calculations. Yesterday's weather is the primary measurement for determining a delivery team's historical *velocity*.

Velocity measures the rate of productivity for a delivery team by tracking how much of the work for an iteration has been completed, and how much work is outstanding. This becomes both a tool for teams to monitor and measure their own levels of productivity, as well as an indication of their ideal delivery pace for scheduling future iterations. Like yesterday's weather, a delivery team's velocity will vary depending on a number of factors, including the nature and complexity of the work required, and the availability of stakeholders when needed. *Chapter 12: Immediate Status Tracking* provides further detail on the use of velocity as a measurement for delivery teams; *Section 4: Making Agile Work in Your Organization* provides tools that can be used to track the velocity of the delivery team's work in an iteration.

Determining the *relative complexity* of the work being undertaken (as compared with equivalent historical work) can be a more difficult undertaking. External factors, such as stakeholder availability, can significantly vary depending on their other commitments, their scheduled vacation leave, even their level of interest in the deliverables. This is why determining the potential rate of productivity for a delivery team is usually only a reasonable estimation. The actual rate of productivity for a delivery team is best measured by a combination of their velocity and their daily updates (*see*

Chapter 11: "Just-in-time" Communication for details on how delivery teams use daily stand-up meetings to track and progress their work).

Using yesterday's weather and velocity measurements enables each Agile team to base their selection of the optimal iteration timeframe on their delivery track record. Factoring in the complexity of the work being undertaken allows the team to reasonably adjust the duration where planned work is much more (or less) time-consuming. In some cases, Agile teams may vary the duration of each iteration as part of the ***O**utcomes review* and the ***N**ext iteration* steps of the ACTION plan.

For example, an Agile team that normally schedules iterations every four weeks may jointly decide that the highest-priority work required for the next iteration should not require more than two weeks to be completed. In this circumstance, the Agile team may agree to either reduce the forthcoming iteration to a two-week duration, or to add more priority work to that iteration in order to maintain consistency and the team's optimal delivery pace in a four-week iteration. At any point in time in these sessions, it is at the Agile team's discretion to determine how long it will reasonably take the delivery team to produce outputs that will provide genuine business value to the organization.

CHAPTER 10: MANAGEMENT BY SELF-MOTIVATION

"I'm not going to do it – and you can't make me"

Employee motivation is an incredibly difficult thing to quantify, let alone influence. There are some employees who are extraordinarily self-motivated; no matter what circumstance they are put in, they always find a way to be challenged by (and be productive in) their work. Conversely, there are employees who cannot be motivated to do even the simplest tasks without heavy supervision or substantial rewards. For most organizations, employees fall within the spectrum of these two extremes, with management forever searching for ways to move them in the direction of self-motivation.

One factor that inevitably influences the level of employee motivation is the work environment. Common sense dictates that organizations that distrust their employees, provide little recognition or reward for their work, and discourage staff initiative are breeding grounds for disgruntled employees and high turnover; whereas organizations that encourage and support their employees, maximize the utilization of their skills, and give them opportunities to succeed are likely to attract (and retain) highly self-motivated employees who genuinely care about their work and the welfare of the organization overall.

So, how do Agile approaches help organizations create an environment that encourages employee self-motivation? By creating an environment that combines the best features of top-down and bottom-up management styles with the power of self-organized teams.

The top-down and bottom-up management myths

The top-down management style of dictating what work needs to be done – and expecting employees to do the stated work, simply based on management's orders, is based on several false assumptions:

Top-down management myths

- **Myth 1: Employees in the 21st century are willing to "take orders" without challenging them.** As each younger generation joins the workforce, the notion of blindly obeying authority becomes more and more antiquated. There are exceptions (such as the highly structured management style of the military), but employees in private and public sector organizations tend to expect a more collaborative management style.
- **Myth 2: Management alone knows what is best for the organization.** Management generally has the experience (and access to information) that can provide them with greater insight into the big picture of the organization than most employees, but lower-level employees have a level of insight from being on the "coalface" of the organization that management rarely gets to experience. It is counter-productive (even foolhardy) for management to minimize the value of input from the people who actually do the work.
- **Myth 3: Employees will understand exactly what management needs based on an initial conversation, an e-mail or a memo.** Giving employees skeletal information about the organization's requirements – and assuming that no ongoing input from management is required – is a recipe for miscommunication and low business-value outputs. It is also a virtual guarantee that

rework will be required in the future, costing the organization two to three times the original amount for management to receive what they had originally envisaged.

There is another more subtle factor hidden in the top-down management myth: the correlation between receiving management orders and employee self-motivation. The less involved employees are in controlling the work that they do, the less motivated they are likely to be to want to do it (or do it to a high level of quality). Receiving management orders as irrefutable mandates can make an employee feel valueless, even *trapped* in their work, which can make them resent both their jobs and their employers. It is also likely to make them focus on giving the *appearance* of productivity (in order to appease management), instead of focusing on adding real business value to the organization.

Equally damaging is the bottom-up management style of empowering employees to unilaterally make key decisions on behalf of the organization, based on their hands-on knowledge of the work required. ("No one knows what the customer needs better than the people who work with them day to day"). This logic is similarly faulty to the one-sided perspective that underpins the top-down management myths.

Bottom-up management myths

- **Myth 1: As employees are in the "coalface" they understand the requirements of the organization better than management.** Most employees do have a more realistic understanding of the operations of the organization than their managers. What they generally lack, however, is a big picture understanding of all of the other facets that can influence corporate decisions, including cross-departmental work, industry drivers and market trends.

- **Myth 2: Decision by consensus is more meaningful than decision by management.** Decision by consensus is wonderful in theory – and a logistical (and strategic) nightmare in practice. On a purely practical level, is the amount of work that is required to get everyone involved in a corporate decision familiar with all of the implications of each option available (which is one of the key reasons why countries choose to use a government-by-representation model). On a strategic level, there are often hard decisions that management must make for the greater good of the organization. Deciding to reduce (or eliminate) a product line based on diminishing market demand may not be a popular decision, but it could be a necessary one for the long-term survival of the organization.

Bottom-up management styles may have less of a detrimental effect on the motivation level of the employees, but they can result in significant damage to the organization overall.

The problem with top-down and bottom-up management styles is that they are based on extremes; either give all of the authority to management or give all of the authority to the employees. Agile approaches take a middle ground between the two management styles by empowering the delivery team (employees) to do the work required under the guidance and oversight of the business owners (management).[40]

The power of self-organized teams

The following quote from General George S. Patton, Jr. is an amazing testament to the power of self-organized teams:

> Never tell people how to do things. Tell them what to do and they will surprise you with their ingenuity.

Even in a military environment, General Patton understood the value of directing his troops and then trusting them to get the job done. Agile approaches are based upon the same underlying premise of both guiding and empowering people in order to get the most value from their work.

Chapter 5: Responsive Planning identified the first three core steps in the ACTION plan as:

- *Actionable goals* where business owners break down their strategic objectives into smaller actionable business goals and communicate these goals to the delivery team.
- *Communicating priorities* where business owners identify their highest-priority business goals (i.e. those that require the most immediate action).
- ***T****ell us what can be done* where the delivery team advises the business owners on how much high-priority work they can reasonably deliver in that iteration.

The ***A****ctionable goals* and ***C****ommunicating priorities* steps of the ACTION plan are where business owners manage

---

[40] This is not a literal metaphor, as the members of the delivery team generally report to their operational managers, not the business owners. But it draws a parallel between business-driven and staff-driven approaches to work.

and guide the work that is required by the organization. They set the goals. They assign the priorities. They advise the delivery team on *what* needs to be accomplished, but not *how* the work will be done. They understand that no one is in a better position than the delivery team to identify the work required, to assign an estimated time for each task, and to assess the amount of work that they can realistically achieve in the iteration, given their current workload and other commitments.

The ***T****ell us what can be done* step of the ACTION plan is where the delivery team is empowered to determine what work they are willing (and able) to commit to over the course of the iteration. They estimate work (and their own velocity) based on their intimate knowledge of the team's strengths and weaknesses. This not only provides the Agile team with a realistic path forward for the iteration, it gives the members of the delivery team a sense of control over their own destiny. Their direct involvement in the decision-making process motivates them to want to achieve the work they have committed to – and, because they were part of the decision, they feel personally responsible for the outcomes.

Interestingly, there is another benefit to self-organizing teams that is generally not available through top-down management styles: natural skills and strengths compensation. When delivery teams are empowered to produce outcomes, they tend to divide and conquer the work required based on the relative skills and strengths of each team member. This no longer becomes an ego-building exercise of individuals taking on work to impress management. Nor does it become a "that's not my job" mindset of passing responsibility from one team member to another. Because successful delivery is the responsibility of the team *as a whole*, delivery team members regularly work between themselves to assign work to the most appropriate and/or most available person. They avoid pigeon-holing themselves into exclusive roles in favor of doing whatever the team needs in order to get the job done. This may mean that the marketing specialist on the team needs to analyze data on prospective customers one day, clean up a reporting spreadsheet the next morning and contact the business owners with questions that afternoon. Although each team member is primarily focused on doing the work that aligns to their strengths, they are equally available to take on other roles in the team as needed.

Giving the team a higher purpose

One of the biggest differences between employees in a traditional business environment and those in an Agile environment is that the delivery team's focus is generally not on "doing a task," but on "achieving an outcome" for the organization.

The delivery team's direct involvement with the business owners in the iteration planning session allows them to truly understand how the work that they are doing fits into the overall needs of the organization. It allows them to think strategically about each task and its implications, and to recommend better alternative approaches where needed. This enables the iteration planning session to become a two-way interaction between the people who genuinely understand the needs of the organization and the people who intimately know the complexities of the work.

Employees who are able to see the organizational value in their work may also be more motivated, simply because it makes the work that they do more meaningful than the individual tasks that are assigned to them. They get the satisfaction of working directly with the business areas that benefit from their work. They are empowered to influence the future of the organization.

In my estimation …

One of the most motivating aspects of the ***T****ell us what can be done* step of the ACTION plan is the fact that it empowers the delivery team to decide how much work they can reasonably achieve in the upcoming iteration. In traditional business environments, work is generally delegated to staff with a fixed deadline set by management ("we need the completed report by the end of this month"). In the Agile environment, the organization defers to the delivery team to determine what the team believes is a realistic and achievable timeframe. Not only does this show trust in (and respect for) the delivery team members, it enables them to realize that their input and their expertise *matter* to the organization.

Empowering the delivery team to estimate the work required to achieve an outcome also puts a responsibility on the team to make their estimates as accurate as possible. If the delivery team overestimates the amount of work that they can accomplish in an iteration, they set the stage for under-delivery and business owner disappointment (or, equally damaging, for overworked and burnt out team members). If the delivery team underestimates the amount of work that they can accomplish, business owners will begin to doubt the accuracy of their ongoing estimates – or see reduced business value in their ongoing work – which also undermines the shared trust that drives the Agile team.

Delivery team members are encouraged to use information from previous iterations (yesterday's weather) and ongoing metrics from the current iteration (velocity) to establish and maintain realistic estimates of the work required for each iteration. They are also equally motivated to ensure that their daily levels of productivity align with the estimates that they provided.

Trusting the team

In many traditional organizations, empowering employees to self-manage is a difficult challenge for management. Many managers were trained in corporate environments that fostered an "us and them" mentality between management and staff members. So, it is hard for them to believe that employees can – and will – get the job done without their constant supervision. In their minds, it is safer to keep close tabs on the employees, in order to ensure that they are working hard and that work is being done correctly.

What these managers fail to realize is the incredible motivational power of entrusting a person with a responsibility, particularly one that they were able to influence. (It is the emotional equivalent of the first time that parents hand the keys to the family car to their teenager.) This does not mean that every employee is able to handle this responsibility equally (in the same way that not every teenager takes the same level of care with the family car), but *most* employees will thrive amazingly well in an environment that empowers them to influence and manage the work that they do.

Agile approaches entrust the delivery team to do the work required during the course of the iteration, in order to achieve the outcomes that were agreed in the iteration planning meeting. Business owners are encouraged to be involved in the delivery process as advisers and reviewers of work undertaken by the delivery team, but they are *not* there to oversee the work. This independence allows the delivery team to become self-managing in their work, pacing themselves against the activities that need to be completed in the short iteration timeframe.

Along with the independence that accompanies Agile approaches, comes a responsibility for the delivery team to communicate with the organization regarding the status of their work. Delivery teams use team management tools such as *delivery backlogs* and *burndown charts* to provide the organization with status information regarding their work. *See Chapter 12: Immediate Status Tracking* for further detail on the use of these tools.

These tools can be made available to anyone in the organization with an interest in the delivery team's work; which means that business owners, operational managers and executives are able to get a daily update on the work that the delivery team has accomplished, along with an understanding of what work is remaining.

As long as the delivery team continues to produce the required results in each iteration (including providing reasonably accurate estimates in the iteration planning meeting), the organization can confidently continue to entrust the team to self-manage. Furthermore, because delivery teams realize that this authority is contingent upon their ongoing production of valuable outputs, they continually strive to deliver work that meets the requirements of the organization.

Why shorter deadlines lead to happier employees

The power of imminent timeframes section in *Chapter 9: Immovable Deadlines* described the value of organizing work to be delivered in shorter timeframes. Imminent timeframes create a sense of urgency that longer deadlines lack. Delivery team members become more focused on valuable outputs than paper productivity (e.g. status reports). Shorter deadlines allow employees to see the results of their efforts more quickly, which can create a momentum that encourages them to continue producing valuable outcomes for the organization. They provide employees with a sense of real accomplishment and progress.

The Agile world understands that shorter deadlines can provide a strong motivational environment for employees. In the ACTION plan, delivery team members are able to see the value that they are bringing to the organization through regular review sessions with business owners. The positive feedback that can come from the outcomes review sessions encourages the members of the team to continue producing value (unlike the 12-month gap between annual reviews). Even constructive criticism in these sessions gives the delivery team members a path forward to progress their work without feeling as though they have wasted months of effort.

It is important to recognize that simply setting shorter deadlines in an organization, without including the other facets of Agile approaches, does not provide a sufficiently motivating environment (and, in fact, may have the opposite effect). Employees are motivated by a *combination* of shorter deadlines with achievable tasks and regular feedback. The Agile world encourages realistic goals for each iteration to ensure that delivery team members can feel a sense of *accomplishment* at the outcomes review sessions, not burnout.

The end of overtime

Employee overtime can be a dangerous thing for an organization. Beyond the potential cost implications of salary loading and "time in lieu," are the physical and psychological effects that the extra hours can have on employees. Extra hours in the office lead to less time with family and less time to unwind. This can create excessive internal stress for an employee and eventually lead to complete burnout. Overtime can also seriously affect the quality of the work that the employee produces, in both the extra hours that they work and the impact of losing sleep on the next day's work.

On rare occasions, employees may have to put in a few extra hours than they originally anticipated to meet a deadline, but planning for overtime (and expecting it from employees on a regular basis) can be a formula for low-quality work, mistakes due to fatigue and losing good employees due to burnout.

Agile approaches strongly discourage delivery teams from planning for overtime. This is not only to ensure that the delivery team members are able to continually deliver high-quality outputs, it is also to ensure that they are able to stay motivated and excited about their work.

Estimates provided in iteration planning sessions are deliberately designed to consider the activities that can be achieved in *normal working hours*. If the work scheduled for an iteration requires overtime in order to be completed by the end of the iteration, the Agile team needs to either:

- scope down the scheduled work for that iteration (i.e. raise the line in the requirements backlog) so that work can be completed in normal working hours, or
- break down larger tasks into smaller ones that can be achieved in the iteration without requiring overtime.

The equivalent guideline is true as work is progressing throughout the iteration. If the delivery team's velocity is slower than expected for that iteration, the team will need to scope down the work that they are doing by postponing lower-priority activities until there is sufficient time. (Or by supplementing the team with additional resources where needed.) Aiming to deliver the pre-determined list of outcomes through evening and weekend work should only be an option in extremely rare circumstances.

One other factor to consider when an organization needs employees to work overtime is, why was the situation created in the first place? Quite often, the need for overtime comes from a combination of unrealistic deadlines and lack of ongoing employee productivity. Agile approaches combat both of these circumstances by creating an environment where deadlines are achievable and where delivery team members are motivated to be continually productive. This combination maximizes the potential for activities to be completed in normal working hours, thereby reducing the need for management to choose between the delivery requirements of the organization and the welfare of their employees.

Success breeds motivation

Everything about Agile approaches is designed to create an atmosphere where employees can *succeed* in their work. Delivering successful outcomes in a supportive working environment can create an enormous positive energy that motivates employees to *want* to continue producing value for the organization.

Agile approaches create delivery teams that are:

- empowered and entrusted to self-manage
- aware of how the work that they are doing fits into the overall requirements of the organization
- provided with regular feedback on their efforts
- encouraged to remain continually productive to reduce the potential that they will need to put in overtime hours
- truly positioned to respond to the changing needs of the organization.

Most importantly, Agile approaches allow employees to see the impact of their work as *real outcomes* for the organization, not as paper productivity reports that sit on a shelf. Knowing that the work that they do really makes a difference can be the greatest employee motivator of all.

CHAPTER 11: "JUST-IN-TIME" COMMUNICATION

When was the last time you attended a valuable meeting?

"I can't get that proposal to you until tomorrow ... I'm in *meetings* all day today."

It is no wonder that meetings have earned a bad reputation in the corporate world. They are often seen as non-productive time-wasters that stop employees from getting their *real* work done. Which is reasonably due to the fact that, most of the time, meetings *are* time-wasters.

The meetings themselves are not actually the problem. In fact, the graph from Alistair Cockburn,[41] shown in Figure 3, identifies face-to-face discussion as one of the most effective forms of communication.

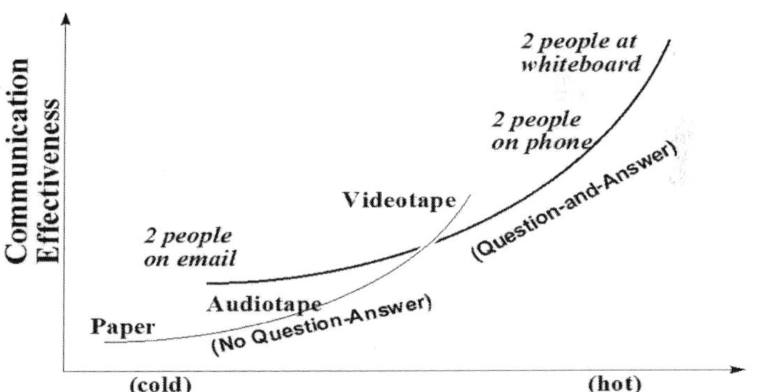

Figure 3: Richness of communication channel

---

[41] Reprinted with permission from Alistair Cockburn: *http://alistair.cockburn.us/*.

So, the problem is not with the use of face-to-face communication; it is often due to a combination of *why* the meeting is held, *who* attends and *how* it is conducted.

Organizations generally hold meetings to provide a status update on current and planned activities, to propose and plan for an idea/activity, or to address issues. Often, for convenience sake, meetings become a combination of two or more of these objectives (since "we have everyone in the room anyway"). This means that meetings generally include a combination of the people who genuinely need to be there and the "incidental" attendees who are there for convenience sake.

In most circumstances, the person calling the meeting comes in with a formal (or rough) agenda of what needs to be covered in that session. The brave ones even endeavor to allocate times for each agenda item, with the intention of ensuring that *this* meeting (unlike the last eight meetings) is going to end on time. An organization that is really focused on productive meetings may even hire a professional facilitator to run their meetings. All of these approaches are well intentioned, and all seem to overlook the fact that meetings, by design, are inherently flawed.

Why the meeting is held: Meetings tend to try to cover too many topics in the one session, which often results in a cursory review of the key discussion points and not enough time to deliver conclusive results. Meetings may also be held for the sake of consistency ("we have our weekly sales update every Thursday afternoon, no matter what"), which is especially important when the meeting is really intended to compensate for not having sufficient day-to-day communication within the organization.

Who attends: Meetings tend to focus on being as inclusive as possible, inviting anyone and everyone who could possibly benefit from (or add value to) the information covered. The people who are often the most valuable contributors in these meetings, however, are the *key decision makers*, i.e. the people authorized to make a decision on behalf of the organization, so that actions can progress. Even though key decision makers are often too busy to attend the meeting – or to stay throughout the entire meeting – meetings are likely to go ahead without them.

How it is conducted:

- Status update meetings are notorious for allocating too much time to cover each topic. Presenters put together extensive slideshows to say in 30 minutes what could have been sufficiently covered in 10 minutes or less. "Going around the table" to get an update from each attendee generally results in an endless sea of unprepared statements and *ad-hoc* comments, with an occasional point of interest that digresses the meeting for at least 10 minutes.
- Concept and planning meetings tend to encourage open discussion and brainstorming, which can be beneficial in these circumstances. However, once the initial brainstorming is complete, the remainder of the meeting is rarely contained to a fixed set of topics for discussion, so that decisions can be made and work progressed. Instead, these meetings can result in a white board filled with great ideas and no committed path forward to turn these ideas into reality for the organization.
- Issue review meetings often go from being a pointed discussion of key items (in order to determine a reasonable path forward), into an interactive free-for-all

where attendees digress on topics indefinitely. Meeting facilitators will often try to time-box these discussions (and warn the attendees when the time to discuss an issue is running out), but rarely will they enforce a decision to be made on the next steps required to resolve the issue. It may be cathartic for attendees to have a forum to air their concerns, but it has little value for the organization unless something constructive comes from the discussion.

It is the combination of all of these factors that can make traditional meetings frustrating for attendees, and often less than valuable for the organization overall.

Redefining the corporate meeting

Agile approaches take a different position on corporate meetings, specifically:

- Meetings are meant to *supplement* not *substitute* for day-to-day communication in the organization.
- Meetings should have *one specific area of focus* with the success or failure of the meeting being measured solely on whether the area in focus was sufficiently addressed.
- Meetings should be time-boxed to allow for reasonable levels of discussion around the area of focus, without encouraging attendees to go too far off-topic.
- Meetings should include all necessary participants, including key decision makers who are able to attend the *full duration* of the meeting. If key decision makers cannot attend, then attendees will not be in a position to transform the discussion into actionable work. Therefore, the meeting should be rescheduled.

The responsive planning process detailed in *Chapter 5: Responsive Planning* identified two key meetings that are used in Agile approaches:

- the iteration planning session
- the outcomes review session.

The iteration planning session, held at the start of each iteration, is the meeting where business owners communicate their goals and priorities, and delivery team members advise on what priority work they can reasonably deliver in the forthcoming iteration.

Depending on the nature and complexity of the work, the iteration planning session can take as little as one hour (especially if it is a continuation of previously reviewed requirements) to as much as eight hours (if there are a large number of new requirements that require substantial discussion). In most cases, however, iteration planning sessions will take two to three hours each iteration (i.e. every two to four weeks). It is critical that decision makers attend these sessions to ensure that the delivery team receives clear and decisive direction from the business before the iteration begins.

The outcomes review session, held at the end of each iteration, is where business owners review the work that has been completed by the delivery team in the previous iteration, discuss any questions or concerns, and update the requirements backlog to reflect any changes to the business requirements, based on the result of this review. Like the iteration planning session, the duration of an outcomes review session will vary depending on the scope and complexity of work completed; however, it is reasonable to allow between two and four hours for this session. As with the iteration planning session, outcome review sessions require decision makers to attend, so that feedback received is definitive and work can confidently progress.

It is worth noting that because Agile approaches minimize the time commitment for business owners to less than a day each iteration (e.g. one day every four weeks), it is more likely that key decision makers will be able to commit their time to these sessions. Moreover, the more successful Agile work is within the organization, the more that these decision makers will be encouraged to make time for these meetings in their schedules.

In situations where the business owners and the members of the delivery team are expecting to continue working together in the next iteration, it may be efficient to schedule the iteration planning session to *directly follow* the outcomes review session. This can reduce the meeting commitment for the Agile team to one business day each iteration (or less). However, this approach may not always work, especially if the outcomes review session results in follow-up work that the business owners need to do off-line, including discussion around re-prioritizing the requirements backlog.

What can you do in five minutes?

For business owners, the iteration planning session and the outcomes review session are the only two formal meetings that they are required to attend in support of the Agile process. For delivery team members, there is one additional type of meeting that they are required to attend: the *daily stand-up meeting.*

The daily stand-up meeting is a five-minute session that occurs every morning where delivery team members get together to review:

- the work that they completed the previous day
- the work that they are planning to do today
- any hurdles or issues that they have encountered (or expect to encounter) in their work.

The term "stand-up meeting" is inspired by the fact that, in many cases, delivery teams will *physically stand up* throughout the entire meeting duration, to help ensure that the five-minute timeframe is adhered to. In addition, each attendee is expected to come *prepared to address* the three bullet points above, both to avoid wasting the other attendees' time and to minimize the chance of improvised responses resulting in key items being overlooked. Delivery teams can opt to use the delivery backlog as a tool to facilitate these discussions and reduce the amount of redundant information being covered in the little time that is available.

Daily stand-up meetings do not only provide a forum where delivery team members can get real-time updates on the status of their work, they also create an interesting dynamic to inspire team member motivation by:

- asking team members to think about (and account for) the work that they do each day
- allowing team members to regularly air their concerns and issues, so that they are not left unaddressed for an indefinite period of time
- encouraging delivery team members to self-manage by knowing what work is scheduled and, where appropriate,

negotiating tasks so that the most skilled (and/or most available) resource can take on that work.

The Agile facilitator guides daily stand-up meetings both to ensure that the information addressed achieves the intended objectives and to make certain that the meeting time does not extend to a "one hour stand-up meeting" to address issues that can be handled offline. The Agile facilitator is also responsible for taking ownership of resolving any issues or impediments to delivery that the team identifies. This frees up the delivery team members' time to focus on their key activities, without being preoccupied with issues and obstacles.

It should also be noted that, in the interest of open communication, business owners are invited to attend daily stand-up meetings *as an observer* any time they choose, throughout the iteration. To keep to the five-minute timeframe, business owners are encouraged not to attend as advisers (to avoid the potential for the meeting to digress too far into one topic). However, their attendance at these meetings may give them insight into the work that the team is doing (and the hurdles that they are encountering) which, ideally, will inspire them to make themselves more available to the delivery team outside the meeting to address these topics.

Further information on conducting iteration planning sessions and outcomes review sessions is detailed in *Chapter 12: Immediate Status Tracking*.

Knowledge transfer through pairing, co-location and cross-training

One of the key principles that underpins the Agile approach to meetings is that meetings are meant to *supplement* not *substitute* for day-to-day communication in the organization. Throughout each iteration, delivery team members may hold any number of informal discussions with business owners, from *ad-hoc* telephone calls, to e-mails, to one-on-one detailed reviews of their requirements. In addition, the delivery team itself requires regular, ongoing communication between team members to ensure that their work is consistent, to jointly overcome hurdles and to collectively address the activities in the delivery backlog.

Agile approaches address this need for ongoing communication within the delivery team by encouraging *pairing, co-location of delivery team members* and *cross-training.*

Pairing is having two members of the delivery team working together on assigned tasks, even for work that would normally be assigned to only one person on the team. The logic behind pairing is:

- *Increased accountability*: delivery team members are more likely to be productive and focused if they are working with someone, even if that person is only acting as an observer.
- *Better quality outputs*: having a second person working with a team member encourages communication of ideas, discussion of questions, explanation of decisions and critiquing of work undertaken.
- *Knowledge sharing*: pairing of team members allows more than one person on the delivery team to be aware

of the work that has been undertaken and the logic behind decisions that are made. This can ensure that the delivery team is not overly dependent on the availability of any one resource for this knowledge.

Having work done jointly by two members of the delivery team is likely to result in an increased upfront resourcing cost to the organization. Although, the level of quality of the resulting work – and the minimized need for rework – often more than compensates for this initial overhead. (*See Chapter 14: Constantly Measurable Quality* for information on how much low-quality outputs can truly cost an organization.)

Co-location of delivery team members is a strategic way to encourage day-to-day communication, sharing of ideas and real-time awareness of the status of the team's work. Not only are team members physically near each other, facilitating *ad-hoc* discussions and face-to-face reviews of work, the resources of the team (e.g. documents, whiteboard diagrams, models) are in a central location, which is immediately available to anyone on the team who requires access to these materials. Logistically, this may not always be possible in an organization, particularly where delivery team members are on different floors, in different offices or even in different countries. However, *virtual co-location* through videoconferencing, shared workspaces on the intranet, and "presence" tools can provide a reasonable alternative in most situations.

On rare occasions, an organization will be forward-thinking enough to co-locate the *business owners* with the delivery team for the duration of the iteration. This is the ideal model for ensuring that deliverables align with the business requirements, but it is not always feasible. The alternatives are having the business owners be available to meet with the delivery team at their desks on an "as required" basis, or enlisting the help of a highly qualified business analyst to represent the interests of the business owners on a day-to-day basis.

Cross-training is distributing work across all members of the delivery team (where possible), so that team members have hands-on knowledge in all facets of the work that the team is doing. Like pairing, cross-training also provides cross-fertilization of knowledge to minimize the potential for the delivery team to be overly dependent on the availability of any one resource. It also fosters an environment of knowledge-sharing and multi-disciplinary skills development across team members, which makes them more valuable both to the delivery team and to the organization overall.

Pairing, co-location of delivery team members and cross-training are all designed to create an environment where delivery team members communicate regularly and work together towards a shared goal. They are work practices that negate the need for excessive formal meetings. This means that the only required meetings for the delivery team during the course of iterative work are the five-minute daily stand-up meetings that take less than half an hour of each resource's time per week.

Documentation is no substitute

Organizations (especially large organizations) love documentation. People's in-trays are filled with memos, status updates, discussion papers and 200-page doctrines from professional consulting firms. Their e-mail inboxes are overflowing with attachments and embedded document links. There is something about having a large document in one's hands (or on one's computer) that feels as though the organization is being productive. It is one of the most deceptive aspects of the corporate world.

Every time a document is created in an organization, there are likely to be a number of related activities that take up the organization's time, staff and resources *in addition to the physical creation of the document*, such as:

- input from other staff members in the content of the document
- quality review of the document
- physical printing and collation of paper documents
- distribution and storage of the documentation (electronic and paper documents)
- time required for other staff members to read through the documentation
- repetition of all of the above activities for each new version of the documentation that is released.

Finding the time to review these documents can be a challenge for most employees – and, when they finally *do* find the time to read the materials, it is likely that the content will have been superseded by more recent information in the organization.

Chapter 1: Agile in a Nutshell describes the pitfalls that organizations can fall into when they rely too heavily on upfront documentation to communicate their business requirements. Because specifications can take months to produce (and even longer to get approved for release), formal documentation on business requirements almost inevitably reflects outdated information about the state of the organization. In a cutting-edge marketplace, organizations cannot afford to work from old information – or to continually repeat work based on outdated requirements.

Documents *do* have a place in the corporate world. They provide a record of agreed communication after the fact. Organizations cannot exist without documented contracts and recorded agreements. However, formal documents are not as effective as face-to-face discussions when it comes to communicating business requirements.[42]

In the Agile world, the key to "just-in-time" communication is a combination of short, targeted meetings and ongoing discussions between Agile team members. These approaches focus on *face-to-face communication* as the most effective way of reviewing and discussing business requirements. Agile approaches replace the need for extensive documentation with interactive meetings (such as iteration planning sessions) where participants can discuss business requirements in detail, ask targeted questions and provide feedback to refine these requirements.

Requirements backlogs are used to record the high-level details and relative priority of each business requirement. Supporting information (including documents) can be linked to individual entries in the requirements backlog as needed, but business owners are responsible for ensuring that this supporting information reflects the most current requirements details prior to the iteration planning session.

---

[42] As shown in the "Richness of communication channel" graph at the beginning of this chapter.

Agile work can be formally documented *after the fact* to reflect the deliverables. Depending on the requirements of the organization, Agile teams may choose to allocate a day or two in between iterations to capture the work that was completed. This allows documentation to serve as a record of agreed outcomes, instead of a substitute for face-to-face communication.

The most valuable meeting of all

Because there are so few formal meetings in the Agile process, Agile team members are encouraged (and expected) to attend each meeting. However, what if you were an executive who only had time for one meeting a month?

The most valuable meeting in the Agile approach is arguably the outcomes review session at the end of each iteration. This is where business owners see the tangible outputs from the delivery team. It is their hands-on opportunity to review the completed work, critique deliverables and ask targeted questions of the delivery team.

The outcomes review session is where the business owners determine whether the original business requirements have been met, and collectively decide how the organization should move forward. It is where the value of Agile approaches is most evident.

CHAPTER 12: IMMEDIATE STATUS TRACKING

The end of the monthly report

For many organizations, status reporting is an *en masse activity*, generally allocated to time-based increments where employees *stop what they are doing* in order to provide management with a "snapshot" of their work progress (e.g. monthly status updates). This monthly reporting cycle is intended to provide frequent enough updates to keep management aware of the status of the work in their area – without overloading the team with reporting activities (or the manager with paperwork to review). It creates a *paper productivity* trail where managers can confidently take action based on the *appearance* of productivity provided in these reports – and employees can continue focusing on their "real work" for the next 30 days.

In the Agile world, status reporting is an *ongoing activity*. The same environment that enables delivery teams to be self-managed also creates an *obligation* for the delivery team members to keep others in the organization aware of the status of the work that they are doing. This obligation is not just for their managers, it is equally important to keep the *business owners* aware of the delivery team's progress – and, more than anything, it is a tool for the delivery team to manage *itself.*

The Agile world has found that the best way to incorporate status reporting in delivery team work is to allow teams to use the *same tools* to manage and track their own day-to-day work as their managers use to oversee their progress. This means that reporting does not need to be an added step in the delivery team's work; tracking the progress of their activities is an inherent part of their daily routine.

It is important to emphasize that progress reporting on Agile activities is *not* the daily tracking of hours in a timesheet. Agile approaches are far less focused on what time has elapsed, and far more focused on what *actual business value* has been produced. That is why the Agile world uses tools that track the progress of *work completed* and *effort remaining* to achieve the agreed objectives.

The four tools that are most commonly used in Agile approaches are:

- requirements backlogs
- delivery backlogs
- burndown charts
- executive dashboards.

The requirements backlog

The *requirements backlog*[43] (described in *Chapter 5: Responsive Planning*) is a tool where business owners can record and prioritize their business requirements for each iteration – and where delivery teams can record the progress of their work during each iteration against these requirements.

---

[43] The requirements backlog is known more commonly in the Agile world as a "product backlog" because Agile approaches have tended to focus on the delivery of software products.

The delivery backlog

The *delivery backlog*[44] is a tool used by the delivery team to track the details of their day-to-day work for each iteration, including breaking down each business requirement/activity into *specific tasks* that the delivery team members need to complete for that requirement to be met. For example, if one of the activities in the requirements backlog for planning a corporate event is "reserve a venue," the corresponding task entries in the delivery backlog may be:

- visit potential venues
- select the preferred venue
- negotiate the contract for using the selected venue.

The executive dashboard

Executive dashboards are used to summarize the progress within (and across) Agile teams against their stated objectives. These tools provide management with an "at-a-glance" view of the key metrics that the organization requires to monitor productivity levels (and business-value generation) across the organization.

Burndown charts

Burndown charts are visual tools within the requirements backlog, the delivery backlog and the executive dashboard that enable Agile teams to track their rate of productivity (their *velocity*) for the current iteration, to self-manage their

---

[44] The delivery backlog is known more commonly in the Agile world as a "sprint backlog" because in the Scrum methodology, where responsive planning is most commonly used, each iteration is called a sprint.

productivity levels based on this information, and to use it as input in estimating the amount of work that they can reasonably achieve in future iterations.

Each of these tools is described in further detail later in this chapter.

Backlogs, burndown charts and executive dashboards are valuable tools for monitoring the progress of the work that is undertaken by the delivery teams, particularly for day-to-day status tracking. Most important, however, is the progress reporting that is done as part of the outcomes review session at the end of each iteration.

Where a monthly paper report describes completed (and pending) work using text, bar charts and graphs, the outcomes review session at the end of each iteration provides the business owners with *hands-on outputs* in an *interactive discussion forum*. Unlike the graphs and charts in a monthly report that can be handcrafted to portray work in the best possible light, outcomes review sessions put this work under the microscope, leaving little opportunity for the delivery team to embellish their accomplishments.

With the outcomes review sessions, issues that are impacting organizational productivity are no longer resigned to be red text on page three of a paper report; they are addressed (and ideally resolved) hands on with key decision makers. This makes the outcomes review session a much more valuable and meaningful source of progress information for the organization than any two-dimensional report (including the Agile tracking tools) can provide. The delivery team is positioned to get *direct feedback* on their work from the business owners – and the organization is positioned to get *ongoing value* from the delivery team from the minute that the outcomes review session is completed.

It is interesting to note that the timing of four-week iterations aligns closely with the timing of monthly reports. This means that Agile teams are also able to use outcomes review sessions to report on their progress in conjunction with the standard reporting cycles for the organization overall (if required). The information that is recorded in the requirements and delivery backlogs can even be used to feed data into these corporate reports to minimize the overhead of monthly report generation for the delivery team.

Measuring productivity by outputs

If productivity is the measurement of how much *business value* the delivery team brings to the organization, then status reporting of Agile work needs to be able to track how much business value the delivery team has produced in each iteration – and when additional business value is anticipated to be delivered.

As described in *Chapter 6: Business-value-driven Work*, Agile approaches initially use expected business-value measurements as part of the iteration planning sessions in order to determine:

- the work that should be undertaken by the delivery team
- the order in which work should be completed (i.e. the top-down priority order in the requirements backlog).

The expected business-value calculation formula in that chapter identified that one of the ways to assess the value of an actionable goal was to determine the percentage of work that the goal represents within the *value of an overall initiative*. Conversely, the progress (and the corresponding business value) of the overall initiative can be determined by measuring the progress of *each of the actionable goals* within that initiative.

For example, if the business value of a new product that the organization is launching is projected to be $3.2 million – and the website for that product is expected to generate 75% of that revenue ($2.4 million) – then the work required to deliver that website can be tracked as a percentage of the overall business value of each requirement being delivered:

- build the website structure = 40% of the business value ($960,000)
- create an e-commerce capability to process orders = 30% of the business value ($720,000)
- provide an interactive service that allows website users to customize the product to their requirements = 20% of the business value ($480,000)
- build additional features to make the website more usable (e.g. a reusable customer profile) = 10% of the business value ($240,000).

These metrics allow the organization to use Agile tools such as executive dashboards to track how much *business value* has been delivered – and how much is remaining – based on the amount of work completed for each of the actionable goals at the end of each iteration.

Using the above example, at the end of the second iteration, the delivery team advises that they have completed building the website structure (100%) and have also completed one fifth of the e-commerce capability (20%). Based on this status update, the organization now knows that they have received approximately $1.1 million worth of business value from the completed work[45] – and that $1.3 million worth of business value is vested in the remaining work.

It should be noted that the above example is a *simplification* of the actual business-value calculations required in Agile approaches. The simplified model is intended to highlight the underlying difference between Agile tools and standard corporate reports. There are two areas in particular where the real-world application of Agile approaches is more complex than the example provided:

- The requirements listed in the bullet points above are too broad to be considered user stories (see *Communicating actionable goals and priorities* in *Chapter 6: Business-value-driven Work* for details on what makes an effective user story).
- The correlation between a partially completed requirement and its relative business value is subject to the nature of the work, e.g. a half-completed website may (or may not) be releasable in its current form. Therefore, the organization may prefer to calculate earned business value only on *completed* requirements.

Organizations need to use discretion when applying these calculations to ensure that the expected business value is not significantly over- or under-estimated, or misinterpreted by people who are less familiar with Agile approaches.

---

[45] Based on 100% of $960,000 plus 20% of $720,000 ($144,000).

Tracking overall progress in the requirements backlog

The requirements backlog is a simple reporting tool that enables both business owners and delivery teams to monitor the progress of work against the agreed business requirements (including activities) in each iteration. Although requirements backlogs can vary in format and complexity, depending on the nature of the work that the team is doing, the basic components of a requirements backlog are:

- a top-down priority list of the requirements that the team is scheduled to work on
- grouping of these requirements into iterations that indicate when the work for each requirement/activity is scheduled to be completed
- tracking the progress of each requirement by recording:
  - when the work is actually undertaken
  - the amount of work remaining to complete (i.e. fulfill) the requirement
- graphical tools that visually depict the amount of overall work remaining for the delivery team and the estimated time in which the work will be completed (i.e. *burndown charts*).

Figure 4 shows an example of a simple requirements backlog.[46]

---

[46] Adapted from simple product backlog example, courtesy of *http://agilesoftwaredevelopment.com*.

Charity golf day requirements backlog

ID	Value (x$100)	Description	1	2	3	4	5	6
		Iteration #	1	2	3	4	5	6
		Effort needed for minimum event requirements	107	48	28	0	0	0
1	50	Get an agreed event date	5	0	0	0	0	0
2	50	Reserve a venue	12	0	0	0	0	0
3	20	Organize response tracking with Customer Service	2	0	0	0	0	0
4	30	Design and print invitations	12	0	0	0	0	0
5	20	Organize catering	4	0	0	0	0	0
Iteration 1		*Goal: Set up event venue and invitations*						
6	80	Invite customers and partners	16	6	2	0	0	0
16	10	Set event agenda	2	1	0	0	0	0
17	10	Organize an alternative date for the event if it is raining	-	2	0	0	0	0
7	50	Notify media of event	16	3	1	0	0	0
8	20	Order trophies	2	2	0	0	0	0
9	50	Organize for all executives to attend the event	4	3	3	0	0	0
Iteration 2		*Goal: Send invitations and organize event logistics*						
10	80	Track invitation responses	16	15	6	0	0	0
11	40	Match customers with sales team members	8	8	8	0	0	0
12	20	Fill empty spots with additional employees	4	4	4	0	0	0
13	50	Arrange venue and caterer pre-payments	4	4	4	0	0	0
Iteration 3		*Goal: Track invitations and finalize logistics*						
Milestone: Minimum requirements for event								
14	5	Order golf balls with custom logos	8	8	8	8	8	8
15	3	Order golf shirts for employees	4	4	4	4	4	4
18	2	Organize a golf cart for each foursome	4	4	4	4	4	4
Iteration 4		*Goal: Add more services and promotional items*						
Milestone: Enhanced event options								
		Effort in the whole backlog	123	64	44	16	16	16

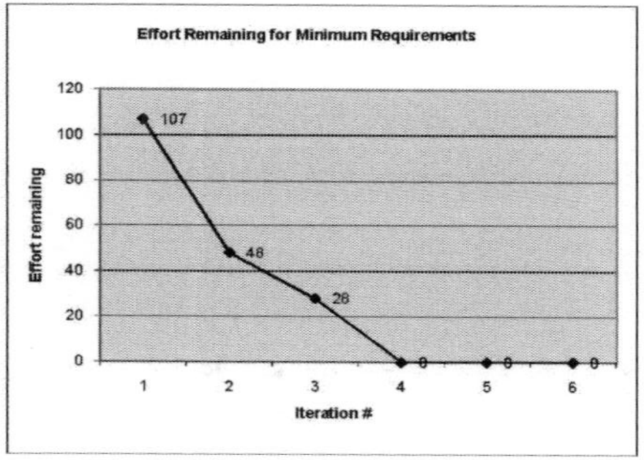

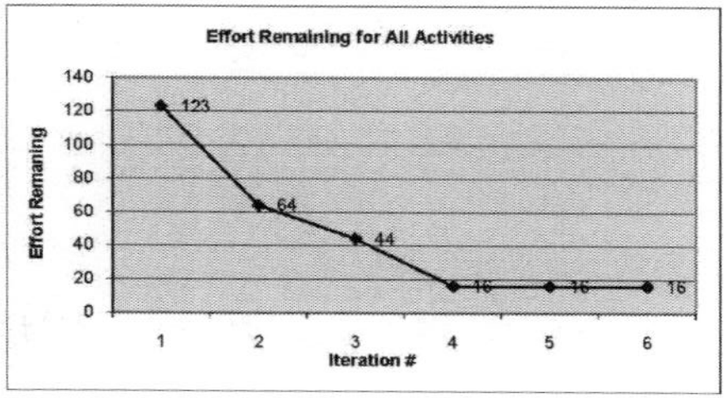

Effort Remaining for Minimum Requirements

Effort remaining (0–120) by Iteration # (1–6): 107, 48, 28, 0, 0, 0

Effort Remaining for All Activities

Effort Remaining (0–140) by Iteration # (1–6): 123, 64, 44, 16, 16, 16

http://agilesoftwaredevelopment.com/scrum/simple-product-backlog

Figure 4: Simple requirements backlog

The content of the requirements backlog is managed and updated by all members of the Agile team.

- Business owners are responsible for maintaining the list of requirements in top-down priority order.
- The business owners and the delivery team collectively determine the iteration in which each requirement will be delivered as part of the iteration planning session.
- Progress tracking on the work for each requirement is maintained by the delivery team through the day-to-day recording of their work in the *delivery backlog*. (Where the details in the delivery backlog are rolled up to provide the overall calculations used in the requirements backlog. See *Tracking day-to-day work in the delivery backlog*, below, for further details.)

The requirements backlog becomes a shared tool for all members of the Agile team (and their managers) to keep track of the overall status of their work. It combines textual detail (on the left) and visual indicators (on the right) to give the organization a "snapshot" of the Agile team's progress, at any point in time, *without* requiring the team to develop separate corporate status reports.

Chapter 19: Using Agile Tools provides a step-by-step explanation of how requirements backlogs are used by Agile teams.

Tracking day-to-day work in the delivery backlog

The delivery backlog is a dynamic reporting tool that enables delivery teams to monitor and manage their *actual day-to-day work* in far more detail than the requirements backlog allows. Where the requirements backlog is a tool for business owners to record, prioritize and track the progress of business requirements overall, the delivery backlog is a tool for delivery team members to record and track their actual work and progress against the *detailed tasks* for each iteration.

At the end of each iteration planning session, the business owners and the delivery team agree on the subset of high-priority business requirements/activities that will be actioned in the upcoming iteration (i.e. "drawing the line" in the top-down priority order of tasks).

These agreed requirements are transferred from the requirements backlog to a list of *corresponding tasks* in the delivery backlog, for the delivery team members to action. For example, if the entry in the requirements backlog for creating a new product sales tracking report is "design the tracking report", the corresponding entries in the delivery backlog may be:

- review detailed report information requirements with key stakeholders
- confirm that all report data is available in current corporate information
- design mock-ups of report layouts
- present report layouts to stakeholders for feedback.

The actionable goals that are listed in the requirements backlog become *actionable work* in the delivery backlog. These are the specific tasks that the delivery team will need to do in order to deliver each agreed requirement for that iteration.

Figure 5 shows an example of a simple delivery backlog.

Charity golf day delivery backlog

Iteration 3 goal: Track invitations and finalize logistics

ID	Task	Day in iteration / effort remaining													
		1	2	3	4	5	6	7	8	9	10	11	12	13	14
		32	32	31	28	26	22	22	21	18	16	16	16	16	16
10	**Track invitation responses**														
	Get daily reports from Customer Service	8	8	7	6	6	5	5	5	4	3	3	3	3	3
	Keep VP of Sales appraised of key customers who respond	4	4	3	3	3	3	3	3	3	3	3	3	3	3
	Keep venue updated if numbers look much smaller or larger than expected	1	1	1	1	1	1	1	1	1	1	1	1	1	1
	Check with the mailroom for any returned invitations	3	3	3	2	2	2	2	2	1	1	1	1	1	1
11	**Match customers with sales team members**														
	Confirm strategic matches with VP of Sales and CEO	2	2	4	4	4	4	4	4	4	4	4	4	4	4
	Confirm which sales team members are attending the event	2	2	2	2	1	1	1	1	1	0	0	0	0	0
	Get more current copy of sales team client list	1	1	0	0	0	0	0	0	0	0	0	0	0	0
	Match customers from invitation responses	3	3	3	3	2	2	2	2	1	1	1	1	1	1
12	**Fill empty spots with additional employees**														
	Identify employees who are best positioned to meet with customers	3	3	3	2	2	2	2	1	1	1	1	1	1	1
	Confirm preferred employee list with VP of Sales	1	1	2	2	2	2	2	2	2	2	2	2	2	2
13	**Arrange venue and caterer pre-payments**														
	Confirm purchase order approval with Finance	1	1	0	0	0	0	0	0	0	0	0	0	0	0
	Hand-deliver certified checks from Finance	3	3	3	3	3	0	0	0	0	0	0	0	0	0

[47]

Figure 5: Delivery backlog example

[47] Adapted from simple sprint backlog example, courtesy of *http://agilesoftwaredevelopment.com*.

The content of the delivery backlog is managed and updated by all members of the delivery team on a daily basis. Maintaining the progress information in the delivery backlog is not an added overhead for the delivery team members; it is an essential part of their own self-management. The fact that management and business owners can also use the delivery backlog tool (and the corresponding requirements backlog) to track the team's progress is an added benefit from the delivery team's perspective. It means that they will have little (or no) additional paperwork to complete at the end of each month.

Chapter 19: Using Agile Tools provides a step-by-step explanation of how delivery backlogs are used by Agile teams.

The power of the "burndown" chart

The requirements backlog and delivery backlog examples shown in the previous sections both include graphical charts, known as *burndown charts*, that indicate the delivery team's progress (and effort remaining) for each iteration. This enables the delivery team to *track the velocity* of their work, as described in the *Setting the next deadline* section of *Chapter 9: Immovable Deadlines*.

In the requirements backlog, the burndown chart on the top right-hand side provides a visual representation of the *amount of work (effort)* that is remaining for the delivery team to achieve the *minimum* event requirements; the burndown chart on the bottom right-hand side provides a visual representation of the *amount of work (effort)* that is remaining for the delivery team to achieve *all* of the listed event requirements.

In the delivery backlog, the burndown chart at the bottom left-hand side provides a visual representation of the *amount of work (effort)* that is remaining for the delivery team to achieve all of the tasks within that iteration.

Combined, these burndown charts enable the business owners and the delivery team to track productivity rates (i.e. velocity) within and across iterations. This provides the Agile team with two valuable tools:

- A ***self-management tool*** that allows delivery teams to track their delivery pace during each iteration.
- An ***estimation tool*** that can assist delivery teams in determining the amount of work that they can reasonably expect to deliver in future iterations (based on the "yesterday's weather" productivity rates for work done by the delivery team that was of an equivalent size and complexity).

The *In my estimation ...* section of *Chapter 10: Management by Self-motivation* described the powerful effects that can occur when delivery teams are empowered to manage their own work commitments. The use of velocity information provides a tool for these teams to confidently make estimations based on *real accounts* of their historical productivity levels (not "guesstimates"). It assures the delivery team that the work that they have committed to is achievable – and it generally results in far more realistic productivity levels in the actual work completed for each iteration.

The power of velocity tracking, however, is not limited to estimations of future work. It is an equally valuable tool for delivery teams to track and manage their work during each iteration against the levels of productivity that they committed to at the start of the iteration.

Tracking velocity in current iterations allows the delivery team to check its own status by comparing the level of outputs that they had expected to deliver (doing similar work) against the level of outputs that they are currently generating. If the delivery team is producing fewer outputs than expected, this may be a red flag for the team members to step back and see what might be causing this slowdown. For example, in the current iteration, business owners may not be as responsive to delivery team member questions as they had been in the past due to end-of-year financial reporting commitments. Equally, if the team determines that they are moving at a faster pace than expected, they may be able to confidently commit to a greater number of tasks at the next iteration planning session.

The content of these burndown charts can be *automatically* updated based on the progress information that the delivery team records in the delivery backlog each day. This enables the delivery team to review and track their velocity without requiring additional work to collect this information.

See Setting the next deadline in *Chapter 9: Immovable Deadlines* for further information on measuring a delivery team's velocity.

The real-time executive dashboard

In addition to progress reporting through requirements backlogs, delivery backlogs and burndown charts, Agile approaches provide senior management with *executive dashboard* reports that summarize the work within (and across) Agile teams for easy progress monitoring across the organization. Executive dashboards are similar in design to standard dashboards in corporate reporting tools. Corporate reporting dashboards provide management with an "at-a-glance" visual summary of key activities in the organization (usually actual progress against financial KPIs). Agile executive dashboards also provide "at-a-glance" visual summary information, but the focus is on measuring *real productivity gains* by summarizing the work completed and the work remaining for each Agile team across their iterations.

Figure 6 shows an example of an executive dashboard tool that management can use to monitor the progress of Agile work.

Charity golf day executive dashboard

At-a-glance core requirements

Core requirement	% complete	Value earned	Value remaining	Estimated completion
Finalize date	100	$5,000	$0	Iteration 1
Organize venue	80	$9,600	$2,400	Iteration 3
Invite customers	93	$10,300	$700	Iteration 3
Notify media	94	$4,700	$300	Iteration 3
Track responses	67	$6,700	$3,300	Iteration 3
Match customers	0	$0	$4,000	Iteration 3

Requirements burndown charts

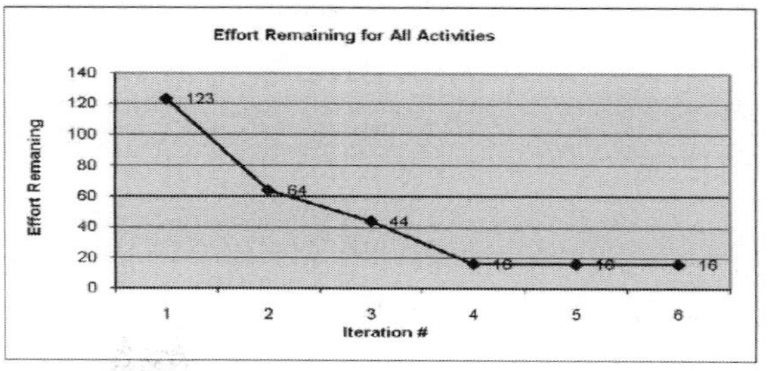

Expected *versus* earned business value

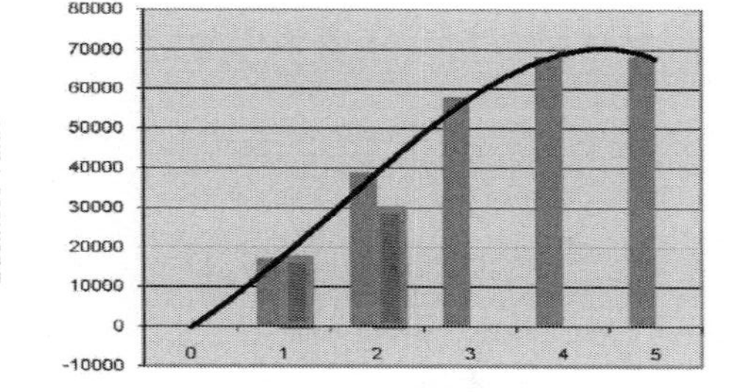

Figure 6: Executive dashboard tool example

In this executive dashboard tool, summary information is broken down into three mandatory sections:

- *At-a-glance core requirements*: shows the progress of Agile work against each key executive-level objective for the Agile team.
- *Requirements burndown charts*: show the overall progress of the Agile team based on the *amount of work* that they have completed and the amount of work that is remaining against each milestone.
- *Expected versus earned business value*: shows the overall progress of the Agile team based on the *business value of the work* that they have completed and the business value of the work that is remaining.

There are other optional sections which Agile teams may choose to include, if they are relevant to the work that the team is doing, such as:

- a "work breakdown structure" (WBS) that visually depicts the correlation and dependencies between each key executive-level objective for the Agile team
- a "key information" text area for other important status and context information that executives need to be aware of, including:
    - key achievements
    - key decisions
    - known issues
    - critical risks.

Agile teams can adapt the executive dashboard for each initiative to suit the specific requirements of their work, the standards for the organization overall, or the preferences of individual executives.

As with the velocity tracking tools, most of the information in the executive dashboard tool is *automatically* generated, based on the progress information that the delivery team records in the delivery backlog each day. However, some of the optional sections (such as the WBS and the "key information" area), where included, can require manual updating by the Agile team.

The WBS, which can be handcrafted by the Agile team at the start of the work, only requires updating when the status (or nature) of the key objectives changes – which is generally apparent at the end of each iteration planning session. The "key information" area, however, may require more frequent maintenance based on the critical information that arises during the course of each iteration. In some cases, Agile teams have opted to link this section of the executive dashboard to a dynamic issues log that is maintained in a centralized area, which the Agile team updates every time key information arises (versus waiting until the end of each iteration to update these details). This enables executives to get a realistic "snapshot" of the Agile work at any point in time, not just as part of their monthly reports. (How many corporate reports are you aware of that are able to give you real-time updates on the amount of business value that employees are – and are not – generating in their ongoing work?)

It is important to note that the example provided shows the work that is being tracked for *one Agile team*; however, executive dashboards can provide tracking information at any level of detail, including a visual summary of the work being done by *all* Agile teams.

Early and continuous delivery tracking

The *Early delivery means early payback* section in *Chapter 9: Immovable Deadlines* explained that one way in which Agile approaches differ significantly from traditional business practices is in their ability to deliver business value to the organization from the first iteration. Because the work that the Agile team delivers is *functional* outputs (not thought papers or prototypes), the work that is delivered at the end of each iteration is often available for the organization to use immediately. This means that the organization can expect to receive early and ongoing benefits from their Agile work.

Similarly, the nature of Agile tracking and reporting tools means that the organization receives early and continuous status information regarding their Agile work. Management does not have to wait for a monthly report to know that there is substantial progress in (or key issues with) the work that the Agile teams are doing. The business owners and delivery team members do not have to wait until the end of the month to see status information that can indicate significant problems in the work that they are doing. Instead of status reporting being a one-off retrospective view of work each month, Agile tracking and reporting tools provide the team members (and the organization) with real-time feedback on their progress – and real-time flags when action is required.

Redefining risk management

The real-time tracking of work progress in Agile approaches provides the organization with another significant advantage over traditional business practices:

Immediate risk identification and mitigation. The benefits of using Agile approaches for risk management are not only evident in the work that the delivery team produces. The delivery of functional outputs forces team members to confront and resolve real issues in their work (*see Mitigating risk* in *Chapter 7: Hands-on Business Outputs* for further detail) – it is an inherent part of the nature of the tools that Agile teams use to track their work.

Key issues that can affect the delivery team's productivity levels are immediately apparent in the tools that track the *velocity* of the team's work. If the delivery team is producing outputs in an iteration at a significantly slower velocity rate than they did in a previous iteration with equivalent work, this could be a strong indication that the team is encountering issues that are limiting their productivity. Although Agile tracking and reporting tools cannot determine whether the source of the issue is a lack of skilled resources, insufficient participation from key stakeholders, inadequate tools or other organizational factors, they *can* prompt the business owners, the delivery team members or their management to take action to investigate the source of the problem. Furthermore, the real-time nature of these tools means that the investigation and mitigation did not need to wait until the end of the calendar month (or quarter) before being actioned.

The executive dashboard provides the Agile team and their management with tools for real-time monitoring of ongoing business value in the work that is being undertaken. This allows for risk management of a different sort: mitigating the risk that the organization's resources will focus on work that brings relatively little business value, in favor of work that could deliver significantly greater business value. Although the risk of low business-value work may not invoke the same sense of urgency that a critical issue would, it is one of those insidious problems that can slowly erode the value of an organization by chipping away at its real productivity levels.

Similarly, the executive dashboard allows senior management to view the relative business value of remaining work *across* Agile teams, to determine where ongoing resource efforts should be focused to provide the greatest benefit to the organization. It also provides executives with an exceptional level of accountability for the work that their employees are doing.

This accountability is *not* due to the fact that the day-to-day tracking of Agile work provides a "big brother" opportunity for executives to track every detail of their employees' work. In fact, Agile approaches can produce the *exact opposite* effect, by instilling an unprecedented level of trust in the work of their employees. It means that senior management can see at any point in time what the Agile team has produced – and the work that is remaining. They can know whether or not each Agile team is producing business value. They can confidently report to their executives about the work that their area is doing with documented proof for every claim. Most importantly, the information that senior managers are working from when making key decisions about the organization's future, is a reflection of the *real work* that the organization has (and has not) achieved – far more accurate than a handcrafted (and strategically positioned) *paper productivity* report could provide. This means that the organization is better protected from the risk of executives making decisions based on faulty (or misleading) information.

Finally, there is the risk management that naturally occurs as a result of providing Agile tools that enable delivery teams to self-manage their work. The responsibility of estimating work, and then using tools to record the actual work against these estimates, compels delivery team members to try to make their estimates as realistic as possible. The delivery team knows that their ongoing self-management is contingent upon management's confidence that Agile approaches are delivering business value to the organization. If they regularly *overestimate* their ability to produce valuable outputs, they run the risk of senior management losing faith in their ability to self-manage. If they regularly underestimate their ability to produce valuable outputs, they run the risk of senior management stopping their work because the projected business value of their scheduled activities is not producing enough ROI against the overheads of their resource costs. This creates an imperative for Agile teams to remain vigilant in their ability to accurately report on and deliver business value to the organization. The fact that the process is *self-correcting* can give senior management the confidence of knowing that risk is being actively managed at all levels of the organization.

CHAPTER 13: WASTE MANAGEMENT

What is waste management?

Waste in an organization can take many forms. It can be an *overt* waste of:

- budget funds (e.g. equipment that is purchased, but is never used)
- skilled resources (e.g. a product that staff dedicated eight months of their time to, which did not meet the needs of the marketplace)
- available time (e.g. staff spending three months developing a discussion paper, leaving them only one month to act on the resulting decision).

Or it can be a much *more subtle* waste of finances, skilled resources and available time by having:

- products and services that are "over-delivered" to provide more than the target audience needed (or even wanted)
- employees who are in a "holding pattern," waiting on input from others before they can progress their work
- people who have so many different tasks assigned to them that they are unable to spend meaningful time (or focus) on any one task
- staff members who end up *recreating* work that already exists in the organization because of ineffective communication channels.

All of these circumstances can result in wasted time, budget funds and resources for the organization. These are the very issues that Agile approaches are designed to address.

The ultimate goal of every Agile approach is to increase the delivery of *high business-value outputs* in an organization by optimizing the organization's resource and budget utilization (i.e. by reducing its waste). Agile approaches argue that anything an organization does which does not lead to high business-value outputs, is likely to be wasting that organization's time, money and resources. Therefore, the goal of an organization should be to maximize the value of its current resources by *reducing* and, where possible, *eliminating* low business-value activities. The Agile practices of *waste management* are based upon this very assertion.

Waste management is based upon the *lean manufacturing* approaches that were pioneered decades ago as a way of maximizing resource utilization in the manufacturing sector. Since the introduction of lean manufacturing approaches, other industry sectors have adopted quality improvement methodologies (e.g. SixSigma) in an effort to better measure, improve and control their business processes. (Further detail on the history and evolution of lean approaches is provided in the *Popular Agile methods* section of *Chapter 1: Agile in a Nutshell*.)

One of the quality improvement methodologies that extended from lean manufacturing is *lean thinking*,[48] which advocates that productivity is most effectively addressed when you combine continuous improvement techniques with a "respect for people" (e.g. empowering the staff). Lean thinking sees waste management as the natural outcome of an organization that promotes the value of

---

[48] From *Lean Primer*, Larman C & Vodde B (2009): www.leanprimer.com/downloads/lean_primer.pdf

people and the importance of improving their work practices, business processes and overall work environment.

Agile approaches combine the best of both worlds by valuing staff members (*see Chapter 10: Management by Self-motivation*, improving their work environment (*see Chapter 16: Continuous Improvement*) and optimizing their work practices and business processes through the waste management techniques described in this chapter.

It's what you *don't* do that matters

There are a number of areas where organizations can have inefficiencies (i.e. waste) in their work practices and business processes, including:

- ***Overproduction***: by producing *more than is needed* to satisfy the customer's requirement.
- ***Waiting***: where work cannot progress due to the unavailability of required resources, materials, information, management decisions and/or management approvals.
- ***Non-value-added processing***: which includes over-inspection, reworking and other added tasks to compensate for a lack of effective quality control in the overall process.
- ***Defect handling***: where the organization's resources are wasted addressing problems in their products, services and business processes, instead of focusing on core business activities. Note that this also includes "damage control" to protect the reputation of the organization when these defects are visible to external audiences.

- ***Under-utilized people***: where staff cannot work to their full mental and physical potential due to ineffective workflows, restrictive organizational cultures and inadequate training.
- ***Excess movement***: where the organization's resources (staff, materials, etc.) are moved from activity to activity without adding value to the business process. This includes *mental* movement where staff members cannot focus on their work because they are constantly moving from task to task. It also includes unnecessary movement due to a lack of effective communication channels in the organization (e.g. recreating an existing procedures manual).
- ***Over preparation***: where the organization hoards resources or prepares materials "just in case" the organization might need them in the future.

The key to successful waste management is ensuring that the organization does not squander its time, budget or resources using wasteful approaches that add minimal business value to the organization. Productivity gains in an organization can equally be achieved by *not* doing things that are wasteful as by doing things that are more productive.

The power and peril of the value stream

At the heart of lean techniques (and, consequently, waste management) is a focus on the *value stream* – those activities that *directly result* in business-value generation for the organization. Any work that is done which does not add to the value stream – or which impedes the flow of the value stream – is considered waste. This is similar in concept to the "critical path" in traditional project management techniques: there are core activities that the organization needs to do in order to get from Point A to Point B; anything that delays or detracts from these activities will directly impact the organization's ability to deliver the intended outcomes within the agreed time, cost, resource levels and/or quality.

In the manufacturing sector, the value stream is a relatively straightforward thing to analyze and measure. Is the equipment working? Are the people sufficiently trained? Do we have the components that we need in hand at the exact time that they are needed? Do the manufactured products meet the quality standards? *Monitoring* the value stream in the manufacturing sector is also reasonably straightforward: a hold-up in the production line is visible to the floor manager; a flawed product (ideally) gets picked up in quality testing. However, in other industry sectors, leaks in the value stream may not be as evident.

What if the "hold-up in the production line" is a business process that requires six people's signatures to approve an employee expense form before the employee can be reimbursed? Or an employee who cannot distribute an analysis report of current market trends until their manager has reviewed it – and their manager will not be in a position to read through it for at least three more weeks (at which point, the "current" information is already becoming historical information).

What if the "flaw" in your product or service was its inability to meet customer needs? It may function as intended, meet every criterion in the original design, pass all of the physical quality checks in the organization – but if the product does not meet customer needs and is, therefore, put away on the shelf to collect dust, has the organization achieved business value from this work? (Beyond, of course, the important – and expensive – lesson of learning from one's mistakes!)

An equally dangerous "flaw" can be where your product or service *exceeds* customer needs by "over-engineering" or "over-delivering" the solution to their requirement. This can result in inflated costs, increased training requirements and a greater potential for human error. (See *Over-delivery is wasted money* in *Chapter 6: Business-value-driven Work* for further information on the risks of over-delivery.)

The following sections identify areas of waste that are common across *all* organizations – activities that take employees away from the value stream of their core business activities. These are the "insidious problems," referenced in *Chapter 12: Immediate Status Tracking* that can slowly erode the value of an organization by chipping away at its real productivity levels; although most of them are far too subtle to be noticed by the organization.

The waiting game

When a patient in cardiac arrest enters a hospital, every second counts. Emergency workers are trained in critical response techniques to address the life-threatening circumstances. They are positioned to take *immediate action* to ensure that no time is wasted. They will *drop everything* that they are doing to ensure that the urgent situation is handled.

When a patient enters a hospital with a sore throat, however, the reaction from hospital staff is markedly different. Because this is not a critical situation, the imperative for staff to respond does not need to be as strong. So, the patient is added to the queue, behind all of the cases that came in earlier that day, as well as any urgent cases that may come in while the patient is waiting. It does not matter how long someone has been waiting, critical issues will always take precedence.

For most organizations, almost *every* business process is a patient with a sore throat. Unless the situation is truly critical (or a top-down directive from the Chief Executive), people are not likely to drop everything that they are currently doing just to meet your requirements. Consequently, people in an organization will often find themselves waiting for the materials, staff, information, decisions and management approvals that they need to progress their work. These delays and hold-ups are so common that they have become an expected part of business.

The *inconvenience* of waiting becomes a *problem* when the input that the staff members require is part of the value stream (i.e. the critical path) of activities, which means that work *cannot continue* until the input is received. In these circumstances, the lack of essential input at the required time can result in a work stoppage for the rest of the value stream. These are the most critical delays for the organization to address; the issues that cause skilled staff members to be *under-utilized* while they wait for the resources that they need.

Waste management approaches specifically target the points in the business process where the organization is most vulnerable to work stoppage (or resource under-utilization) due to delays. The three most effective approaches for reducing the potential for work stoppage (i.e. avoiding the "waiting game") are:

- ***Business process modeling and improvement***: this involves documenting the current business processes that an organization uses and assessing them to determine where inefficiencies exist. One of the most effective ways of modeling business processes is by using Business Process Modeling Notation (BPMN), which is an industry standard for documenting business processes in visual diagrams with supporting textual information.
- ***Effective communication***: ensuring that the key participants in the business process are aware of both their role in the process and the timing of their involvement, so that they are better prepared to respond when they are required. This includes providing advanced notice to the areas of the organization (or to the external suppliers) who have the information, staff and materials required, in order to minimize last-minute "fire-fighting" for the resources needed – and the inevitable delays that ensue when your urgent requirement is put in a queue behind everybody else's needs.
- ***Facilitation***: proactively working with the areas that have the resources that you need, in order to address any delays or impediments in their involvement. (This is so critical that Agile approaches assign a dedicated member of the team – the Agile facilitator – to be responsible for overcoming delivery hurdles. See *Chapter 5: Responsive Planning* for more details on this role.)

Techniques for addressing waste management through *business process modeling and improvement* involve addressing the most common inefficiencies in business processes, such as over-handling, decentralized information, serial tasks, over-management and overuse of decision points.[49] These are addressed in the following sections.

Techniques for addressing waste management through the use of more effective communication and facilitation is explained in *Chapter 11: "Just-in-time" Communication.*

Movement without added value

Although *movement without added value* originated from the literal movement of materials on the production line in a manufacturing plant, the "movement" referred to in this section does not always involve the physical movement of materials from Point A to Point B. In most other industry sectors (particularly services sectors), the "materials" being moved can be documents and information – and "wasted movement" can take the form of:

- unnecessary steps or people in the process (i.e. *over-handling*)
- excessive management involvement, including unnecessary approvals (i.e. *over-management*) and excessive use of decision points (i.e. creating checkpoints at every step of a business process instead of allowing core work to be progressed without interruption – and establishing a mechanism for escalating exceptions and problems when they arise).

In the previous section, business process improvement (BPI) was identified as a key approach for eliminating waste in an organization. One area where organizations can

[49] From my research paper, *Using Business Process Modeling Notation (BPMN) to Identify and Reduce Inefficiencies in Business Workflows*, adapted with permission from the University of Canberra (www.canberra.edu.au).

achieve significant BPI benefits is by removing the *non-value-added middle man* from a business process. When modeling a business process (using BPMN or equivalent modeling tools), this non-value-added middle man can take the form of:

- an administration staff member who is solely responsible for routing a deliverable from one staff member to another
- the third and fourth staff members in a review and approval process.

In these circumstances, this added movement in the business process is generally endeavoring to compensate for ineffective quality controls in the overall business process (*see Chapter 14: Constantly Measurable Quality*) or for a lack of effective communication (*see Chapter 11: "Just-in-time" Communication*). Therefore, improving these underlying issues in the work environment will often negate the need to have these extra non-value-added steps in the business process altogether.

Another area where organizations can achieve significant BPI benefits is by reducing the amount of *documentation* that employees need to produce. The *Documentation is no substitute* section of *Chapter 11: "Just-in-time" Communication* identified the issues associated with using documentation in lieu of more effective forms of communication. Ironically, this means that all of the added time that an organization spends creating documentation can actually result in a *sub-standard* outcome for the organization when the documentation endeavors to provide communication which would be better handled through face-to-face discussion.

As explained in *Documentation is no substitute*, the key to reducing the waste caused by over-documentation is to provide alternative methods for staff communication where the same degree of formal documentation is not necessary. Organizations can significantly reduce waste in their business processes by making documentation an activity to document decisions and outcomes *after the fact* – and only when having that information formally documented would truly provide business value to the organization.

Task-switching and time leakage

When the "material" being moved in a business process is physical (e.g. equipment), the organization can easily use tools such as BPMN modeling to identify and address inefficiencies. However, what if the "movement without added value" is a much more subtle activity, such as the constant movement of a staff member's *mind* from one task to another? In these circumstances, the organization risks losing a little bit of that staff member's time – and momentum – every time that their focus needs to shift from one activity to another. This is particularly true in circumstances where the staff member is over-committed to work and, consequently, cannot "take the time" to properly focus on the work that they are doing. This means that task-switching does not only risk time leakage for the organization; task-switching by over-committed staff can result in low-quality outputs and burned out employees.

Agile approaches address the issue of task-switching in three ways:

- allowing the delivery team to estimate and self-manage their work, so that they control their levels of commitment in each iteration
- providing the Agile facilitator as a resource who is dedicated to addressing issues that the team encounters, so that they do not need to waste their brainpower on activities other than their core work
- using daily stand-up meetings (described in *Chapter 11: "Just-in-time" Communication*) as a tool to highlight potential over-commitments from delivery team members (even if they are too caught up in the work that they are doing to notice it themselves).

This does not mean that every member of the delivery team will have the luxury of focusing on only one activity for the duration of the iteration. For most organizations, it is realistic to expect that employees will be required to take on some level of concurrent work, even mandatory corporate communication activities such as department meetings. (This reality of competing commitments in the corporate world is why this section is called waste *management* and not waste *elimination*!) Agile approaches are designed to *minimize* the occurrences of these distractions, so that the *majority* of each delivery team member's time can be spent on their core work.

Doing it right the first time

Defects in an organization can be extremely costly. Organizations that produce consumer products (such as the manufacturing sector) are well aware of the legal and financial implications of producing bad quality outputs. Most service organizations are equally aware of their liability if they provide low-quality services to their customers. This is why customer contracts are filled with liability waivers and indemnity clauses to protect the provider and/or the customer from the impacts of sub-standard outputs. The financial impacts of bad quality outputs in an organization are, however, far beyond the monetary damages that may be awarded in a courtroom (and the associated legal costs).

When a bad quality output is identified *before* it leaves the organization, there are often a number of wasteful *churning* activities that occur between areas of the organization. This can include everything from urgent "all hands on deck" staff meetings, to stand-offs between department managers (the "blame game"), to endless analysis work to determine the source of the problem. As costly as these activities are, however, they are *minuscule* when compared with the cost of a bad quality output that is identified *after* it leaves the organization. When a defect leaves the organization, the cost can include everything from undertaking damage control with current customers, to addressing unflattering media coverage, to the often unquantifiable loss of prospective customers – not to mention the potential legal liability for the organization.

The problem is that most organizations perceive quality control as a checking activity that occurs *at the end* of the production line, not as an *intrinsic part* of the organization's business processes, work practices, corporate culture and work environment. The inherent flaw in this approach is that the end of the process is the time when resolving defects in a product or service can often be the most costly for the organization, especially if the resolution requires a full replacement of the output (100% rework cost), or a partial replacement (with a corresponding percentage of rework cost). Furthermore, the additional costs of rework do not include the potential damage for missing a delivery deadline (or for incurring staff overtime costs to meet that deadline) – let alone the greater likelihood that a rushed replacement deliverable at the end of the process is likely to have even more extensive quality problems than the original.

The reality is that bad quality outputs (i.e. defects) in an organization are often the result of the *flawed approaches* that preceded the actual delivery of the outputs. These flawed approaches can take the form of:

- inefficient (or insufficient) work practices
- ineffective business processes
- miscommunication that causes errors and rework
- outputs that do not meet the needs of the internal or external customer (and, therefore, require partial or full rework).

All of these factors contribute to the overall potential for outputs to cost more, to take more time to deliver, to require more resources, and to be produced at a sub-standard quality. This is why building in quality *upfront* is a core principle in Agile approaches.

Chapter 14: Constantly Measurable Quality focuses on the key facets that can affect the quality of an organization's outputs, including their business processes, work practices and communication channels. Agile approaches understand that instilling quality in *every aspect* of an organization can redirect employees from the frustration of addressing problems, repeating their work and "fire-fighting," to the satisfaction of focusing on their core business activities and delivering valuable outcomes for the organization.

"Just-in-time" versus "just-in-case"

Chapter 5: Responsive Planning explained that upfront plans are destined to fail because everything in an organization is subject to change – and that even the best planning cannot predict every possible situation that a business team may have to face. Part of responsive planning is using *flexible business processes* that are able to adjust to fluctuations in market demand, staff shortages, equipment failures and competing resources.

Just-in-time planning is strategically designing business processes to adapt the work that employees do to react to the evolving circumstances of the organization. It is positioning the organization to have sufficient staff, suppliers and product available to handle high demand periods, but equally being able to reduce and reallocate these resources in low demand periods. It is ensuring the continued supply of resources when (and if) they are needed without incurring added overheads for storing excess materials, having staff members in a "holding position" waiting for work, or committing to minimum purchase levels from suppliers.

Conversely, *just-in-case* planning is spending excessive time, resources and funds trying to prepare upfront for *every possible contingency* – even when the majority of these situations never arise. It is the excessive stockpiling of materials that *may* be required in the future – and the associated storage costs. It is hiring permanent call center employees to support a sales campaign that may (or may not) occur six months down the track. It is preparing four different variations of the same management report in the hope that one of the variations is what the executives are looking for.

Contingency planning is a risk versus reward game. If you spend all of your time planning for every possible eventuality, you will most likely be prepared for everything – and accomplish nothing. For example, if a team prepares for four potential outcomes "just in case" they occur – and only one of those outcomes eventuates – the team has effectively wasted 75% of its efforts.

That is not to say that contingency planning is a waste of time. Any organization that does not keep up-to-date backups of their computer systems (including off-site backups) is significantly risking the ongoing operations of the organization. However, there is a difference between reasonable contingency planning and planning for every possible eventuality that might occur.

The thinking behind just-in-time (versus just-in-case) planning is straightforward:

> Control what you know – and be well positioned to respond to what you don't know.

The concepts that underpin just-in-time approaches emerged in the manufacturing sector as a way of ensuring that materials were delivered as close as possible to the point in the production line when they were required. This reduced the need for organizations to invest in long-term storage (e.g. utilize costly warehouse space) and, consequently, reduced the need for excess movement between temporary storage locations. *Stockpiling* was identified by just-in-time approaches as an added overhead that results in increased operating costs, including wasting both storage space (physical and virtual) and the resources required to manage the excess stock until it is needed. The prevailing logic was that, unless the overhead costs of stockpiling are offset by a corresponding cost savings (e.g.

discounted prices for purchasing bulk materials in advance), the organization was paying a substantial price simply to avoid the potential for prospective customer orders not being fulfilled in time.

Just-in-time planning enables the organization to establish processes that allow the supply chain and the production line to increase or decrease their levels of productivity, based on the level of customer demand. For example, having active arrangements with four different suppliers of product components, so that the organization can double or triple its levels of productivity in a high demand period – and ensuring that equipment, staff and distribution centers are equally positioned to handle magnitudes of increased activity.

The converse to this is positioning the organization to be equally prepared for low demand periods by avoiding minimum purchase commitment clauses in supplier contracts and by having sufficient levels of alternative value-added work for production line staff to do during the downtime; in other words, by establishing a *process* that allows the organization to effectively respond to changing demand in the marketplace, without incurring the significant overheads of preparing for every contingency. This is at the very heart of Agile approaches.

In Agile approaches, just-in-time planning is delivering *what* the customer needs *when* they need it – no more and no less. It is not focusing the delivery team's energy on predicting what the customer *might* need (e.g. four different variations of the management report); it is working hands on with the business owners to find out what they *do* need – and then focusing all of the team's efforts on delivering the required outcomes in the agreed timeframes.

Maximizing your resources

Every aspect of lean techniques is designed to *maximize* the human, physical and financial resources of the organization:

- it is increasing the upfront quality of work to minimize resource time spent on addressing problems, reworking and damage control after the fact
- it is making better use of existing resources by reducing the amount of unnecessary work that they do, including the overheads associated with "over-management" and "just-in-case" preparation
- it is reducing "task-switching," so that staff are able to properly focus on the work that they are doing, instead of being physically (and mentally) pulled in different directions
- it is improving communication channels within and between areas of the organization, so that employees are all working from a shared understanding.

One aspect that has not been addressed sufficiently, however, is the waste that results from the *under-utilization* of resources.

By definition, under-utilization implies that a resource has greater capacity to produce value than the business process (or the organization) is using. This could be as simple as:

- a photocopier that is only used twice a day
- an empty office space
- surplus corporate funds in a non-interest bearing account
- employees who cannot progress their work because they are waiting on information, management approvals or materials.

For many organizations, however, under-utilization of people is a much more subtle activity where the physical, mental or creative abilities of employees are not used to their fullest potential. This can be a result of under-employment (hiring someone whose skill set exceeds their responsibilities); ineffective workflows or inadequate training (so that people are not able to perform as efficiently as they could); or high turnover (where people spend so much time focusing on knowledge transfer and new hire training that they are unable to focus on their core work). No matter what the cause, under-utilization of people is both a waste for the organization (who could be better leveraging their capabilities) – and a risk for the organization (as it has the potential to reduce employee motivation, satisfaction and pride in their work).

Ideally, organizations should endeavor (where possible) to implement hiring practices, business processes and training programs that allow employees to perform at their fullest potential. Realistically, however, even the most skilled employee needs to be available (and willing) to do work that the organization requires, even if it is not the best use of their skills (e.g. status reporting). A good metric is for the organization to aim for at least two-thirds of an employee's work to be suited to their skill levels; and to accept that the remaining third of their time is likely to be spent addressing organizational administration requirements, supervising other people or undertaking supplemental work for the team.

The ACTION plan described in *Chapter 5: Responsive Planning* identified the ***T**ell us what can be done* step as the point in the responsive planning process where the delivery team translates the highest-priority actionable goals into the specific activities that will be required to achieve these goals – and then advises the business owners on the work that can realistically be achieved in the upcoming iteration. Not only does this approach empower the members of the team to manage their responsibilities and workload, it allows them to identify the subset of work that will utilize the team's *collective* physical, mental and creative abilities to their fullest capacity. This enables the delivery team to divide the work amongst themselves, to compensate for each other's strengths and weaknesses, and to use their velocity as an indicator of their optimal levels of productivity.

Under-utilization of employees has two comparable circumstances that can result in equivalent levels of waste for the organization: the *over-utilization* and the *mis-utilization* of employees.

Both *over-utilization* and *mis-utilization* of employees can occur when employees focus their time and skills on work that has limited (or no) business value for the organization. This can include redundant or repeated work (due to a lack of effective communication channels), work that does not meet the needs of the target audience (requiring rework), and work that *exceeds* the needs of the target audience (over-production and over-delivery). The ACTION plan provides approaches for encouraging communication (see *Chapter 11: "Just-in-time" Communication*) and confirming that the work that the delivery team is doing meets the needs of the business owners (see *Chapter 8: Real-time Customer Feedback*), but how does it ensure that the delivery team does not fall into the "just-in-case" trap, focusing on the work that the business owners *might* need, instead of the work that they *do* need?

The very nature of Agile approaches means that teams do not have the time (or luxury) of focusing on hypothetical situations. The short iterations and "Apply, Inspect, Adapt" mindset of Agile approaches mean that delivery teams are not in a position to go too far down the wrong path before the business owners (or other factors in the organization) get them back on track. It also means that delivery teams are not in a position to over-deliver in preparation for what the customer *might* require; they have just enough time available to deliver what they know the customer really needs.

If the ACTION plan requires that everything the delivery team does is *in response to* what the business owner needs, then what happens when team members (who are closest to the work) have their own suggestions to improve the outcomes for the organization, such as the addition of a "shopping cart" feature on the website that the business owner did not ask for? Do lean techniques allow the organization to consider additional (or alternative) activities beyond the most basic work required to respond to the immediately identified needs of the business owners?

Agile approaches encourage the delivery team to think about what the business owners might need beyond what was already recorded in the requirements backlog, and to bring these ideas to the iteration planning sessions for discussion with the business owners. The biggest difference in the Agile approach is that the business owners are given the opportunity to approve, postpone or reject these suggestions *before* substantial organizational resources are utilized – and the delivery team resources have not sacrificed their time and energy on an outcome that is likely to result in minimal business value for the organization.

For more examples of how *lean techniques* can be applied to maximize staff productivity, see *Section 3: A Case Study*, which compares two organizations that have exactly the same business objectives, but take very different approaches to achieve these objectives.

CHAPTER 14: CONSTANTLY MEASURABLE QUALITY

How much does quality cost?

Although *how much does quality cost*? is not a trick question, it does have three different answers – particularly where the *cost* of quality is considered against both the *value* that high-quality outputs can bring to the organization, and the *issues* that producing low-quality outputs can create for the organization:

- ***Benefits for the organization***: high-quality outputs can deliver strong *external* benefits for an organization, including a positive public image, repeat customers and competitive advantage in the marketplace. However, it can also deliver significant *internal* benefits, such as reduced overheads, more satisfied employees and fewer last-minute "fire-fighting" activities that create unnecessary stress in the workplace.
- ***Risks to the organization***: low-quality outputs, on the other hand, can represent a significant liability for the organization, particularly if people outside the organization (e.g. customers, competitors) become aware of them. These external exposures are compounded by the internal impacts of low-quality outputs, including the overhead costs of rework, defect handling and damage control, as well as the effects that poor outputs can have on staff motivation, stress levels and camaraderie (e.g. pitting employees against each other in the "blame game").
- ***Implementation costs***: these are the overhead costs for the organization in establishing quality processes and

practices, and ensuring that there are sufficient resources (e.g. staff, equipment, education, management tools) for employees to use them.

The *Doing it right the first time* section of *Chapter 13: Waste Management* explained that resolving defects in a product or service *at the end of the process* is often far more costly to the organization overall than resolving the issues *throughout the process* that caused the defect in the first place. Issues within a process can include:

- ineffective business processes
- inefficient (or insufficient) work practices
- miscommunication that causes errors and rework
- outputs that do not meet the needs of the internal or external customer.

Although identifying a bad quality output before it leaves the organization can protect the organization from exposure and liability, it does nothing to stop the same problem from occurring again the next time, and the time after that ...

Organizations will often weigh the costs of implementing quality management and control processes against the potential internal and external risks for the organization. For example, a company which produces clothing may be willing to absorb the cost of an occasional faulty product leaving the organization, against the expenditure that would be needed to install better quality production equipment in the factory. A company that produces baby formula, however, will invest significant corporate funds in infrastructure to ensure that every product the organization ships meets stringent industry standards. The cost (and time) investment that an organization is willing to make to ensure quality outputs is in direct correlation with the potential exposure (and financial liability) that bad quality outputs can create for the organization.

For many organizations, "quality control" is a series of *checkpoints* that occur towards the end of a process to confirm whether or not the outcomes match expectations. Where physical outputs are produced, these checkpoints can be physical measurements, visual inspections and stress tests; where intellectual outputs are produced (such as documents) these checkpoints can be quality reviews by other employees. The intent of the checkpoints is to catch problems in the outputs *before* they reach their intended recipients, particularly when those recipients are external to the organization. There is, however, a distinction between:

- ***passive quality checkpoints*** that check a completed (or near completed) deliverable at the end of a process
- ***active quality checkpoints*** that review a deliverable early enough in the process to be able to impact (and improve) its quality.

Using passive quality checkpoints to catch a faulty output at the end of a process does not resolve the underlying issues that caused the quality problem in the first place (in the same way that treating a symptom is not the same as curing the disease). Organizations often spend countless resource hours "chasing their tails" trying to ensure better quality by instituting more frequent (and more stringent) passive quality checks at the end of a process. However, if the quality issue is in *the process itself*, then no amount of passive checks will stop the problem from occurring (and recurring) indefinitely.

Weight control and the bathroom scale

Steve McConnell wrote a guide for software developers that included an exceptionally powerful statement about how employees can ensure ongoing quality in their work:[50]

> If you want to lose weight, don't buy a new scale; change your diet.

At the heart of McConnell's statement was the critical premise that quality management is *not* a series of measurements at the end of the process to see how well the work was done; it is the establishment of a work environment (and corresponding business processes), which ensure that quality is a consideration in every activity along the way. McConnell was not telling readers to ignore the bathroom scale (as weight loss, like quality, needs to be measured in order to be managed effectively); he was telling readers not to assume that measurement alone will improve a situation if the underlying causes of the problem are not addressed.

This chapter identifies a number of approaches that organizations can use to build quality into their work environment and business processes, and explains how Agile practices use *active quality checkpoints* to maximize the quality of outputs throughout the process.

True quality requires a culture change

Quality is not a coincidence. It is the result of a work environment that:

---

[50] *Code Complete*, McConnell S, Microsoft Press (1993) ISBN 1556154844, 9781556154843.

- promotes high communication and information sharing within (and outside) the organization
- creates tools for knowledge capture and knowledge transfer that de-centralize expertise in the organization – and equip less experienced staff to deliver more reliable and consistent outcomes
- encourages employees to look for and recommend areas of improvement throughout the organization (including management procedures that are designed to elicit this information)
- structures work to be done in pairs and teams for greater accountability and cross-training
- recognizes and rewards employees for "getting it right the first time"
- supports skills development and continued education, so that employees are able to introduce and implement best practices in their work.

No amount of business process improvement is going to significantly change an organization where employees are rewarded for building silos of knowledge, are individually recognized (i.e. singled out) for the work that they did as part of a team, or are encouraged to do their work "the way things have always been done around here," instead of regularly looking for ways to improve the organization.

The impact of high communication

Agile approaches, such as the ACTION plan detailed in *Chapter 5: Responsive Planning*, are designed to create high communication, team-based environments. *Chapter 11: "Just-in-time" Communication* identified a range of techniques that Agile approaches use to encourage communication within and between areas of the organization, including:

- iteration planning sessions
- outcomes review sessions
- daily stand-up meetings
- pairing of delivery team members
- co-location of delivery team members
- cross-training of delivery team members.

All of these techniques are designed to promote information sharing and knowledge transfer, not just within a team, but across the organization.

One of the key outcomes of this multi-faceted communication approach is the establishment – and ongoing confirmation – of a *shared vision* and *shared expectations* for the work that is being done. This means that delivery teams can use the business owner's ongoing input to guide and shape the work that they are doing – and business owners can be confident that the outcomes at the end of the process will be as close as possible to what the organization requires. It also means that one key measurement of quality (customer satisfaction) is built directly into the process.

Each outcomes review session is an *active checkpoint*, where business owners assess the ongoing work of the delivery team against both qualitative and quantitative measurements. In some cases, the measurement of outputs is a subjective assessment by the business owner regarding whether the outputs align with their initial expectations (their "vision"). In other cases, the measurement of outputs is based on defined metrics, such as increases in sales orders or reduced overhead costs.

The intent of the review session is not for business owners to accept or reject the outputs presented by the delivery team based on these quality measurements – the intent is for both teams to use the session as an opportunity to *communicate* with each other, so that they can refine the outputs together.

This is not to say that the use of high-communication practices in one area of the organization is going to address significant communication deficiencies across an organization. A deeply-embedded culture of knowledge silos and "business as usual" mindsets is not going to change overnight, but the adoption of Agile practices in organizations has historically been the result of successful outcomes getting the attention of upper management. Even the most steadfast organizations are strategic enough to leverage approaches – even dramatically different approaches – as long as they can deliver proven results.

Quality by design

Having a work environment that encourages and promotes effective work practices is half the battle for building quality within the organization; the other half is designing the business processes within the organization to have *active quality checkpoints* throughout.

The lean techniques described in *Chapter 13: Waste Management* do not just enable business processes to be run more efficiently, they can also result in higher quality outputs by:

- reducing the amount of unnecessary work (including "just-in-case" work), so that staff can focus on their core business activities (i.e. the value stream)

- eliminating excess movement within the process, so that there are fewer hands involved in each step of the process – and, therefore, less opportunity for work to get lost between physical locations – or in the stack of papers on an employee's desk
- allowing employees sufficient time to focus properly on their work by minimizing task switching.

The fewer complexities there are in a business process (e.g. decision points, unnecessary tasks), the less potential there is for things to go wrong at each step of the process. This does not mean that a complex business process should be over-simplified, just to reduce the potential for error – but it does encourage organizations to look closely at what activities are core to the value stream, and which activities can be pared down (or eliminated) to reduce both costs and complexity in the process.

The IT industry uses an Agile approach called *refactoring* to continually review and, where required, restructure software solutions to be *as simple as possible* to meet the required business objectives. In some cases, this means *discarding* most (if not all) of the work that they have currently done, in order to establish a "more elegant" solution that will be easier for the organization to manage and extend upon in the future.

For some organizations, the thought of "throwing away" an existing business process would be impossible to sell to upper management. This is, however, not wholly different to a homeowner's decision to tear down and rebuild a house on their property, instead of extending the existing one. There are times when it is more cost-effective for an organization to achieve its longer-term objectives by architecting an environment that is specifically designed for that vision, rather than by trying to retrofit an existing process – especially if that process was established 10 years ago to meet the needs of the organization at that time.

So, once the process itself is as simple as it can reasonably be to achieve its intended business objective, how does the organization create *active quality checkpoints* throughout the process – and avoid the expense and exposure of only finding issues at the end? The key to implementing active quality checkpoints in a business process is making the measurements of success an *intrinsic part* of the process.

Fit-for-purpose outputs

Agile practitioners in the IT industry have made both a science and an art form of building quality into their business processes.

One of the Agile techniques that the IT industry uses to manage the quality of software *while it is being developed* is a practice called *test-driven development* (TDD). The basic premise of TDD is simple (and readily transferable to any business activity):

> Identify your measurements for success upfront – and design your work around these measurements.

In the IT industry, this involves having the software development team (literally) build all of the tests that they are going to measure their software against *before* they begin writing the first line of programming code for the solution. This enables the delivery team to both design their work around these measurements – and regularly check their ongoing work to confirm that they are delivering outputs that will achieve the required results.

Other industries can achieve an equivalent outcome for their business activities by identifying and structuring their end outputs (e.g. products, reports, services) against their measurements for success *before* beginning the work required to create these deliverables. For example, if a delivery team is required to put together a report that identifies changing trends in customer demand over the past 24 months, the team members would first confirm the measurements for a successful report with the business owners:

- the customer demand report will achieve its objectives if it can accurately document:
    - the historical and current quantity of customer orders
    - upward and downward trends in customer orders over the past 24 months
    - external factors that might influence fluctuations in customer orders, such as seasonal variations.

The delivery team may even do some background research and preparation with stakeholders before confirming these measurements for success with the business owners, such as:

- identifying what specific information is required to accurately capture customer orders (e.g. number of orders per month, products being ordered) and confirming that this information is available within the organization
- laying out the structure of the proposed report in a draft form, including all of the information that they believe will be needed.

Presenting these proposed measurements for success to the business owners (before any significant work has been done) results in the following feedback:

- customer orders within the organization need to be benchmarked against overall industry trends, in order to isolate variations in market behavior that are specific to the organization (critical priority)
- identifying the ordering trends of individual customers (particularly the ones with the largest orders) would help to identify the behavior of repeat customers – and to determine whether repeat orders can be reasonably predicted in sales forecast reports (high priority).

This initial feedback from the business owners alone has enabled the delivery team to extend their initial measurements for success to also include accurately documenting comparable industry figures and individual customer behavior.

With these measurements for success in hand, the delivery team endeavors to collect the required information and put together a report with real production data by the next outcomes review session. In putting together the report, the delivery team finds that the organization's internal systems also track the number of times that a customer *cancelled* an order before it was fulfilled. Before the team members spend time gathering and formatting this new information, they assess it against the original measurements of success that were agreed with the business owners: will knowing how many orders were cancelled assist the organization in accurately determining trends in customer demand?

In this situation, the delivery team realizes that they are not in a position to make this decision on their own. They contact the business owners to confirm whether this added detail will add value to the report. This discussion with the business owners identifies that cancelled orders are not a good indicator of customer demand, as their experience indicates that most customers who cancel an order subsequently resubmit an equivalent order soon after. This means that including this data in the report could artificially inflate the customer demand trends.

Instead of including this additional information in the report simply because it was available, the delivery team assessed the work that would be required to include the information against their originally agreed measurements for success. The subsequent decision *not* to include this new information in the report resulted in additional time that the delivery team is able to spend focusing on the true criteria for success (e.g. the behavior of repeat customers), which is likely to result in a higher quality output for the organization overall.

The interesting thing about designing business processes around measurements of success is that it is one of the triggers for the delivery team reviewing and restructuring their current work (i.e. refactoring) to better align the activities that they are doing with the business owner's objectives.

For the customer demand report, the delivery team knowing upfront that the organization may need to track individual customer orders as part of their analysis, means that they can request (and prepare for) this level of detail from the beginning; and knowing that the organization *does not* require detail about cancelled orders means that they can *simplify* the report to only include the required information for *completed* orders. Realigning the report to better suit the needs of the organization may mean that the delivery team needs to discard (or revise) some of the draft report layouts that they were working on (which had included cancelled customer orders in the overall totals). However, the delivery team also realizes that making this change will result in significantly less work in the report development process overall than if they were to restructure the report (and report data) at the *end* of the process.

The (almost) real-time measuring stick

In the IT industry, monitoring and measuring the quality of outputs is a much more straightforward (and quantifiable) activity than it may be for other industries. Software developers have the benefit of tests which clearly identify when a defined outcome has been achieved (e.g. when a website feedback form has been sent to the customer service department) and when it has failed (e.g. the website feedback form was *not* sent because the phone number field was left blank). Software developers even have the benefit of *automated testing harnesses*, which enable them to run *all* of their quantifiable tests *every day* as a constant measure of the quality and progress of their work. Any non-quantifiable quality measurements that they have (e.g. usability) can be measured as part of the outcomes review sessions with the business owners. The fact is that daily quality checking is one of the few circumstances in which the IT industry may be better positioned than other industries in using Agile approaches.

For other industries, the degree to which an organization can monitor and measure the quality of work through regular (e.g. daily) quality checking is often more limited. In *Chapter 12: Immediate Status Tracking*, several reporting tools were identified for regularly monitoring and managing Agile work, including:

- requirements backlogs

- delivery backlogs
- velocity trackers
- executive dashboards.

These tools are primarily designed to track the *progress of work completed* and the *effort remaining* to achieve the agreed objectives; they are not specifically designed to monitor the *quality* of the work that has been done by the delivery team.

Unless you are in an industry (like the IT industry) where work is so quantifiable that quality checking can be automated, it is unlikely that there will be tools available for business owners to easily monitor the quality of outputs on a daily basis. Therefore, the best quality management tools that an organization can use in their Agile work are the communication methods detailed in *Chapter 11: "Just-in-time" Communication*, particularly pairing and co-location of delivery teams, daily stand-up meetings, and outcomes review sessions at the end of each iteration.

Pairing and *co-location* of the delivery team establishes a high-communication environment where delivery team members are encouraged to work together, check (and critique) each other's work, and jointly overcome challenges. In addition, the *daily stand-up meetings* provide a forum for the delivery team to step back and assess the work that they are doing as a group, as well as raise any issues that they have encountered for the Agile facilitator to resolve. These communication tools help the delivery team to regularly monitor the work that they are doing against the objectives (and measurements) agreed with the business owners at the start of each iteration – and to continually assess whether they are delivering high-quality outputs based on these measurements. They also provide a mechanism for escalating exceptions and problems when they arise, which allows the core work of the delivery team to be progressed without interruption.

Equally, the *outcomes review session* is a dedicated opportunity for *business owners* to regularly assess the quality of the delivery team's work. When the ACTION plan is done in four-week iterations, the organization has at least *one time each month* where key stakeholders can get a hands-on review of the delivery team's work – and track the completed work against the originally agreed objectives. For organizations that require more stringent monitoring of the quality of the delivery team's ongoing work, the ACTION plan can be reduced to two-week iterations. This allows the business owners to get a hands-on review of completed work every other week – and to request rework if the quality of the outputs does not meet their expectations.

The communication tools in Agile approaches provide both the business owners and the delivery team with mechanisms for including *active quality checkpoints* in their ongoing work. These active checkpoints position the organization to respond more quickly (and more cost-effectively) to issues that arise than traditional quality reviews at the end of the process. They allow the delivery team to focus its efforts on producing high business-value outcomes, instead of rushing at the end of the process to fix the problems that were found just before the deadline.

Exponential returns on your quality investment

This chapter began by identifying the costs of quality, including the benefits that high-quality outputs can bring to the organization – and the protection that these high-quality outputs can provide for the organization against internal issues and external liabilities. It also identified that there are overhead costs in implementing quality processes, practices and tools within the organization – and that organizations need to weigh these costs against the potential internal and external risks for the organization. So, is the investment in high quality simply a way for the organization to avoid litigation? Or, is there a return on investment that makes investing in quality a sound business decision, beyond risk aversion?

An organization that truly implements high-quality practices and processes is likely to receive the following returns on their investment:

- market position:
  - more reliable products and services
  - quicker time to market (due to less rework)
  - more positive public image
  - competitive advantage over less stringent organizations
  - more satisfied customers
- financial:
  - reduced "total cost of production" overheads (costs, time and staff) – including the ongoing benefits of having more simplified, fit-for-purpose business processes
  - increased sales
  - less work required to win customers
  - greater likelihood of repeat customers
- human resources:
  - more satisfied employees
  - more motivated employees

- greater employee confidence and pride in their work
- better employee retention rates
- a working environment with less stress and negativity (due to the minimized need for "blame game" assignment and last-minute "fire-fighting" activities).

In addition, organizations that institute high-quality practices and processes are well-positioned to be formally certified to industry quality management standards (such as ISO9001), which can significantly strengthen their credibility and competitive position in the marketplace – including making them eligible to undertake work that can *only* be done by quality certified organizations.

Most importantly, the high-communication tools and active quality checkpoints in Agile approaches can position an organization to achieve high-quality outputs *without a significant upfront investment*. This means that the ROI equation is resolved quickly, so that the benefits listed above can become pure gain for the organization.

CHAPTER 15: REARVIEW MIRROR CHECKING

Slight imperfections

No process is perfect. Agile approaches endeavor to create a more perfect environment by focusing on high business-value outcomes, establishing regular communication channels, encouraging hands-on teamwork and directly involving stakeholders – but even the most well-run business activities can always be improved. This is why the Agile world includes *retrospectives* as part of the outcomes review session at the end of each iteration.

Retrospectives are a dedicated time when the Agile team can step back and review the work that was undertaken in the previous iteration. Retrospectives provide the business owners and the delivery team with a chance to collectively reflect on both the good and bad aspects of the work that they did. The intent of the exercise is to recognize those processes (and people) that were particularly effective in the previous iteration; and to identify challenges and problems that need to be addressed in order to improve the work in subsequent iterations.

The structure of a retrospective is quite simple. An hour (or so) is allocated at the end of each outcomes review session for the participants to:

- review the work that was done
- acknowledge the positive outcomes
- discuss where work could have been done better
- use this information to identify "opportunities for improvement" which can be actioned, in order to make the work in subsequent iterations more effective.

Once opportunities for improvement are identified (and listed on the whiteboard), the Agile team members then assess each item to determine:

- Who is in a position to take action on this improvement? For example, a communication issue within the delivery team can most likely be resolved by the team members themselves, but the need to purchase better equipment needs to be escalated to management.
- What is the urgency (i.e. priority) of the improvement? Is it something that is going to completely stop work from progressing (such as lack of support from a key stakeholder), or is it something that the team can postpone until the next iteration in favor of more critical activities?

At the end of the retrospective, the Agile team takes ownership of actioning the highest-priority items that they are in a position to address; these improvement items are then added to the requirements backlog for consideration, in conjunction with the other commitments that the delivery team has in the coming iteration. Where there are high-priority action items that need to be addressed by people *outside* the Agile team, the Agile facilitator takes ownership of following up on these items with the relevant people.

Not surprisingly, the approach that Agile teams use for assessing and actioning opportunities for improvement in a retrospective is similar to the way in which business requirements are reviewed and prioritized as part of the iteration planning session. The intent of the retrospective is *not* to create mounds of paperwork in order to effect the necessary improvements; the intent is to identify and action improvements in line with the other priority work that the team is doing.

You only need to glance at the mirror …

People check their rearview mirrors when they are driving in order to get a 360-degree perspective of the road conditions. They know that looking ahead alone will not give them all of the information that they need in order to proceed confidently. Equally, they know that focusing on the rearview mirror for too long can put them in even greater danger.

There is a reasonable balance between *glancing* at a rearview mirror, in order to get perspective, and *focusing* on it. Retrospectives are not intended to be blaming sessions, or endless discussions on why something did not go as expected. They are opportunities for Agile teams to glance at the mirror, adjust their ongoing work, and (in extreme circumstances) reconsider their travel plans altogether based on the information gathered.

This is why retrospectives should not be day-long activities. (In most cases, they take about an hour.) Keeping the retrospective timing to an hour avoids the potential for them becoming extended "think tanks" where teams spend endless amounts of time contemplating the meaning of life. Retrospectives are brainstorming sessions where issues (and resolutions) get identified, prioritized, assigned ownership and actioned.

What a retrospective is – and is not

In order for the retrospective to be a constructive and valuable exercise for the Agile team, there are some basic guidelines to follow:

- ***Keep it to the time limit***: generally, retrospectives should run for an hour, except for rare circumstances (e.g. particularly complex work), where they can run for up to two hours.
- ***Stay on topic***: the discussion needs to stay focused on the core objectives and not digress too far into any one issue.
- ***Balance the good and bad observations***: it is tempting for attendees to focus on the issues encountered in the previous iteration, but this is also the forum for the good work and effective work practices from the delivery team to be recognized.
- ***Use constructive language***: the language of the retrospective needs to be professional and respectful, so that team members are comfortable discussing (and resolving) issues together.

It is the job of the Agile facilitator to ensure that retrospectives follow these guidelines, so that these exercises can provide the greatest ongoing value for the team.

One last comment about the structure of retrospectives: although managers are welcome to attend these sessions, they need to respect the fact that retrospectives are *team-driven* exercises. The intent of the retrospective is for the business owners and the delivery team members, who have been actively involved in the process, to be able to freely discuss (and resolve) their issues. This is why, if managers choose to attend retrospectives, they need to be prepared to go there as observers only.

There is an argument to say that the mere presence of managers or executives in a retrospective (even as observers) may unintentionally affect the dynamic of the exercise, by making attendees feel more self-conscious about discussing their concerns – or less likely to want to expose what may be perceived by management as weaknesses in the process. Therefore, managers need to make a judgment call on whether it would be more valuable for them to attend retrospectives, or to be briefed on the outcomes of the exercise after the fact. Why put a speed bump on an otherwise smooth racing track?

The self-correcting team

The Agile team is not just empowered to self-manage the work that they do; they are equally empowered (and equipped) to *monitor* and *correct* their work before, during and after each iteration.

The iteration planning session that takes place before each iteration includes estimation activities that allow the delivery team to identify how much work is involved in each high-priority requirement, which then enables them to determine the amount of work they can reasonably commit to in the upcoming iteration. (*See* the *In my estimation ...* section of *Chapter 10: Management by Self-motivation* for details on how delivery teams estimate their work.)

As part of these activities, the team uses estimation cards as a "checks and balances" way of confirming their estimates across all delivery team members, including (when necessary) checking the velocity of the equivalent work that the team has completed, to assess how their actual work time compared against their previous estimates. This confirmation of historical performance against current estimates allows the team to have a quick glance at the rearview mirror as a "sanity check" on the numbers that they are using in their estimates.

Within each iteration, the team members use the tools detailed in *Chapter 12: Immediate Status Tracking* to monitor their ongoing work and "get it back on track" when needed. This allows both the business owners and the delivery team to *regularly check* their rearview mirror as the work is progressing and self-correct where their productivity level (i.e. their velocity) is not on track with their original estimates. One Agile thought leader has even introduced the concept of a cut-down *five-minute retrospective*[51] as an extension of the delivery team's daily stand-up meetings. In these quick retrospectives, the delivery team asks itself two key questions:

- What have we improved?
- What do we still need to work on?

The premise of the five-minute retrospective is to enable a time-pressured team to have the high-level benefits of a retrospective, without asking them to commit one to two hours of their time. However, it also encourages the delivery team to reflect on (and self-correct) their work more often than once an iteration, which, for a team that is struggling with serious communication or productivity issues, may enable them to address the problem well before it impacts the overall outcomes from that iteration.

At the end of each iteration, the retrospective session is the mechanism for more formally reviewing the work that was done as a focused team activity. The fact that retrospectives

---

[51] *No time for reflection? Try a 5 minute retrospective*, Stevens P (2008): *http://agilesoftwaredevelopment.com/blog/peterstev/no-time-reflection-try-5-minute-retrospective*.

are deliberately run *by* the Agile team *for* the Agile team allows them to take ownership of the improvements that are needed to make their work more productive. The team members are the ones responsible for identifying (and prioritizing) the extent to which each issue impacts their ability to deliver ongoing business value to the organization – and they are equally responsible for following through on the action items that they commit to.

Changing your travel plans

Although retrospectives are intended to provide an opportunity for Agile teams to reflect on their work, so that actionable improvements can be identified, there are occasional situations in which the outcomes of the retrospective will reveal a more significant (and potentially insurmountable) problem, such as:

- an essential business owner who is no longer available to participate in the process due to other commitments
- a problem with equipment or facilities that cannot be resolved quickly (e.g. faulty machinery)
- a substantial issue within the dynamic of the delivery team that is jeopardizing their ability to work together.

In some cases, resolving the issue identified could be as simple as changing the members of the delivery team. However, in other cases, the resolution may require more money, resources or time than the organization is in a position to spend.

Where the issue cannot be resolved in the near term, the retrospective may indicate to the business owners that ongoing work needs to be cancelled (or postponed indefinitely) until the core issue is resolved. Although this may not be the preferred outcome for the Agile team (or the organization), it is better for the issue to be addressed directly than to drag on and affect the ongoing productivity of the delivery team.

The *When to walk away* section of *Chapter 5: Responsive Planning* identified that ending the ACTION planning process (even if it has not yet achieved its intended objectives) is, in reality, an extremely positive outcome for the organization. It avoids having the organization spend significant budget funds, time or resources on a process that is not going forward in the most effective way for the organization. In this way, the retrospective becomes another *active quality checkpoint* for the organization, addressing (and, ideally, resolving) core issues in the process before they can significantly impact the productivity levels of the team.

CHAPTER 16: CONTINUOUS IMPROVEMENT

Become better – or become obsolete

At the very start of this book, the following challenge was put forward to readers: how is your organization going to sustain its current business processes and practices in an ever-increasing high-technology global marketplace? Organizations that want to survive (and thrive) in a rapidly changing marketplace need to focus on *continuously improving* the way in which they do work.

It does not take an enormous crack in your organization's business process pipeline to cause it to burst. Even small leakages can lead to compounded issues in the long term.

Everything about Agile approaches is designed to provide *continuous improvement* for the organization:

- The high-communication, business-value-driven prioritization and team-driven estimation activities in iteration planning sessions can ensure that the delivery team is continually focused on delivering the highest business-value outcomes for the organization within allocated time, budget and resource constraints.
- Daily stand-up meetings, pairing, co-location of delivery team members, refactoring, velocity checking and five-minute retrospectives all encourage the delivery team members to focus on continuous improvement *within* each iteration.
- The outcomes review sessions and retrospectives when the work is completed, encourage continuous improvement *between* iterations.

The time, cost and resource efficiencies that Agile approaches deliver are compounded by the improved results that they can generate for the organization:

- A high-quality product or service that more closely aligns with a customer's requirement does not just save your organization from having to do rework, it can encourage repeat customer sales with minimal opportunity costs for the organization to absorb.
- A business process that was made more efficient through the use of refactoring can produce ongoing savings for your organization every time that process is used.
- Motivated and satisfied employees can reduce turnover rates, which not only saves your organization from the overheads of acquiring and training new staff, it also encourages people with the strongest corporate memory – including hands-on experience in making Agile approaches work within your corporate culture – to continue to apply their knowledge for the ongoing benefit of the organization.

Continuous improvement benefits are able to be delivered by a range of Agile approaches, from employing lean techniques in order to optimize your business processes (see *Chapter 13: Waste Management*), to changing your corporate culture in order to create a work environment that encourages high quality (see *True quality requires a culture change* in *Chapter 14: Constantly Measurable Quality*), through to using retrospectives to continually review and improve the work that is being done by Agile teams (*see Chapter 15: Rearview Mirror Checking*). Any one of these approaches alone can protect your organization from running out of time, money, resources and customer good will as you grow to meet the ever-increasing global demand. All of these approaches *combined* can position your organization to achieve real productivity gains that will keep you well ahead of the competition as market demand evolves.

One step back – five steps forward

Taking the time to implement Agile approaches – with minimal upfront costs – can position the organization to receive exponential returns. Adopting and using Agile approaches within your organization is likely to require:

- strategies to convince decision makers to endorse these approaches
- initial overheads in training and equipping your staff to apply Agile practices and techniques most effectively
- a culture change that moves the organization from knowledge silos and passive quality checkpoints to high communication, responsive planning, lean techniques and quality-driven processes.

It is for these very reasons that the adoption of Agile approaches will not happen overnight. Even if you are fortunate enough to work for an organization (like BT) that is willing to mandate the shift to Agile approaches across the organization, there will be additional time required to get employees familiar (and comfortable) with these practices. For most organizations, however, the adoption of Agile approaches is likely to be a slower process where the success of individual Agile projects gives others in the organization the confidence to try these approaches within their own areas. This "grassroots campaign" strategy can eventually result in the broader adoption of Agile approaches across the organization, but you need to allow time for the grass to grow.

In the *Exponential returns on your quality investment* section of *Chapter 14: Constantly Measurable Quality*, it was identified that Agile approaches can position an organization to achieve high-quality outputs *without a significant upfront investment*, which means that the ROI equation can be resolved quickly – enabling the subsequent benefits of Agile approaches to become *pure gain* for the organization. This assertion does not just apply to the benefits of high-quality outputs; it equally applies to the benefits of having more efficient business processes, a more responsive corporate culture, greater employee retention and a more satisfied customer base. Once Agile approaches are in place, the infrastructure needed to sustain these approaches is relatively small (mostly ongoing staff education and resource allocation to participate on Agile teams).

Added to these benefits is the fact that there is a groundswell of resources available for Agile teams to learn from the community of Agile practitioners who have been refining these approaches for the past three decades (see *More Information on Agile* for a list of these resources). So, even the costs of ongoing staff education can be reduced by leveraging the expertise (and generosity) of others in the Agile community who are working together to improve these processes for all organizations.

All of this means that introducing Agile approaches within your organization can be a relatively low-cost activity with significant ongoing returns. Perhaps the most important return for the organization, however, is not the reduced overheads or increased profit margins that the organization can achieve; it is the *resiliency* and *sustainability* of the organization to grow – and *thrive* – in changing market conditions.

Regular review and adjustment

The aspects that make responsive planning so effective in meeting changing stakeholder needs are the same ones that make continuous improvement techniques so powerful as market conditions evolve. In a static market, the regular review and adjustment of business activities is a mechanism for ensuring that work is being done as efficiently (and effectively) as possible. In a dynamic market, the regular review and adjustment of business activities is a *necessity* to ensure that the organization is continuing to meet market demand.

In a world where technology is growing in *dog years* and the physical barriers that used to impede global trading are rapidly being torn down, *annual reviews* of the organization's performance will not suffice. Most organizations are strategic enough to keep a close eye on their competitors, to monitor industry trends and to try to predict (and plan for) changes in market behavior. Yet, how many of these organizations are equally diligent in ensuring that internal staffing levels and business processes are in a position to support these changes? What if these changes do not indicate *potential increases* in the levels of work that the staff is currently doing, but the likelihood of *long periods of downtime*, or shifts *away from* your organization's core activities? Are your internal resources equally positioned to be productive in a lower demand period, or to retrain staff skills (and retool equipment) to support a changing market demand?

Continuous improvement techniques are designed to provide an organization with pulse point checks of the work that is being done against the *most current information* in the marketplace. This means that indications of increasing market demand can be adapted to in small increments, instead of mad dashes to hire more staff. It also means that indications of decreasing market demand can be addressed through normal staff attrition, instead of mass layoffs.

The Agile approaches detailed in this book (such as direct stakeholder engagement) do not only provide organizations with a mechanism for keeping a finger on the pulse of the market; they equally provide organizations with tools (such as lean techniques) to adapt internal business processes and work practices to accommodate the results of these pulse point checks – and with techniques, such as refactoring, that create simpler, more efficient business processes that can minimize the overheads in making these changes.

Quantifying and measuring improvement

Throughout this chapter, the terms *efficient* and *cost-effective* have been used to describe the benefits that continuous improvement techniques can bring to an organization. How does the organization quantify and measure these improvements, in order to both confirm that they are achieving the intended results, and to use this information to acquire ongoing executive support for these techniques?

The *Measuring cost/benefit* section of *Chapter 6: Business-value-driven Work* provides a formula that organizations can use to assign a cost-driven expected business value to each planned actionable goal, in order to assign it a relative priority against other goals that are competing for the same resources. A similar approach can be used to measure the business value of previous work activities against improved work activities, by applying the following steps:

- ***Baseline***: in order to measure comparative improvements, the organization needs to assess and record the business value of work activities prior to the introduction of continuous improvement techniques. This snapshot represents the *baseline* for future comparison.
- ***Isolate***: to the largest extent possible, the organization needs to *isolate* the work activities being measured against factors in the organization that could also impact these activities. For example, an expected reduction in staff due to scheduled vacation leave.
- ***Apply***: once the targeted work activities have been baselined and isolated from other factors in the organization (to the largest extent possible), the organization can then apply the proposed continuous improvement techniques to the targeted work activities.
- ***Measure***: after a pre-determined period of time, the organization can then use the business-value formula to take another snapshot of the targeted work activities and compare relative business values using the applicable KPIs (overhead costs, net profits).
- ***Repeat***: as continuous improvement techniques are regularly used to improve ongoing work activities, the same formula can be applied at regular intervals to measure the ongoing business-value impact of these techniques.

Organizations can use an equivalent approach for estimating the business-value impacts of proposed continuous improvement changes using *predictive analysis*. In this situation, the *baseline* is taken, using the *current work activities*, and the measurement is against models for *proposed future changes*, which can be documented through the business process modeling described in *Chapter 13: Waste Management*.

Bringing it all together

One of my most favorite quotes is the following observation from George Eliot:

> It is never too late to be what you might have been.

Everybody has the ability to improve, no matter how old, or how set in their ways they are – and organizations are no different.

Section 3: A Case Study demonstrates the impact that implementing Agile approaches can have on business value generation for organizations in *every* industry, including the most traditional ones.

Section 4: Making Agile Work in Your Organization provides pathways for *any* organization to trial Agile approaches, from the most change-averse established organizations, to the most forward-thinking new start-ups. This section includes:

- a workflow tool to guide you through selecting the most appropriate Agile approaches for your organization's activities
- guidelines for introducing Agile approaches within your organization, and
- tools for your organization to actively apply, manage and track the effectiveness of these approaches.

The key to Agile success is to start by selecting and implementing the most effective Agile practices and techniques to suit the specific needs of your organization, and, then, focus on *continuous improvement*, so that the ongoing value of these approaches can be adapted to suit the evolving needs of your organization.

Describing the benefits of Agile approaches on paper can be valuable, but seeing the power of Agile approaches in action is far more compelling. The best way to illustrate both the power and the value of Agile approaches for every organization is to compare them side-by-side with traditional business approaches, using common business scenarios that organizations *in any industry sector* can appreciate.

The following section provides a composite case study of two competing pharmaceutical companies that need to prepare for the launch of a new product that they are offering. Each pharmaceutical company has to build a product website, make consumers aware of the website and fulfill customer orders using the *same budget allocation*, and the *same number of employees*, in the *same timeframe*. One company uses traditional business approaches to achieve these objectives, the other uses Agile approaches; and the two companies achieve vastly different results.

SECTION 3: A CASE STUDY

A CASE STUDY: TRADITIONAL VERSUS AGILE APPROACHES

The following composite case study describes a common scenario for many organizations: preparing for the launch of a new product. In this scenario, two pharmaceutical companies approach the same business challenge in two very different ways. One company uses the traditional process that most organizations would follow, the other uses an Agile approach; and there is a marked difference in the outcomes.

Website building in a competitive marketplace

The best way to start illustrating the value of Agile approaches is to use an example that bridges both business and technology drivers: building a product website in the pharmaceutical industry, a highly competitive (and often volatile) sector, where public image and time to market are critical.

Two competing pharmaceutical companies – let's call them Traditional Approaches, Inc. and Agile Approaches, Inc. – have each discovered a medical breakthrough pill that is guaranteed to cure the common cold. Both companies are currently in the final stages of government-regulated testing, with the expectation that the pill will be available to go to full market distribution in six months. Each pharmaceutical company has done significant market research indicating that their target demographic for purchasing this product:

- is between the ages of 25 and 55

- is distrustful of broad marketing claims, such as "cures the common cold"
- sees the Internet as a convenient way to research and confirm information
- is willing to provide their personal details via the Internet, but only on a trusted website with a secure connection.

Therefore, in order to capture the target demographic audience, both pharmaceutical companies decide to build a secure website for their product, which will be released as part of the product launch. Given the exceptional results that were achieved in the initial testing of the pill, both pharmaceutical companies realize that the best way to gain credibility in the marketplace is to provide prospective customers with free trial samples of the pills. Each company is convinced that once people are able to see firsthand how effective the pill is, word-of-mouth networking and viral marketing is likely to create the ongoing sales momentum that they need.

In order to meet the six-month timeframe for the product launch, each pharmaceutical company establishes an urgent internal initiative for building the product website. Based on market research and government regulations, both companies identify the following minimum core requirements for the product website:

- the website must contain credible product information
- the website must enable people to request a product sample, so that they can see the powerful results of the new drug firsthand
- in order to request a product sample, customers must prove that they are at least 18 years old (to comply with

federal regulations on the controlled distribution of pharmaceuticals)

- the website must be able to process up to 10,000 concurrent orders
- any information gathered on the website must be sent through secure communication channels.

So, the two competing pharmaceutical companies – Traditional Approaches, Inc. and Agile Approaches, Inc. – both lock themselves behind closed doors to deliver the best website possible in time for the product launch. However, the executives in these two organizations take very different approaches on how their staff will meet this requirement.

The traditional approach

The first pharmaceutical company, Traditional Approaches, Inc., decides to brand the pill "Cold Riddance," with a full media campaign to encourage customers to request a sample pack from their website. The CEO of Traditional Approaches publishes a press release announcing that "Cold Riddance" will be in the marketplace by January 1st – and issues an internal memo to all executives to treat this product as their topmost priority.

The information technology (IT) department is allocated a budget of $180,000 and 12 full-time employees for the website development over the next six months. The only directive from the CEO is for the IT department to do "whatever it takes" to make sure that the January 1st deadline is achieved.

Budget	\$180,000
Number of employees	12 full-time employees
Delivery date	December 31st
Scope of deliverable	Fully functional and tested website with: • credible product information • secure sample pack order form • confirmation that the customer is over 18 years old • the ability to process up to 10,000 concurrent orders

Figure 7: Website development constraints

July

Acting on the CEO's announcement, the Vice President of Marketing at Traditional Approaches writes a memo to the IT Director, detailing the core requirements for the website. Given the especially critical nature of this product launch, the Marketing Vice President also organizes a face-to-face meeting with the IT Director to emphasize the importance of:

- the website supporting all of the stated requirements
- the website being delivered within the stated budget
- the website being delivered on time.

It is clear to both the Marketing Vice President and the IT Director that the future of the company could depend entirely on the success (or failure) of this product.

The Traditional Approaches IT Director is understandably concerned about the high visibility of this website. A hugely successful product launch can make a career; a disastrous product launch can just as easily destroy one. So, to be safe, the IT Director instructs the website development team to put together a detailed specification for the product website, including proposed screen designs and descriptions of functionality. (This way, the IT department is guaranteed to produce exactly what the company needs – or at least have somewhere else to put the blame if the website is a failure.) The IT Director instructs the website team *not to take any further action* until the Marketing Vice President has signed off on their website specification.

The traditional approach

- Put together a detailed upfront specification.

Get sign-off on the full specification before undertaking any work.

August

Five weeks (and several updates) later, the Traditional Approaches Marketing VP signs off on the product website specification, on the understanding that the website will be available for testing at least one month before the product launch. The website development team now has a little less than four months to deliver a fully functional website that meets the signed-off details in the website specification.

The next four months ...

The Traditional Approaches website development team proceeds with their standard process for building websites. They lock themselves away with their computers, following the specification as far as technically possible.

At the direction of the Marketing Vice President, the website development team limits their contact with the marketing department to only the most urgent questions, so that the marketing team can focus on their other campaign work for the product launch.

It is technically challenging, but the Traditional Approaches website development team is committed to delivering a product website that will meet the specification in the agreed timeframe. Late nights, weekend work, postponing vacations – whatever it takes.

The traditional approach

- Have the website team work independently from the business areas.
- Discourage communication with the business areas during the process.
- Wait until the end of the process before showing the business the work that has been done.

December (one possible outcome)

Four months later, the Traditional Approaches website development team announces that the product website is ready for testing. They organize a meeting with representatives from the marketing department to walk them through the website screens. They proudly demonstrate all of the required features, including how the customer sample request form securely integrates with a centralized identity confirmation database, to confirm that the customer is at least 18 years old. They even show the marketing department the "shopping cart" feature that they decided to add to the website, which they hoped would make it easier for customers to order both sample packs and full product packs on the site in the future.

Overall, the marketing department representatives are satisfied that the product website meets the requirements detailed in the specification. They do, however, have one strong concern about the behavior of the sample request form:

- The form only advises customers if there are problems with their information after all of the form screens have been completed. This means that users will need to go back to each screen one-by-one to correct errors before the form can be re-submitted. The marketing department representatives are concerned that this will frustrate customers and deter them from completing the form.

Additionally, they have some smaller concerns that:

- the colors on the screen are visibly different to the colors on the printed materials for the product launch
- the graphics on the screens are not being displayed consistently on some browsers.

However, these concerns are minor in comparison to the overall usability issue with error handling on the forms.

The website development team advises the marketing department that they can fix some of the screen colors; but, with only four weeks left before the product launch, it is too late in the process to make any significant error-handling changes to the website.

The marketing department representatives agree that, although the usability issue is important, it is not worth the risk of jeopardizing the product website release date. They are happy to progress website testing based on what they have seen to date (and to deal with the usability issues in the next release of the website). So, with the marketing department's approval, the Traditional Approaches website development team now has four weeks to fully test and implement the site in time for the product launch.

The traditional approach

- Business issues are identified that cannot be resolved before the deadline.
- The only options are to go forward with a less than optimal website – or risk having no website at all.

One week into product testing, the Traditional Approaches quality assurance team finds a significant problem with the website. The identity confirmation function slows down to a halt if more than 100 people are trying to submit the sample request form at the same time. In some cases, this delayed response is causing the user's system to crash. The quality assurance team knows that the website cannot be released without the identity confirmation function. An urgent resolution meeting is called.

The website development team members offer their IT Director three options to resolve the problem:

1 Replace the automated identity confirmation function with a pop-up screen that asks users to verify that they are at least 18 years old before continuing.
2 Rebuild the identity confirmation function, so that there is a queue to hold confirmation requests until the system is ready to receive them.
3 Increase performance by adding extra servers and network bandwidth, so that each identity confirmation can be processed in 20% of the original time.

The IT Director knows that something must be done to resolve this issue. Postponing the website launch is not an option. The first two suggested resolutions require programming changes that could jeopardize the integrity of the sample request form functionality overall (especially as there will be little time to test the changes once they are done). The third suggested resolution does not require programming changes, but will cost the organization over $60,000 in additional equipment – not to mention a significant amount of staff overtime to get the new machinery in place (and tested) in time for the launch. This is not an ideal option for the organization, but it is the safest one. Most of all, it allows the IT Director to confidently go forward with a website that is launched in time. So, budget allocations for future IT work are moved to this initiative, and the department gets the funds needed to acquire the additional equipment.

The traditional approach

- Testing at the end of the process results in significant performance issues that cannot easily be resolved.
- The business must choose between allocating additional emergency funding or risking the availability of the entire website in time for the launch.

In the end, Traditional Approaches, Inc. launches their website on time. It is not as usable as they would have liked, staff had to put in over 200 hours of overtime and the budget blew out by over $60,000, but the website is ready for the product launch and the IT Director's job is safe until the next major disaster occurs.

Yet, what if the problems found in website testing could not be resolved simply by shifting budget allocations?

December (an alternative outcome)

What if Traditional Approaches, Inc. had used exactly the same process to build the product website, but this time the quality assurance team found a *significant security issue* in the website one month before the product launch? In this alternative outcome, the testers find that users can *bypass* the identity confirmation function altogether by bookmarking (and jumping directly to) the second screen in the sample request form. This exposes Traditional Approaches, Inc. to breaching the terms of their license by knowingly allowing the product to be distributed to minors. At a minimum, the organization would be exposed to significant fines and a public relations nightmare; at a maximum, they risk having their license to distribute the product revoked altogether.

As before, an urgent resolution meeting is called. Except, this time, the website development team advises the IT Director that fixing this problem will require significant programming changes to the sample request form that will take at least six weeks to develop and test. Throwing additional resources at the problem will not solve it – it will take too long to get new staff familiar with the work. The website development team members are already putting in over 60 hours a week to meet the deadline, so additional overtime is not a realistic option. This means that Traditional Approaches, Inc. has two choices:

- delay the launch of the product website until the problem is fixed
- release the product website without the sample request form (or with a far less functional sample request option, such as a downloadable form that customers have to print out and mail in with proof of age).

In both of these circumstances, Traditional Approaches, Inc. risk losing a significant amount of competitive advantage in the marketplace. Not having a product website means losing a key communication channel with prospective customers; and having a product website that makes it difficult for customers to request sample packs means that they are likely to go to a competitor's website instead.

The traditional approach

- Testing at the end of the process results in significant website issues that cannot be resolved in time for the launch.
- The organization must choose between:
    - releasing a website that could jeopardize their product licensing
    - releasing a website that is much more difficult to use than their competitors' sites
    - not releasing a website at all.

Either way, the problem has been found *too late in the process* for the organization to properly respond and address the issue. This is one of the key advantages that Agile approaches offer over traditional approaches.

The Agile approach

The second pharmaceutical company, Agile Approaches, Inc., decides to brand the pill as "NoSneezium" with a full media campaign to encourage customers to request a sample pack from their website. The CEO of Agile Approaches publishes a press release announcing that "NoSneezium" will be in the marketplace by January 1st – and issues an internal memo to all executives to treat this product as their topmost priority.

As with Traditional Approaches, the IT department of Agile Approaches is allocated a budget of $180,000 for the website development over the next six months. However, unlike their competitor, the CEO of Agile Approaches, Inc. directs the organization to use *Agile practices and techniques*, such as responsive planning, direct stakeholder engagement, management by self-motivation and real-time productivity, to make sure that the deadline is achieved.

Budget	$180,000
Number of employees	12 full-time employees
Delivery date	December 31st
Scope of deliverable	Fully functional and tested website with: • credible product information • secure sample pack order form • confirmation that the customer is over 18 years old • the ability to process up to 10,000 concurrent orders

Figure 8: Website development constraints

July

Acting on the CEO's directive, key representatives from the Agile Approaches marketing department, the customer service department and the website development team lock themselves away in a conference room for four hours to jointly map out the requirements for the website. The aim of this session is not to produce a detailed specification which the marketing team will sign off on – it is to effectively *communicate* and *prioritize* the business requirements for the website, so that everyone in the room has a shared understanding of the required functionality.

Each core requirement is described on a 3x5 inch index card which is pinned on the conference room wall. The marketing department talks through their expectations for each requirement with the attendees. The customer service representatives ask questions about usability. The website development team members ask detailed questions about the intended behavior of each function. Once all of the attendees' questions have been addressed, the website development team members provide the group with an estimate of the amount of effort that will be required for them to deliver each function. Each requirement is then assigned an expected business value based on:

- the benefit that it will bring the organization
- the cost of the resources required to achieve the desired outcome
- the complexity (i.e. risk) of delivery.

The marketing department representatives order all of the requirements in a top-down priority list, based on their expected business values. The website development team then advises the marketing department representatives on how much of the highest-priority work they can reasonably achieve in the *next four weeks*. The website development team is particularly concerned about the more complicated functionality on the website (most notably, the sample request form), so they encourage the marketing department representatives to include researching this functionality as one of the most urgent priorities.

At the end of the four-hour session, the marketing, customer service and website development team representatives all have an agreed understanding of the highest-priority work to be done – and a commitment from the website development team for an interim deliverable of this work to be available by the end of July.

The Agile approach

- Key participants in the process meet at the beginning to establish a shared understanding of the work that is required.
- The website team and the business team work together to identify the highest-priority work for the organization.
- Both teams jointly agree on the high-priority work that can be achieved in the next four weeks.

Over the next four weeks, the website development team uses Agile techniques, such as:

- ***Pairing***: having two members of the delivery team working together on assigned tasks (even for work that would normally be assigned to only one person) to increase accountability, knowledge sharing and quality of outputs.
- ***Refactoring***: allowing the team to regularly review the existing system and modify it, where required, so that future changes can be implemented more easily.
- ***Co-location of team members***: physically locating team members near each other to facilitate *ad-hoc* discussions, encourage face-to-face review of work and share team resources (e.g. documents, whiteboard diagrams, models) in a central location.
- ***Daily stand-up meetings***: holding *five-minute* update sessions every day for the team to quickly review required work and address any hurdles.

These Agile techniques enable the team to deliver a *fully functional* and *comprehensively tested subset* of the product website's capabilities. The team is *not* building prototypes or screen mock-ups; they are doing the *actual work* that is required for the production release of the product website at the end of December.

August

In the first week of August, the marketing, customer service and IT department representatives reconvene to get a detailed walkthrough of the work that the website development team has done. The website development team members show the group *real working functionality* for the product website. They ask the marketing representatives targeted questions to clarify the requirements based on their work. They also identify two potential concerns regarding the functionality required for the sample request form:

- Their initial research indicates that the current hardware and network environment would not be able to handle more than 100 users trying to submit the sample request form at the same time.
- In the current proposed design, it is possible for users to *bypass* the identity confirmation function altogether by bookmarking (and jumping directly to) the second screen in the sample request form.

The marketing representatives confirm that each of these is a significant issue that needs to be addressed urgently.

As in the early July meeting, the attendees put each core requirement on a 3x5 inch index card, which is pinned on the conference room wall. This process includes:

- removing any requirement where the marketing representatives are satisfied that all required work has been completed
- updating previously identified requirements to reflect any information obtained through the work done in the previous month, such as the issues that have been identified regarding the sample request form
- adjusting the expected business value assigned to each requirement, based on the updated benefits, costs and risks.

This meeting also allows the organization to do something which is *not* generally available through traditional approaches:

- *adding* and *updating* the product website requirements to reflect any *changes* that have occurred in market conditions, government-regulated testing, organization priorities, etc. since the original requirements discussion was held.

In traditional approaches, the signed-off specification is the "bible" – any changes to the approved requirements are likely to involve extensive document reviews, delays in authorization and frustration for the team affected by these changes, especially if they are requested at the last minute. In Agile approaches, changes to requirements are not only accommodated in the process; they are *welcomed.*

So, if further product testing reveals a potential issue with people who have Type 2 Diabetes using the new pill – and government regulations, therefore, require a warning to any customers with this condition – Agile Approaches, Inc. is in a position to meet this new requirement well before the product launch date.

With the updated information (and expected business values) reflected on the index cards, the marketing department representatives again order each requirement in a top-down priority list, based on the most currently determined business value. The website development team subsequently advises the marketing representatives on how much of the highest-priority work they can reasonably achieve in the next four weeks.

The website development team then proceeds to create *fully functional* and *comprehensively tested features* for the product website, based on the priorities identified by the business.

The Agile approach

- The website team spends the first four weeks building *fully functional* and *comprehensively tested* website features.
- Their hands-on work means that risks and issues are identified early in the process.
- The business team is able to review *working* website features and reprioritize ongoing work based on the issues identified.

The next three months ...

Over the next three months, the marketing, customer service and website development team representatives continue to meet at the start of each month to review the real working functionality that has been built and fully tested for the product website. They discuss the work that has been completed and any issues that have arisen. They update the business requirements based on feedback from the website development team's work, along with any other changes to market conditions. They reprioritize the requirements for each month based on the relative business value of each website capability. Each month, the website development team delivers a greater set of fully functional and comprehensively tested high-priority capabilities in the product website.

November

The marketing, customer service and IT department representatives meet once again to review the work that the website development team completed in October. Except, this time, the marketing team has an exciting announcement for the group. The government-regulated testing of "NoSneezium" is completed and the product is approved for general market distribution *two months* ahead of schedule. The inevitable next question for the website development team: How soon can the product website be released?

The website development team advises that, if they stopped all new development on the product website and focused only on releasing the work that they have done thus far, the website could be live within two weeks. This means that the organization will be getting the high-priority capabilities that they identified over the past four months, all fully functional and comprehensively tested. This includes the sample request form, which has now been optimized to handle up to 10,000 concurrent form submissions – and updated to eliminate the page-bypass security flaw – based on the research that was done in August.

On November 15th, Agile Approaches, Inc. launches "NoSneezium" to the marketplace, along with a fully functional website that includes a sample request form and warnings to potential customers with Type 2 Diabetes.

> **The Agile approach**
>
> - The website team delivers an increasing number of *fully functional* and *comprehensively tested* website features every four weeks.
> - Even though the deadline is moved up two months, the website team's hands-on work throughout the process means that the organization can *safely* progress with an early release that meets business requirements.

In the same timeframe, Traditional Approaches, Inc. (which was also informed about the early completion of government-regulated testing) is currently scrambling to get their 75% completed – and 100% *untested* – website out to the public to keep up with the competition. This means that the performance and security issues in their sample request form – issues that could have been found in internal testing – are now released on the live website for the public to find. Traditional Approaches has potentially jeopardized both its reputation in the marketplace and its license to distribute pharmaceuticals.

So, using Agile approaches not only enabled the product website to be built in time for the January 1st product launch, it allowed Agile Approaches, Inc. to confidently deliver the website *six weeks ahead of schedule* in response to changing market conditions. Not only did these approaches provide the organization with a significant competitive advantage, the reduced website development time meant that they spent less than 80% of the originally allocated budget – freeing up the website development team resources to work on other value-added activities for the organization.

It should be noted that the majority of communication of the website requirements for Agile Approaches, Inc. was done verbally in meetings, not through formal written documentation. The website development team is required to document the website for future reference purposes (e.g. maintenance), but because requirements are being shared in the monthly meeting, it is not essential that this documentation is done upfront. In fact, where the documentation is done retrospectively, after the website has been released, it allows the team to focus on their core work and to better reflect the actual behavior of the released website.

Traditional Approaches, Inc. Website development outcomes		
	Projected	**Actual**
Budget	$180,000	$240,000
Number of employees	12 full-time employees	14 full-time employees (FTEs) with resources required for additional server installation
Delivery date	December 31st	November 15th
Scope of deliverable	Fully functional and tested product website with: • credible product information • secure sample pack order form • confirmation that the customer is over 18 years old • the ability to process up to 10,000 concurrent orders	An untested product website with: • a sample pack order form (that has potential security issues) • screens to confirm that the customer is over 18 years old (although this feature can be bypassed, putting the organization at risk of losing its product licensing) • the ability to handle no more than 100 concurrent orders

Figure 9: Website development outcomes: Traditional Approaches, Inc.

Agile Approaches, Inc. Website development outcomes		
	Projected	**Actual**
Budget	$180,000	$144,000
Number of employees	12 full-time employees	12 full-time employees
Delivery date	December 31st	November 15th
Scope of deliverable	Fully functional and tested website with: • credible product information • secure sample pack order form • confirmation that the customer is over 18 years old • the ability to process up to 10,000 concurrent orders	Fully tested website with the following functionality: • a secure sample pack order form • secure screens to confirm that the customer is over 18 years old • the proven ability to process up to 10,000 concurrent orders

Figure 10: Website development outcomes: Agile Approaches, Inc.

Now, what about all of the other activities that are required to ensure that the new product is released successfully? How can the organization be sure that the marketing campaign will reach the target audiences with the appropriate message? (So that people will be aware of the new product website.) How can the manufacturing area ensure that it has sufficient capacity to meet the increased demand for this medicine? (So that people who order the sample packs are not waiting for an extended period of time.) Agile approaches can be applied to *all of these activities* to ensure that the same level of quality and effectiveness is achieved throughout the organization.

Product marketing in a competitive marketplace

Both pharmaceutical companies, Traditional Approaches, Inc. and Agile Approaches, Inc., need to put together a highly visible and compelling marketing campaign for their new "cure for the common cold" product. They have each determined that the most effective communication channel for reaching their target demographic is the Internet, but how can they make potential customers aware of the new product website so that they can request a sample pack? As before, the two pharmaceutical companies approach the same business challenge in two very different ways; and, as before, there is a marked difference in their results.

The traditional approach

The first pharmaceutical company, Traditional Approaches, Inc., decides to launch a full media campaign to encourage customers to request a sample pack of "Cold Riddance" from their website. The marketing department is allocated a budget of $520,000 and a staff of six people for promotional activities, including television air time and print publications. The only directive from the CEO is for the marketing department to "get the message out there," so that the public is eagerly awaiting the arrival of "Cold Riddance" – and an opportunity to try this medicine firsthand.

Budget	$520,000
Number of employees	6 full-time employees
Delivery date	December 31st
Scope of deliverable	Promotional campaign that will "get the message out there" so that the public is eagerly awaiting the arrival of the new product

Figure 11: Product marketing constraints

July

The Vice President of Marketing at Traditional Approaches sits down with the entire marketing team to brainstorm how they can best "get the message out there" in time for the January 1st product launch. The marketing team identifies a number of likely channels, based on their previous experience with launching new pharmaceutical products to the public, including:

- a series of 30-second television commercials that will air during national shows that have a track record of reaching the target demographic
- banner advertisements on websites that contain health-related content, particularly on website pages that describe cold symptoms and recommended cures

- publications for medical professionals, so that doctors and nurses can recommend "Cold Riddance" to their patients
- advertisements on buses and trains in major cities, where people are likely to be in close quarters and, therefore, more conscious of the potential for catching a cold
- aligning the content and features of the product website to best meet the interests of the target audiences.

The team breaks down the $520,000 budget allocation on a whiteboard to see how much advertising coverage (e.g. television air time) they can afford. Once they work through the numbers, the media section of the marketing department is allocated, on a full-time basis, to secure the required advertising spaces. The remainder of the marketing department is tasked with creating the 30-second commercials, the print pieces, the website banner content and the billboards for the public transportation advertisements. They also agree to meet with prospective customers in focus groups at the end of August, so that they can get feedback on the work that they are doing.

The traditional approach

- The marketing team undertakes an "all-at-once" approach, directing staff to start work on every media channel that the budget will support.
- Stakeholder consultation (through focus groups) is scheduled to begin eight weeks into the process.

August

While the media section of the marketing department is busily contacting all of the required channels to organize advertising space, the rest of the marketing team has been brainstorming and storyboarding advertisement concepts for focus group testing.

At the end of August, the marketing team meets with 12 focus groups that represent their target demographic (people between the ages of 25 and 55) in different cities across the country. The results of the focus groups indicate that:

- The target audience is particularly distrustful of new medicines in website banner advertisements, because they believe that the Internet has some less than credible suppliers. However, they *are* comfortable with clicking on banner advertisements for products that they are already familiar with. No matter what language was used in the sample banner advertisements, the focus groups unanimously agreed that they would not click on these ads if they were not already familiar with the product.
- The target audience believes that the proposed television commercials are good, but that they need more compelling evidence to show how effective the new medicine is. Marketing claims alone are not convincing enough for them to risk trying a new and unproven medication.
- They also believe that seeing an advertisement for a website on a bus or train is only worthwhile if you have a cell phone (or other portable device) that lets you access the Internet at the time that the advertisement is fresh in your mind – and if there is sufficient coverage to access the Internet at that time. They recommend putting

the advertisements in bus shelters or train stations instead, where people may have more time – and better coverage – to check websites. They also recommend advertising in airport waiting lounges where people would be more likely to be accessing the Internet via their laptops or a public kiosk.

- Finally, they have a number of suggestions for information and features that would be really useful on the product website, including the ability for customers to track the status of their sample pack order.

At the end of August, the marketing team reconvenes to assess how the feedback from the focus groups is going to affect their proposed advertising campaign. At this meeting, the media section advises that the purchase of website banner advertisements is already finalized (and non-refundable due to the special pricing that they organized). Traditional Approaches can choose to use this advertising space for another product campaign, but it would need to be relevant to the cold and flu symptom pages where the banner ads are currently scheduled to run.

The media section further advises that they have only organized for public transportation advertisements in four of the major cities, so the rest of the budget can be targeted for airports, bus shelters and train stations in the remaining cities.

They also remind the marketing team that the product website specification was signed off in early August, so there is no way that additional features (like tracking sample pack orders) can be added before the product launch date.

Last, the media section advises that, if the marketing team wants to change the television advertisement – and bring the revised commercials back to the focus groups for feedback – they will need to ensure that there is enough time to produce the commercials and get them approved for airing before the deadlines at each network.

The traditional approach

- Focus group feedback results in significant changes to the original promotional plans.
- The marketing team now needs to reallocate budgets, write-off unrecoverable expenses and change supplier contracts to meet customer needs.
- Some customer feedback (e.g. website changes) cannot be acted upon because work has already been signed off with other areas of the organization.

The next three months ...

The marketing department scrambles to redo the television commercials and organize focus groups to review the revised content. Meanwhile, they try to postpone their deadlines with the production company for the commercials to be as late as possible, to allow for the creative changes that are likely to result from the second round of focus group feedback.

The media section is also trying to renegotiate the website banner advertisement contract, so that the organization can instead use it for their more widely-known and trusted pharmaceutical products – ideally in areas of the website which contain the most relevant content for each type of medicine. The marketing team urgently needs the funding for this contract to be moved to another product's advertising budget, so that they can afford to purchase space in airport terminals (as airport advertisements were not included in the original budget breakdown).

All of these concurrent activities mean that the marketing department will need to reduce (or eliminate) their work in other areas, in order to meet the fixed deadline for the product launch. They are already focused on:

- preparing the copy for each advertisement
- overseeing the production of the commercials
- organizing for public transportation advertising space in the rest of the major cities
- working with the compliance area on product packaging.

The marketing department, therefore, does not have sufficient time to hold focus groups with medical professionals to get their feedback on proposed print ads. However, their experience has been that advertisements in medical publications, which show the results of government-regulated testing in a visible part of the publication, should be sufficient to get their attention and interest. Their workload leaves them no choice but to rely on experience alone for this channel.

In addition to all of their other commitments, the marketing team has to send representatives to meet with the IT department at the end of November, so that they can review the product website that the website development team has built.

The traditional approach

- The allocation of resources to progress the work that can be done (and to fix the things that were done incorrectly) is spreading the marketing team's resources too thin.
- Corners are being cut, compromises are being made, budget allocations are running out and staff are working overtime just to keep their heads above water.

The members of the marketing team know that they will need to work every night and every weekend until the product launch, in order to meet all of these commitments. Then, the marketing department receives the news that the government-regulated testing has finished *two months earlier* than expected – and the CEO wants advertising for "Cold Riddance" to begin as soon as possible so that Traditional Approaches can capture the marketplace before the competition does. The marketing team is stunned by this news; only two of the media channels have copy that is ready to be released, and both campaigns are scheduled to begin in mid-December. This means that the hard work they had already envisaged in order to meet the January 1st product launch date, has now become a mad scramble to get every piece of finished (or even half-finished) copy out to the media outlets as soon as possible. To make matters worse, all of the advertisements point customers to go to a *non-existent* website.

So, the marketing department takes desperate measures to get any media coverage that they can. They quickly put together a press release announcing the new pills; they renegotiate contracts with the media outlets to get their advertisements out as quickly as possible (and pay a little over $24,000 in premium service fees for the privilege);

they convince the IT department to release the product website to the public, even though it has not yet been fully tested. Due diligence is no longer a consideration; getting the word out there, as fast as possible, is the only thing that the marketing department cares about. All of their careful upfront planning is brushed aside, in favor of quickly responding to changes in the marketplace – and the quality of their work clearly reflects that.

The traditional approach

- The unexpected early deadline results in a mad rush for the marketing team to get anything out to the public.
- Emergency funding is required, half-completed work is released, and the organization is exposed to significant potential risks.

The traditional approach to handling marketing campaigns did not allow the organization to be responsive to changing market conditions. All of the work that Traditional Approaches, Inc. did was based on a deadline that was set months beforehand, and the false assumption that this date was immovable. Agile approaches work from the assumption that change is *inevitable*, and the best way to prepare for change is to use a process that is designed to expect it.

The Agile approach

The second pharmaceutical company, Agile Approaches, Inc., also decides to launch a full media campaign for "NoSneezium" to encourage customers to request a sample pack from their website. Like Traditional Approaches, Inc., the marketing department at Agile Approaches is allocated a budget of $520,000 and a staff of six people for promotional activities, including television air time and print publications. However, unlike their competitor, the CEO of Agile Approaches, Inc. directs the organization to use *Agile practices and techniques* (like those used in the delivery of the product website), in order to "get the message out there" as effectively as possible.

Budget	$520,000
Number of employees	6 full-time employees
Delivery date	December 31st
Scope of deliverable	Promotional campaign that will "get the message out there" so that the public is eagerly awaiting the arrival of the new product

Figure 12: Product marketing constraints

Early July

The Agile approach for the marketing campaign work starts in the same way that it did for the website development work, with key representatives locking themselves away in a conference room for four hours to jointly map out the requirements for the marketing campaign for the "NoSneezium" product launch. However, there are two key differences in this scenario:

- ***Preparation before the meeting***: Given the scope and quantity of people who will be attending this meeting, the marketing department decides to hold an internal brainstorming session *prior to* this session, to facilitate the initial discussion with the key representatives. This allows the bigger group to immediately respond to proposed campaign ideas from the marketing department, instead of staring at an empty whiteboard for half an hour (or shouting out 400 different ideas at the same time). However, this preparation work *does not* stop the key representatives from suggesting changes to the marketing activities proposed at the initial session; it just puts a bit of structure around the meeting to make it a more productive session for all attendees.

- ***Key representatives at the meeting***: For the marketing campaign, the key representatives who need to attend this meeting are a *different group* to the ones who attend the meetings for the website development. The marketing campaign specifically requires input from:
    - marketing department representatives, as they are the primary drivers and owners of the marketing campaign
    - sales department representative(s), so that they can provide feedback on how the proposed marketing campaigns will affect product demand and their distribution channels
    - customer service representative(s), so that they can provide hands-on insights into how customers use Agile Approaches' current products, and the concepts to which current customers respond most favorably
    - product research and compliance department representative(s), so that they can advise on the most current results and the overall progress of the government-regulated testing

- IT department representative(s), as they are responsible for delivering the website, which will be a core element of the marketing campaign.

The aim of this first session with key representatives is *not* to produce a detailed campaign plan for the Marketing Vice President to sign off – it is to effectively *communicate* and *prioritize* the proposed marketing campaign activities for "NoSneezium," so that everyone in the room has a shared understanding of the work required.

Each proposed marketing campaign activity is described on an index card, which is pinned on the conference room wall and discussed by the attendees. These discussions include the following:

- Are any of the proposed campaign activities *non-negotiable* priorities (i.e. there is no way that the product launch can occur without this activity)? One example of a non-negotiable priority is likely to be the product website, as it is the primary distribution channel for the sample packs.
- What is the relative importance of each of the *negotiable* campaign activities proposed? What is the real potential value of this channel in reaching (and motivating) the target audience? If the organization has insufficient resources (or time) to complete all of the proposed activities, can any be postponed until after the product launch?
- Can any of the proposed campaign activities be *broken down* into smaller bodies of work that can be completed in a shorter timeframe (e.g. organizing banner advertisements for one of the four targeted websites, instead of all four at once)?

- Which of the proposed campaign activities require the most *lead time* for preparation, such as securing air time on major networks?
- How *late in the process* can the decisions for each proposed campaign activity be made? For example, when do the print publications need to receive finalized input (e.g. creative) in order to meet their production timeframes?
- Can the team organize *flexible arrangements* with media partners, production companies, etc. so that both delivery timeframes and quantity of work can be adjusted as the campaign work progresses?

The responses to the questions above allow the attendees to get a more realistic understanding of the benefits, the costs and the risks of each campaign activity. These discussions also allow the attendees to take a more critical look at each proposed campaign activity, so that the concepts which "looked good on paper" can be prioritized against those that are the most challenging, time-consuming, costly or risky for the organization.

Traditional organizations often endeavor to take on every good idea at once, which inevitably results in half-completed work and staff overtime. Agile approaches know that skilled teams can consistently deliver high-quality work if they are given reasonable quantities of work and realistic timeframes. Late nights in the office, missed lunches and weekend work all set the stage for lower quality outputs and employee burn out. Therefore, Agile approaches are designed to ensure that the most productive use of resource time is focused on the highest-priority work, i.e., the work that will deliver the greatest business value returns for the organization. The questions that were posed above enable the organization to differentiate between the campaign activities which will bring the organization the most business value, and those activities with moderate (or questionable) business value potential that can stretch the marketing team to the point of breaking.

This first session will most likely result in a combination of two outcomes:

- a subset of campaign activities for which a reasonable amount of cost, benefit and risk information is known
- a subset of campaign activities for which further investigation is required before the work can be prioritized (including any new campaign ideas that arose at the first session).

The attendees decide that the marketing team needs more time to investigate the proposed campaign activities before accurate decisions can be made on the relative business value and priority of each activity. As the marketing department is the primary area responsible for doing this investigation, the group defers to the marketing team members to determine how long the team will reasonably expect to need to complete this investigation work. The marketing team believes that they can have all of the required investigation work completed by the middle of July. This will also give them an opportunity to consult with a handful of *actual customers* on some of the proposed campaign ideas.

Although these initial sessions involve a broad spectrum of people, all of the attendees identified above represent *internal* areas of the organization; none is the *actual customer* who is being targeted to use this product. In most traditional organizations, the customer would not get involved in the campaign development process until formal market research activities (such as focus groups) are scheduled. These research activities tend to be *reactive* to predefined ideas (e.g. "which of these three product labels do you find most appealing?") instead of *proactively* seeking their input before predefined approaches are determined.

The *reactive* approach to customer feedback means that most organizations initially rely on:

- the marketing team representatives (who have undertaken market research with current and prospective customers)
- the customer service team representatives (who speak with customers every day)

to be in a position to communicate the interests of the customer on their behalf. However, Agile approaches advocate the value of having real customers (or prospective customers) involved in the brainstorming process *from the beginning*. It may even be worthwhile "hiring" them as advisers *throughout* the six-month process, so that key decisions are not being made in isolation of the target audience.

This does not mean that the customer needs to (or even should) attend the initial session described – as these sessions are as much about internal planning and work assignment as they are about brainstorming campaign ideas – but ideally, they would have been involved in the initial brainstorming work that the marketing team did *prior* to these sessions.

A small number of customers could also be involved in the hands-on work to develop concepts (e.g. creating storyboards) before these ideas are presented to the larger set of customer representatives in formal market research activities. This hands-on involvement of customers throughout the process means that customer-driven ideas (such as tracking the status of sample pack orders on the website) could arise early enough in the process to be incorporated into the first product release – instead of added to the pile of "things to consider" once the product launch is over.

The Agile approach

- Key participants in the process meet at the beginning to establish a shared understanding of the work that is required.
- The marketing team and the other business areas work together to identify the highest-priority work for the organization.
- The team actively involves customers *upfront in the process* to confirm which promotional activities will deliver the greatest business value.

Mid-July

Two weeks after the initial session, the group reconvenes to assess the business value and priority of each proposed "NoSneezium" campaign activity, based on the follow-up investigation from the marketing team. As before, each proposed campaign activity is described on an index card, discussed by the attendees, assigned a business value and then ordered in a top-down priority list based on business value. This time, however, the attendees are in a position to:

- distinguish between non-negotiable campaign activities and negotiable work

- assess the relative business value of each proposed activity based on the benefit, cost and risk of each channel
- break down proposed activities into smaller bodies of work which can be achieved in shorter timeframes (e.g. by the next monthly review session)
- identify where lead times and decision timeframes require a subset of work to be done more urgently, even if the proposed campaign activity is not the absolute highest priority for the marketing team to be working on.

All of this information feeds back into the top-down priority list, so that the work that is truly the most valuable (and time critical) is at the top of the list. The marketing team (that is responsible for undertaking and managing the campaign activities) then advises the meeting attendees on *how much* of the highest-priority work in the top-down list they can reasonably expect to achieve in the next four weeks.

At the end of the four-hour session, the marketing, sales, customer service, product research and IT department representatives all have an agreed understanding of the highest-priority work to be done – and a commitment from the marketing team for a subset of this work to be available by the middle of August.

August

In the middle of August, all of the representatives who attended the initial session reconvene to get a detailed walkthrough of the work that the marketing team has done. The marketing team members show the group a completed creative for one of the five channels with input from customer advisers. The team members confirm that they were able to finalize flexible contracts with three of their suppliers. Also, they advise that four focus group sessions are scheduled for the last week in August, with feedback expected to be available to the team in time for the September review session. In fact, they would like to organize for the September review session to be scheduled in three weeks instead of four, so that they have more time to follow up on work from this session.

As identified earlier, the attendees at these monthly meetings include representatives from the product research and compliance departments, who are monitoring the status of the government-regulated testing, so that they can:

- provide feedback on product testing issues as they arise
- advise the marketing team if there appear to be any changes in the overall product testing timeframe.

At the mid-August session, these representatives advise the marketing team that they are beginning to get information requests from the government testers which indicate that they may be further along in the "NoSneezium" testing process than the research team originally thought. They emphasize that this is just speculation on their part, but it may indicate that the government testing could be finished a couple of weeks earlier than originally expected. Is the marketing team in a position to take action if testing is completed by mid-December, instead of the end of December?

This information from the product research and compliance departments is highly valuable for all attendees. The marketing team now has a stronger imperative to focus on getting a subset of the channels fully ready to go live (instead of spreading their efforts across multiple channels and only having some of them partially completed). The IT department representative can also advise the website development team that the product website may need to go live a couple of weeks earlier than originally anticipated. Plus, the customer service representative can prepare the team to receive calls from customers about the sample pack two weeks earlier than expected.

The attendees use this input to reassess and reprioritize the campaign activities identified for the upcoming month. The marketing team, once again, advises the meeting attendees on *how much* of the highest-priority work in the top-down list they can reasonably expect to achieve before the next monthly review session.

The Agile approach

- The marketing team and the other business areas jointly reassess their original priorities based on the upfront customer feedback that they have received.
- Regular communication channels enable all teams to be aware of – and plan for – the potential for an earlier delivery date than originally expected.

The next three months ...

Over the next three months, the representatives continue to meet to review the work that has been completed (and is in progress) from the marketing team. They discuss:

- any changes in market conditions (such as indications of earlier testing completion timeframes and ongoing customer feedback)

- any new marketing requirements that have arisen (such as the CEO's announcement that there needs to be a press release prepared for the product launch)
- any issues that have arisen (such as one television network's refusal to commit to a flexible contract).

The attendees update the business requirements each month based on this feedback, and reprioritize the ongoing work for the upcoming month based on the relative business value of each activity. Each month, the marketing team delivers a greater set of fully prepared campaigns which are ready to go live whenever the product launch is announced. The IT department representative also announces that they are undertaking equivalent work in their preparations for the product website, so they are confident that they will also be prepared should the product launch date be moved forward.

The Agile approach

- The marketing team regularly meets with the other business areas throughout the process to show them the work that has been completed.
- These regular meetings allow the participants to jointly reprioritize ongoing work based on any new information that has been obtained.

November

As expected, the government-regulated testing of "NoSneezium" is completed and the product is approved for general market distribution *two months* ahead of schedule. All attendees use the November session to determine what work needs to be done in order to finalize the marketing campaigns and the product website as quickly as possible, so that the CEO can make the formal announcement. The attendees realize that some of the planned work (e.g. public transportation advertisements in two of the major cities) is not yet finalized, but they are prepared to make this their highest-priority work directly after the product launch. The most important thing is that the highest business-value channels (e.g. the advertisements in the medical professional publications) are ready to go. Just as importantly, the marketing channels all point to a highly functional product website that is also ready to be released.

At the same time that Traditional Approaches, Inc. is madly rushing around to salvage anything that they can from their partially completed marketing campaign work (and preparing for the onslaught of customer complaints that are likely to arise from issues related to their untested product website), Agile Approaches, Inc. is prepared to go forward with production-ready campaigns and a fully tested product website.

Once again, the responsive planning, business-value-driven and high-communication focus of Agile approaches has positioned the organization to deliver better quality results earlier, and more cost effectively, than their traditional competitors.

Traditional Approaches, Inc. Product marketing outcomes		
	Projected	**Actual**
Budget	\$520,000	\$544,000
Number of employees	6 full-time employees	6 full-time employees
Delivery date	December 31st	November 15th
Scope of deliverable	Promotional campaign that will "get the message out there" so that the public is eagerly awaiting the arrival of the new product	Rushed promotional activities, including: • last-minute press release write-ups • premium service fees for renegotiated contracts • half-completed media campaigns that cannot be released

Figure 13: Product marketing outcomes: Traditional Approaches, Inc.

Agile Approaches, Inc. Product marketing outcomes		
	Projected	**Actual**
Budget	\$520,000	\$520,000 (with some expenditures postponed until after the product launch)
Number of employees	6 full-time employees	6 full-time employees
Delivery date	December 31st	November 15th
Scope of deliverable	Promotional campaign that will "get the message out there" so that the public is eagerly awaiting the arrival of the new product	Top priority promotional activities ready to go, including: • completed media campaigns for the channels with the highest business value • negotiable contracts with suppliers to reschedule other promotional activities for earlier release

Figure 14: Product marketing outcomes: Agile Approaches, Inc.

Order fulfillment in a competitive marketplace

One of the most valuable aspects of Agile approaches is that they take a *holistic view* of required work in relation to the overall objectives of the organization. The use of business-value-driven priority lists at each planning session is designed to ensure that work is done in conjunction with the organization's overarching priorities. The regular review sessions deliberately involve a cross-disciplinary team that represents the areas of the organization that are most likely to be affected by this work, so that decisions are made with consideration for their impact on other business processes and other staff.

This cross-disciplinary approach to working drives the website development and marketing teams to consider more than the work that is in front of them. In particular, they begin to consider the impact of the sample pack ordering capability on the manufacturing area that is responsible for fulfilling these orders. Are they prepared to receive electronic orders from the product website? Are they in a position to respond to both low demand and high demand periods (including the potential for significantly high demands in conjunction with scheduled advertising activities)? Also, just as importantly, will they be positioned to begin manufacturing and distributing sample packs in time for the product launch?

Both pharmaceutical companies, Traditional Approaches, Inc. and Agile Approaches, Inc., need to guarantee that online requests for sample packs from customers are able to be fulfilled by their manufacturing areas as quickly as possible. This means ensuring that they have sufficient internal capacity to meet projected customer demand.

Both companies realize that the best marketing campaign activities and the most effective product website will be meaningless if the people who order the sample packs have to wait for an extended period of time to receive the product. They realize that their competitor could gain a significant advantage by getting their sample product to the customer more efficiently.

Once again, each company approaches this requirement in two different ways, with decidedly different outcomes.

The traditional approach

The CEO of the first pharmaceutical company, Traditional Approaches, Inc., holds a meeting with the Manufacturing Vice President to advise that the organization wants to include sample packs of "Cold Riddance" pills as part of the product launch. The anticipated customer demand is 1.5 million sample packs, but could potentially go as high as 2.5 million if the market take-up is better than anticipated. The CEO advises that the product launch is scheduled for the end of December, and that the manufacturing area has a budget of $760,000 to purchase new equipment and acquire the necessary staff to produce these sample packs.

Budget	$760,000
Number of employees	Current manufacturing and warehouse staff with any additional staff funded within the allocated budget
Delivery date	December 31st
Scope of deliverable	Ability to produce and ship: • 1.5 million sample packs (minimum) • 2.5 million sample packs (maximum)

Figure 15: Order fulfillment constraints

The Manufacturing Vice President is concerned that the current production staff is already struggling to meet the unexpected high demand for another of Traditional Approach's products – and that there are few skilled laborers currently available for hire – but does not want to be the one to disappoint the CEO. So, the production line takes on board this new requirement; even though the Manufacturing Vice President has *no idea* how they are going to fulfill it.

The traditional approach

- Executives issue top-down mandates without factoring in how the work requested will impact staff workloads across all business areas.
- The organizational culture discourages management from providing feedback on executive mandates, even if staying silent puts the entire organization at risk.

Stretching the seams

The Manufacturing Vice President meets with key managers from the production line to advise them of this new commitment. It is now July 1st, and they have six months to increase their capacity to support the potential for up to 2.5 million sample pack orders coming in from January 1st next year. The product packaging needs to be finalized, the equipment needs to be acquired, and the staff need to be trained (and supplemented) to meet this demand.

Two of the best production line managers are pulled from their current responsibilities to focus on the sample pack manufacturing requirement. Selected staff members are promoted to acting supervisors to compensate for these managers being taken offline; and the rest of the production line staff is asked to put in overtime to continue generating the same productivity levels without these staff members.

The human resources area had been focusing on hiring junior production line staff to meet their current staff shortages (for products where training programs and documentation are available). The Manufacturing Vice President now asks them to refocus their efforts on *urgently* hiring more senior production line staff that can work in a new environment where supporting materials are not available.

The finance department begins a selected bid process to find vendors "as fast as possible" who can deliver the necessary production equipment in the required timeframe. The facilities department is taken off the current work of fixing the ventilation in the manufacturing area, in favor of quickly creating floor space for the new equipment. The warehouse area is asked to move current stock offsite as soon as possible to make room for the storage and distribution of the additional product.

The CEO's request of the manufacturing area has thrown most of the organization into a tailspin trying to achieve an impossible requirement. All of the "bird in hand" work that they are doing is potentially going to be compromised by the requirement to "drop everything" in favor of this new product.

The traditional approach

- Meeting the urgent need of one department has drastically changed the priorities for four other departments.
- Corners are being cut to urgently address staff shortages, overtime payments are eating away at the available budget, and *current* customer orders are being delayed in favor of *prospective* customer orders.

Expected (and unexpected) delays

In meeting with each affected area of the organization, the manufacturing area encounters a number of delays which could significantly impact their ability to achieve the December deadline.

The production line managers first sit down with the product research team to review the requirements for manufacturing the pill itself; and then they sit down with the compliance and marketing department representatives to discuss product packaging. The product research team is able to advise on the composition, shape and size of the pill – as well as the necessary storage conditions (e.g. temperature and relative humidity); but the marketing and compliance departments advise that they will need at least two more months to finalize product packaging for the sample packs. This means that the specifications for the packaging equipment (and the corresponding bid to acquire the vendor) both need to be put on hold pending this decision.

The production line managers also know (from their past experience with pharmaceutical products) that government regulation testing is likely to result in last-minute changes to product information (including warnings), so they need to ensure that the packaging equipment for these sample packs can be adjusted – even at the last minute – to accommodate updated wording on these notices. This expected delay creates a constraint in the process, but one which the team can manage more easily because they know about it (and can prepare for it) upfront.

Finally, the Manufacturing Vice President is advised by the Human Resources Manager that there are no qualified candidates currently available to hire for the new production line. Two of the candidates have commitments with their current employers until November; and three more will not be available until January. Can the manufacturing area hold off until these qualified candidates are available; or should the human resources team revisit the junior production line staff candidates from their previous searching to see if any of these workers are available more quickly?

The Manufacturing Vice President knows that hiring junior staff will result in more work for his management staff, greater supervision and less productivity than more senior staff, but the organization cannot wait until November to begin producing the high quantities of sample packs that are required. They have calculated that their machines will need to be fully operational on a near 24/7 basis from mid-October in order to meet the required demand. This means that the organization has no choice but to temporarily hire some of the less experienced candidates for the October / November timeframe and replace them with senior staff as more experienced resources become available.

The traditional approach

- Delays in other business areas are resulting in an inability for the manufacturing team to progress their work.
- The shortage of skilled resources in the marketplace is creating an even greater burden on the manufacturing area team members to supervise junior staff.

Other issues

In addition to all of the challenges already identified, the manufacturing area encounters a number of new issues as the work progresses, each one pushing an already delayed process into further jeopardy.

In early September, the Warehouse Manager advises the Manufacturing Vice President that they only have sufficient temperature-controlled storage areas to support the storage of 100,000 sample packs at a time. Additional storage areas can be built, but they cannot be available any earlier than the end of January. The only other alternatives are for the organization to outsource additional storage spaces (which will create both a cost overhead and a logistical issue for the manufacturing area), or to reduce the supplies of other Traditional Approaches' products that are currently in storage.

In late September, the marketing department decides to include product information sheets in the product packaging to accommodate last-minute testing feedback, instead of updating the product packaging at the last minute. The vendors who have responded to the selected bid process did not include product inserts in the proposed equipment (as it was not a requirement at the time). So, the finance team will need to release an amended bid to the vendors and extend their response date to accommodate this change in requirements. The manufacturing area also needs to pull back on the special features that they had requested to update the product packaging at the last minute, as the inclusion of product inserts means that the external product packaging is not expected to change.

In addition, the manufacturing and warehouse areas had both been working from the assumption that incoming sample pack orders would be processed through the current bulk order system that the sales team uses for other Traditional Approaches products (where high quantities of products are shipped to one address). The Warehouse Manager learns in late October that the sample packs will be ordered through the product website – and that each new order will be submitted to the warehouse one-by-one as it arrives. The warehouse area is not equipped to ship individual products to an address, which means that they will now need to scramble to find a third-party distribution center prepared to fulfill these requests.

The traditional approach

- Lack of communication with other business areas has resulted in wasted work and last minute decision-making.
- Problems which could have been identified and resolved upfront are now creating insurmountable hurdles for meeting the required delivery timeframe.

The end result

The issues and challenges faced by the production line managers mean that, even with third party support, the manufacturing area will only be in a position to produce, store and distribute 200,000 sample packets a month by the end of December. They begin producing sample packs at the end of October with the hope of having 450,000 sample packs available for distribution in time for the product launch (and 200,000 sample packs every month thereafter). This is not the original target agreed with the CEO, but they believe that it should be a reasonable level of production if customer orders come in gradually after the product launch.

Then, the CEO announces that the product launch is scheduled to take place *six weeks* before they had originally anticipated. This means that, in a best-case scenario, they will be in a position to produce 100,000 sample packs in time for the product launch (i.e. less than *seven percent* of the originally projected demand).

The traditional approach to handling manufacturing processes has resulted in the organization being unable to fulfill the vast majority of projected customer requests. This means that Traditional Approaches, Inc. is likely to go into "panic mode" just to meet the expected demand of sample pack orders, let alone if the number of orders is significantly higher than originally projected. Because of these delays, the Traditional Approaches media team will almost inevitably need to do damage control to salvage the organization's reputation and to alleviate the concerns of frustrated customers. Additionally, the staff at Traditional Approaches will be working extensive overtime on an indefinite basis, simply to keep their heads above water.

The traditional approach

- The earlier than expected deadline has resulted in the organization only being able to meet six percent of the originally anticipated demand.
- The organization now needs to prepare for disappointed customers, damage control with the media and increased employee turnover due to the extremely high-pressure work environment.

Compare this outcome to Agile approaches, which combine *lean manufacturing* techniques with *responsive planning* to better prepare organizations for fluctuating levels of customer demand, even when that demand begins *six weeks earlier* than expected.

The Agile approach

The CEO of the second pharmaceutical company, Agile Approaches, Inc., holds a meeting with the Manufacturing

Vice President to advise that the organization wants to include sample packs of "NoSneezium" as part of the product launch. Like Traditional Approaches, Inc., the manufacturing area of Agile Approaches, Inc. is allocated a budget of $760,000 to purchase new equipment and acquire the necessary staff to produce 1.5 million (and up to 2.5 million) sample packs by the end of December. However, the CEO of Agile Approaches, Inc. directs the organization to use *Agile practices and techniques* (like those used in the delivery of their product website and marketing campaigns) in order to meet the anticipated product demand.

Budget	$760,000
Number of employees	Current manufacturing and warehouse staff with any additional staff funded within the allocated budget
Delivery date	December 31st
Scope of deliverable	Ability to produce and ship: • 1.5 million sample packs (minimum) • 2.5 million sample packs (maximum)

Figure 16: Order fulfillment constraints

Early July

The Agile approach for manufacturing the "NoSneezium" sample packs starts in the same way that it did for the website development and marketing campaign work – with key representatives locking themselves away in a conference room for four hours to jointly map out the requirements for producing up to 2.5 million sample packs, before the end of December product launch. For the product manufacturing activity, the attendees include key representatives from:

- the manufacturing department, as they are the primary drivers and owners of the sample pack production requirement
- the warehouse and distribution departments, as they are responsible for the storage and mailing of sample packs
- the product research and compliance departments, as they are advisers on both the product specifications and the product compliance requirements (e.g. warning labels)
- the marketing department, as they are responsible for the product packaging, as well as the wording on the product website regarding ordering the sample packs
- the IT department, as they are responsible for both the product website and the backend systems that will process the customer orders.

As before, the aim of this first session with key representatives is not to produce a detailed sample pack production plan for the Manufacturing Vice President to sign off – it is to effectively communicate and prioritize the proposed manufacturing, storage and distribution activities for “NoSneezium” sample packs, so that everyone in the room has a shared understanding of the work required.

Each proposed sample pack production, storage and distribution activity (and its constraints) is described on an index card which is pinned on the conference room wall and discussed by the attendees. From these initial discussions, it becomes immediately apparent that the current production environment and business processes will never be able to support the demand for up to 2.5 million sample packs in time for the product launch, nor can the level of resourcing be achieved in the specified timeframe without significantly jeopardizing almost every other area of the organization.

The group collectively agrees that the organization has to decide on whether to:

- significantly improve all of the current internal processes to support the expected demand
- outsource the entire sample pack manufacturing and distribution process to a third-party production center which is positioned to handle high quantity order processing
- undertake a hybrid approach, where the processes that can be handled internally are optimized; and the processes that are beyond the capacity of the organization (and are not able to be significantly improved in the six-month timeframe) are outsourced.

The attendees decide that both the manufacturing team and the warehouse team need more time to investigate the potential for improving internal activities before accurate decisions can be made on what portions of the work (if any) will need to be outsourced. As these two teams are the primary areas responsible for doing this investigation, the group defers to these representatives to determine how long they will reasonably expect to need to complete this investigation work. The manufacturing department and the warehouse department representatives advise that they should be able to complete this investigation work within four weeks.

In addition, the IT department representative advises that they may be in a position to enhance their current bulk order processing system to bundle individual product orders for bulk handling (which should make it easier for the warehouse to use their current business processes to ship the orders). The IT team will need at least two weeks to determine whether they can support this additional requirement in conjunction with their current commitment to deliver the product website.

The Agile approach

- Key participants in the process meet at the beginning to establish a shared understanding of the work that is required.
- The manufacturing team and the other business areas work together to identify the highest-priority work for the organization.
- Participants jointly agree that they need to do additional investigation before accurate business value decisions can be made.

Optimizing the business processes

Following the CEO's directive for Agile approaches to be used to meet the anticipated product demand, the manufacturing and warehouse departments decide to bring in a business analyst who specializes in *lean techniques* for optimizing product manufacturing, storage and distribution processes, to advise on the improvements that can realistically be made to their current environment to support the expected production levels.

The business analyst applies *lean principles* to determine where the current manufacturing, storage and distribution processes can be optimized, including areas of:

- ***Overproduction***: where the departments are producing more than is needed to satisfy the organization's (or the customers') requirements.[52] For example, designing equipment which can handle last-minute changes to product packaging when product inserts would suffice.
- ***Waiting***: where work cannot progress due to the unavailability of required resources, materials, information, management decisions or management approvals.[53] For example, where the manufacturing section is waiting for product packaging to be finalized before they can issue a selective bid for the required machinery.
- ***Non-value-added processing***: including over-inspection, reworking and other added tasks to compensate for a lack of effective quality control in the overall process.[54] For example, the warehouse team's current processes for having four different quality checkpoints before an order is shipped – where each of these checkpoints effectively does the same quality review work as the other.
- ***Defect handling***: where the organization's resources are wasted addressing problems in their products, services and business processes, instead of focusing on core business activities.[55] For example, the current warehouse

---

[52] Adapted from *Common Questions Organizations Ask About Lean Manufacturing*, Keberdle CF, Lean Solutions Group, LLC (2008): *www.leansolutionsgroup.com/images/Common_Questions_About_Lean_Mfg.pdf*.

[53] Adapted from *Simulation and the Lean Enterprise*, ProModel: *www.promodel.com/challenge/WP_Lean.pdf*.

[54] Adapted from *Value and Non-value Added Analysis of Incoming Order Process*, Ketkamon K and Teeravaraprug J, Proceedings of the International Multi-Conference of Engineers and Computer Scientists 2009, Vol II, Hong Kong: *www.iaeng.org/publication/IMECS2009/IMECS2009_pp1935-1937.pdf*.

[55] Adapted from *Focus on Processes, Not Operations*, Bodek N: *www.moldmakingtechnology.com/articles/1005lean.html%20* and *The 7 Manufacturing Wastes*, McBride D (2003): *www.emsstrategies.com/dm090203article2.html*.

practices of reprinting shipping labels every time the address is offset due to issues with the printer.

- ***Under-utilized people***: where staff cannot work to their full mental and physical potential due to ineffective workflows, restrictive organizational cultures and inadequate training.[56] For example, the current processes of having senior staff spend 25% of their time overseeing the work of more junior staff.
- ***Excess movement***: where the organization's resources (staff, materials, etc.) are moved from activity to activity without adding value to the business process.[57] This includes unnecessary movement due to a lack of effective communication channels in the organization. For example, the current warehouse procedures of moving stock through three different temporary storage locations before the boxes are loaded onto trucks for distribution.
- ***Over preparation***: where the organization hoards resources or prepares materials "just in case" the organization might need them in the future.[58] For example, the current warehouse allocates 60% of their temperature-controlled storage areas to stockpile products to meet the projected demand for customer orders over the next eight to twelve months.

---

[56] Adapted from *Lean Principles*, Kilpatrick J, MEP Utah (2003): http://yourcareeracademy.com/yca/assets/uploads/lib_file/Lean%20Principles%20-%20overview.pdf

[57] Adapted from *The Seven Deadly Wastes of Logistics: Applying Toyota Production System Principles to Create Logistics Value*, Sutherland J and Bennett B, Lehigh University Center for Value Chain Research (2007).

[58] Adapted from *Lean Manufacturing Principles: A Comprehensive Framework for Improving Production Efficiency - The Evils of Inventory*, Kilpatrick A, Massachusetts Institute of Technology (1997).

By applying lean principles to the current manufacturing and warehouse processes, the business analyst determines that Agile Approaches, Inc. can optimize their current environment to produce and store up to 550,000 sample packs each month. The recommendations for improvement include:

- constraining the marketing department to designing sample pack product packaging that can be produced on the existing equipment, so that the organization does not incur the costs – or time delays – associated with holding a competitive bid process for specialist equipment to be built;
- building better quality controls into the manufacturing and warehouse processes from the beginning, so that fewer quality checks are required (and product defects found) at the end of the process;
- replacing faulty equipment (such as the label printer in the warehouse) to avoid wasting skilled resource time on low business-value activities (e.g. rework);
- reassigning junior staff to less complex (i.e. "safer") production line tasks to reduce the need for constant supervision. Ensuring that these tasks are clearly documented (and that junior staff are sufficiently trained) to reduce the potential for defects. Having senior staff do occasional "spot checks" of the work done by junior staff, instead of regularly watching over them (i.e. empower and equip junior staff members to do high-quality work independently);
- optimizing the warehouse storage and transportation processes by moving long-term product stock to an offsite location, in order to have the most time-critical products close at hand, and by queuing the movement of

stock, so that only one temporary storage location is needed between the storage area and the loading docks.

As part of this review, the business analyst also confers with the IT department to determine the outcome of their investigation into whether they are in a position to enhance their current bulk order processing system to bundle individual product orders for bulk handling. These discussions include the potential for including *contingency plans* in the product website for potential delays in order fulfillment, such as easily changeable values for the number of delivery weeks presented to customers in the sample pack order form.

Based on the discussions with the IT department (and review of the current order distribution processes at Agile Approaches, Inc.), the business analyst advises that there is too much work required for the order distribution processes to be changed in time for the product launch. Therefore, it is recommended that the organization outsources these distribution activities to a third-party shipping house, particularly one that has the technical infrastructure in place to process orders directly from the "NoSneezium" product website.

In order to establish the most flexible outsourcing arrangements, the business analyst advises Agile Approaches:

- to find shipping houses which are willing to offer their services on a variable scale based on fluctuating production levels
- to sign contracts with *multiple* vendors to allow for the potential for significantly increased demand.

These flexible arrangements put Agile Approaches, Inc. in a better position to manage the unknown factors of production quantities and consumer demand, once the product is launched.

The Agile approach

- Lean principles are applied to the current manufacturing and warehouse processes to:
  - optimize work within known constraints; and
  - identify alternative options for those activities that cannot be realistically supported by the organization in the available time.
- Contingency options and flexible supplier arrangements are established to address variable factors (e.g. the quantity of customer orders).

Early August

The attendees from the first session reconvene to review the proposed business process improvements and to determine what (if any) of the current manufacturing, storage and distribution activities need to be outsourced in order for the organization to meet the end of December timeframe for the "NoSneezium" product launch. The business analyst presents the recommendations for optimizing the current manufacturing and storage processes, and for outsourcing the distribution activities. Although the marketing department representatives are concerned about constraining sample pack product packaging to the capabilities of existing equipment, they equally appreciate the risk to the organization overall if the sample packs cannot be produced in time. Based on the outcomes from the investigation, the attendees agree to proceed with a hybrid internal optimization and outsourcing approach to resolving the organization's current limitations for producing sample packs.

The next three months ...

The implementation of change to the internal processes for manufacturing and storage is achieved using the same Agile approaches that the organization used for website development and marketing campaign delivery:

- A cross-disciplinary group of representatives from the organization (and from the selected outsourcer) participate in monthly planning sessions, where they collectively determine the highest business-value work for each month.
- The attendees sub-divide these activities into smaller bodies of work which are achievable in a four week timeframe.
- The manufacturing, storage and outsourced distribution teams aim to deliver completed work products each month (instead of working towards one big outcome at the end of December).
- The group reconvenes on a monthly basis to review the work that has been completed and jointly determine the highest-priority activities for the coming month.

In this way, the highest business-value elements of the optimized manufacturing and storage processes can be in place whenever the product is launched. Additionally, because the cross-disciplinary group of attendees includes representatives from the product research and compliance departments, all of the attendees are advised well in advance that the government-regulated testing is likely to be completed earlier than originally anticipated. This allows the internal manufacturing and storage teams (and the outsourced distribution team) to be as prepared as possible for this potential. The group jointly decides to aim to begin "NoSneezium" sample pack production on a 24/7 basis in early October to allow for at least two months of full capacity sample pack production, even if the product launch is moved to early December.

The Agile approach

- The manufacturing team and the other business areas jointly reassess their original priorities based on the lean principles recommendations that they have received. They agree to pursue a hybrid internal optimization and outsourcing approach to maximize available resources.
- Regular communication channels enable all internal and external participants to be aware of – and plan for – the potential for an earlier delivery date than originally expected.

November

As expected, the government-regulated testing of "NoSneezium" is completed and the product is approved for general market distribution ahead of schedule. The manufacturing, storage and distribution teams did not, however, anticipate that this approval would occur *two months* ahead of schedule and, therefore, the product launch would be six weeks earlier than expected.

The teams' decision to begin sample pack production on a 24/7 basis in early October means that they have a little over 500,000 sample packs already in storage; and they expect to be able to have an additional 280,000 sample packs ready for distribution by November 15th. This represents 52% of the minimum target levels that the CEO had set for sample pack distribution. The team further advises that, at a production rate of 125,000 sample packs per week, they expect to be able to meet the full requirement for 2.5 million sample packs by mid-January. This means that, unless there is an extraordinarily high upfront consumer demand for sample packs, Agile Approaches, Inc. should be able to fulfill all orders within the anticipated timeframes.

The end result

The CEO of Agile Approaches, Inc. realizes that, with the product launch occurring six weeks ahead of schedule, the organization could not have reasonably expected to have 2.5 million sample packs available in this timeframe. However, the Agile approach to handling manufacturing processes has resulted in the organization being well-positioned to meet market demand. If market demand suddenly increases to an unexpectedly high level, the manufacturing and warehouse team now have a long-term solution for high productivity output delivery – not a temporary solution that requires staff to work extensive overtime on an indefinite basis.

Using Agile approaches has also provided the organization with a leaner manufacturing and warehouse area, which is likely to have follow-on benefits for the production of their other products as well. These improvements, along with the flexible arrangements that have been established with the third-party shipping houses, mean that Agile Approaches,

Inc. will be better positioned to increase (or decrease) the production of "NoSneezium," if the product demand differs from expectations.

Traditional Approaches, Inc. Order fulfillment outcomes		
	Projected	**Actual**
Budget	$760,000	$760,000 plus overtime
Number of employees	Current manufacturing and warehouse staff with any additional staff funded within the allocated budget	Current manufacturing and warehouse staff with junior staff to partially supplement the team
Delivery date	December 31st	November 15th
Scope of deliverable	Ability to produce and ship: • 1.5 million sample packs (minimum) • 2.5 million sample packs (maximum)	Ability to produce and ship: • 100,000 sample packs in time for the product launch (less than seven percent of the minimum projected demand) • with ongoing overtime required to produce another 200,000 sample packs per month

Figure 17: Order fulfillment outcomes: Traditional Approaches, Inc.

Agile Approaches, Inc. **Order fulfillment outcomes**		
	Projected	**Actual**
Budget	$760,000	$760,000
Number of employees	Current manufacturing and warehouse staff with any additional staff funded within the allocated budget	Current manufacturing and warehouse staff with support from a business analyst, along with external suppliers for outsourced work
Delivery date	December 31st	November 15th
Scope of deliverable	Ability to produce and ship: • 1.5 million sample packs (minimum) • 2.5 million sample packs (maximum)	Ability to produce and ship: • 780,000 sample packs (52% of the minimum projected demand) • 2.5 million sample packs by mid-January

Figure 18: Order fulfillment outcomes: Agile Approaches, Inc.

But what about *my* organization?

Although the business activities described in the previous case study were specific to the pharmaceutical industry, the benefits that these companies achieved by using Agile approaches can be equally applied to business activities in *every organization* across *every industry sector*.

This is particularly true for those organizations that want to achieve real productivity gains within the constraints of their current budgets and staffing levels, such as:

- government departments that have a fixed budget for improving public transportation services to better meet the needs of the community
- product manufacturers that want to produce products with fewer defects in order to reduce their overheads and improve their corporate image
- insurance companies that want to update their policy structures to better reflect the information that they are gathering on customer needs
- charities that want to increase the breadth of community service activities that they can undertake with their current group of volunteers
- educational institutions that want to reduce administrative overheads for teachers, so that they can maximize their classroom time
- publishers and broadcasters that want to become more responsive to consumer demand and reduce their time-to-market
- small- to medium-sized enterprises (SMEs) that require high productivity levels from a limited number of staff.

Any organization that wants to significantly improve their productivity levels needs to focus on: making their business activities more *responsive to change*; *reducing the waste and inefficiencies* in their business processes; *minimizing errors and repeated work* by having *more effective communication channels*; and establishing *a corporate culture that both equips and empowers its resources* to deliver high business-value outcomes. These are the key principles and core objectives of Agile approaches – and they can be applied with equal benefit to organizations in every industry.

This means that *any* business activity in your organization with a fixed timeframe can be delivered more effectively through the Agile practice of *responsive planning*. It does not matter whether the business activity is:

- a consumer product with a predetermined launch date
- a marketing campaign
- an event that the organization has to plan
- a customer project with a contract-driven deadline
- a sales report that needs to be ready in time for the annual corporate meeting.

Delivery timeframes for all of these activities can be affected by both changes in the organization (e.g. staff departures, business priority shifts, funding reallocations) and changes in the marketplace (e.g. shifts in customer demand, announcements from competitors, the release of new technologies). This is why Agile approaches, such as responsive planning, are designed to help organizations anticipate and react to these changes, instead of being "blindsided" by them.

Equally, *any* business output in your organization can be made more valuable and cost-effective by applying the Agile practice of *direct stakeholder engagement*. Every organization can gain significant upfront and long-term benefits by involving the intended recipients of a business output in its design and development, including:

- commercial products

- consumer services
- internal documents
- corporate events
- promotional activities.

It does not matter whether the target audience for the output is an internal staff member, a corporate partner or an external consumer – the earlier that people are able to provide you with input on whether the work that you are doing meets their needs, the better positioned you (and the organization) are to adapt ongoing work to align with their expectations. Also, the organization wastes less money on outputs that will only need to be reworked or replaced in the future because they do not meet the needs of the intended recipient.

Similarly, *any* core business process in your organization can be optimized by applying *lean techniques* to focus resources (both staff and equipment) on delivering the highest business-value outcomes. Inefficiencies, such as overproduction, excess movement and over-preparation in a business process, can be addressed by optimizing business activities to deliver the highest business-value outcomes. This means that the same lean techniques that were used in the case study to improve the manufacturing and warehouse activities of the pharmaceutical company, could be applied to a wide range of business activities in any organization, including:

- monthly reporting
- expense reimbursements
- customer service work
- budget management
- product and service delivery.

This is not to say that every Agile approach will deliver the same level of business value for every business activity. Some Agile practices and techniques are better suited to situations with unknown factors (e.g. changing customer requirements), while others are ideal for highly predictable and replicable work.

For example, the pharmaceutical company case study used three common business activities of website development, marketing and product manufacturing to demonstrate the breadth of activities that can be improved by applying Agile approaches. Although these were three very different business activities, they had some strong commonalities:

- each activity was *time-constrained* by the product launch
- each activity was assigned a *fixed budget*
- each activity had to be planned around *unknown factors*, such as the potential level of consumer demand
- each activity required *shared responsibility by a team of people* in a *high-communication environment* in order for it to be successful.

The Agile approaches that were applied in these conditions (e.g. responsive planning, business-value-driven prioritization) are particularly designed to deliver results in *dynamic environments*, where unknown factors can impact the organization's ability to deliver required outcomes within fixed timeframes, fixed staffing levels and/or fixed budgets. This means that organizations can expect to achieve more dramatic results by using these types of Agile approaches to improve their business activities in dynamic environments, than in situations where conditions are less susceptible to change.

Conversely, Agile approaches, such as lean techniques, are well suited for highly repetitive and more predictable business activities, such as work undertaken:

- on a manufacturing production line
- in a retail store
- in a call center.

This is because, in these more *static environments*, the risk to the organization is not as much in planning for the unknown as it is in maximizing resource utilization (i.e. minimizing waste) in known activities. This is especially true in high volume industries, where even minor improvements to a business activity can result in exponential increases in real productivity gains as the tasks are repeated.

The degree to which a business activity is static or dynamic generally governs the selection of the most appropriate Agile approaches to apply. However, organizations can choose to apply a *combination* of Agile practices and techniques to suit the specific requirements of each business activity. In the case study, for example, the manufacturing and warehouse challenges were resolved with a combination of lean techniques (e.g. reducing the number of temporary storage locations) *and* responsive planning (e.g. holding monthly meetings to review and adapt the ongoing work to implement these changes within the required timeframe). Similarly, lean techniques can be applied to dynamic environments in conjunction with other Agile approaches (such as business-value-driven prioritization) to ensure that the highest value work is delivered as efficiently as possible. This enables the delivery team to produce more flexible and reusable outcomes for the work that they can control in the short term, even if the activities scheduled for the future may change.

This case study included a number of examples of how risk can be managed effectively through responsive planning, business-value-driven prioritization, direct stakeholder engagement, "just-in-time communication" and immediate status tracking. It equally showed how inefficiencies in the organization can be successfully addressed by reducing overheads, rework and excess movement in critical business areas. Combined, these approaches enabled Agile Approaches, Inc. to release a more functional website, to deliver a more effective marketing campaign, and to produce significantly greater volumes of sample packs using the *same* number of skilled resources, within the *same* budget and the *same* timeframe. This is the very definition of real productivity gains.

SECTION 4: MAKING AGILE WORK IN YOUR ORGANIZATION

CHAPTER 17: SELECTING AGILE APPROACHES THAT BEST MEET YOUR NEEDS

The five fundamental questions

The flexibility of Agile approaches allows organizations to select the most appropriate Agile practices and techniques to suit both their specific business activities and their overall corporate culture. The low overhead costs required for adopting Agile approaches means that organizations can often get started without the usual budget approval processes. This is both the appeal – and the danger – of Agile.

Although it might be tempting for you to want to "dive right in" and start using Agile approaches within your organization, it is valuable for you to step back for a moment and consider the specific needs – and constraints – of your organization. Here are five fundamental questions that you need to ask yourself in order to determine how best to begin.

Question 1: What are the biggest issues that my organization is currently facing?

Is your organization under pressure to achieve difficult deadlines? Are there too few people to get the work done, or insufficient budget allocations? Or is it a combination of all of these factors?

Are staff not as productive as they can (or should) be? Are the business processes, equipment or communication channels that they use slowing them down? Is there too much corporate knowledge in the heads of a handful of employees? Or, are low-quality outputs creating the need for constant "fire-fighting" and damage control?

Every organization can benefit to some degree by using Agile approaches, but those organizations which have the most significant issues also have the most to gain from the Agile approaches that specifically target these issues.

If your organization is trying to meet time, budget and/or resource constraints, particularly in a dynamic marketplace, then Agile approaches, such as *responsive planning*, *business-value-driven prioritization*, and *direct stakeholder engagement* (i.e. the ACTION plan in *Chapter 5: Responsive Planning*) will probably bring you greater returns than waste management approaches, such as lean techniques. In which case, the stakeholders' business-value calculations for prioritizing work will need to be centered on the time, budget and/or resource constraints that are creating the greatest challenges for your organization.

If increasing the productivity of staff, business processes or communication channels is your organization's greatest challenge, then the *lean techniques* described in *Chapter 13: Waste Management* are likely to deliver you the biggest returns.

If your organization is facing *all* of these challenges, then you may need to consider a combination of these approaches, where the organization strives to improve current business processes and communication channels while delivering time-, budget- and resource-constrained outcomes. This may be a bit daunting at first, but the efficiencies that the organization gains by using Agile approaches in one area can be used to reallocate resources to less efficient work until the underlying problems are addressed.

The Agile approaches selection tool at the end of this chapter is designed to assist you in aligning the business activities that you want to implement with the Agile approaches that will be most effective in meeting your specific needs.

Question 2: Are the people in my organization ready for a significant change in the way they currently work?

For most organizations, particularly larger and older ones, the answer to this question is likely to be *no*. In rare circumstances, the management of an organization is so forward-thinking (like the senior executive at BT[59]) that they decide to dramatically shift the corporate culture by mandating the use of Agile approaches across the organization. For almost everyone else, however, the introduction of Agile approaches needs to be a strategically positioned one. *Chapter 18: Introducing Agile Within Your Organization* takes you through the strategies that organizations have historically used to introduce Agile approaches and helps you to decide which strategies are likely to be the most effective in your organization.

---

[59] *Agile Coaching in British Telecom*, Meadows L and Hanly S (2006): *www.agilejournal.com/articles/columns/column-articles/144-agile-coaching-in-british-telecom*.

Question 3: To what extent can I influence the decision to use Agile approaches in the organization?

The key word in this question is *influence*, not control. It does not matter whether you are the CEO of the organization, the manager of a department, or a new starter in a junior position – the key to successfully applying Agile approaches within an organization is to find an internal champion with sufficient influence to support the decision.

If you are the top executive in the organization, you have the discretion to use Agile approaches in the broadest (or most narrow) areas of the organization, depending on your comfort level, the readiness of the corporate culture and, for some organizations, the willingness of the board members. Equally, if you are a department manager, you may opt to trial Agile approaches in one or two selected activities within your department. If you are a project manager or team leader, you may opt to use these approaches within your own project – and to encourage other project managers to consider a broader use of Agile approaches for their projects.

If you are not currently in a formal leadership position, then you may need to be a bit more creative in how you encourage the organization to adopt Agile approaches. Ideally, you can introduce these concepts to someone who is in a position of influence in the hope that they will be willing (and able) to champion the use of these approaches. Otherwise, you may need to go forward with an approach known within the most inner circles of the Agile world as *Agile-by-stealth*.

Chapter 18: Introducing Agile Within Your Organization identifies the most effective strategies that you can use to influence the adoption of Agile approaches within your organization, including *Agile-by-stealth* where needed.

Question 4: Are the intended participants in the Agile approaches sufficiently aware of both the processes and their roles?

In *Chapter 3: Why Don't More Organizations Use Agile?* it was identified that one of the biggest hurdles to the successful adoption of Agile approaches in an organization is the historical *misapplication* of these approaches as techniques not principles. It is not enough for the people who participate in Agile work to understand the mechanisms of these activities; they also need to understand the *intent*, in order for them to most effectively utilize these approaches.

In the example that was provided, the misapplication of Agile approaches related to organizations using iteration-based project planning against a *predefined upfront specification*, which only served to provide them with more frequently delivered misaligned outcomes. Another common misapplication of Agile approaches is the mistaken belief that optimizing a business process means cutting out the most costly activities (or resources), instead of refocusing the work on the core value stream.

For the ACTION plan, it is essential that business owners understand their role in the process. This includes undertaking the necessary research beforehand to correctly assess the actual business value of each proposed activity (otherwise, the process may only deliver *perceived* business value). It is equally important for business owners to genuinely defer to the delivery team's advice on how much work can be completed in each iteration. Imposing undue pressure on the delivery team to over-commit only serves to position the process for failure, either in missed deadlines, overworked employees or low-quality outputs.

Chapter 18: Introducing Agile Within Your Organization includes information on the best ways to educate participants in the intent and mechanisms of Agile approaches, including the importance of their roles.

Question 5: Which Agile approaches are best suited to my organization?

The Agile approaches selection tool in the following section provides you with a workflow tool for determining which Agile approaches can best meet the specific needs of the activities in your organization.

The Agile approaches selection tool

The workflow tool in Figure 19 takes you through the key questions that you need to ask in order to select the most appropriate Agile approaches to meet the needs of the activities in your organization.

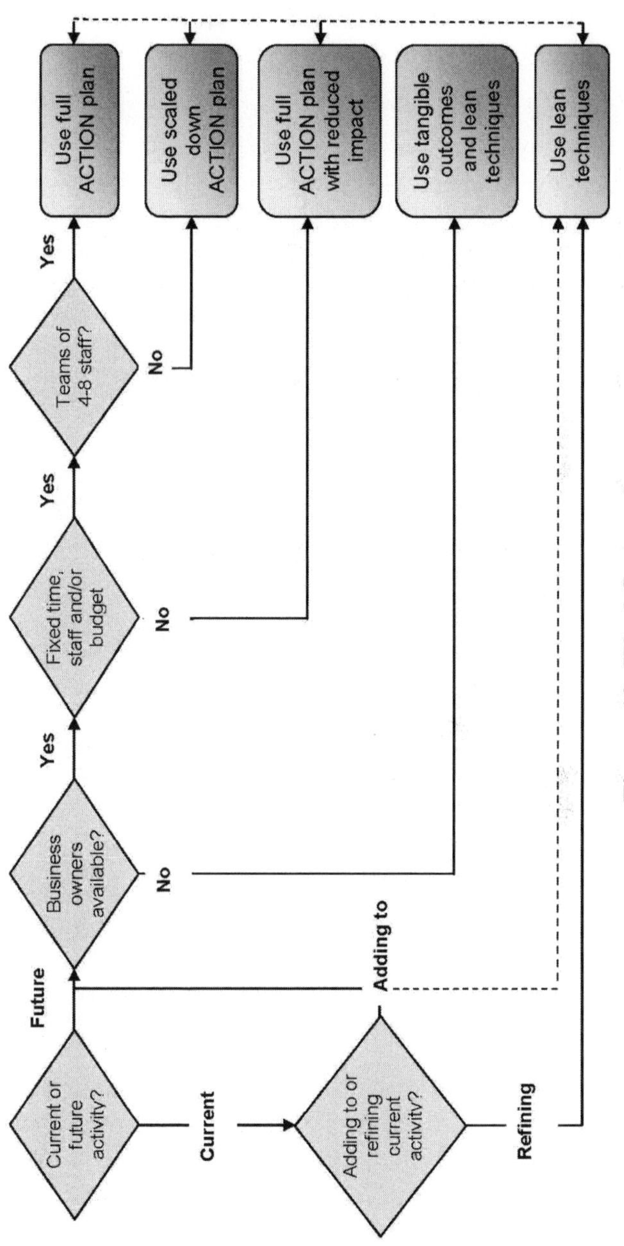

Figure 19: Workflow tool

To use this tool, start with the question in the upper left-hand corner:

Current or future activity? Are you interested in using Agile approaches on a business activity that your organization is *currently doing* or one that it is *planning to do in the future*?

Using Agile approaches for future activities

If you are interested in using Agile approaches on an activity that your organization is planning to do in the *future*, then the three key questions to ask yourself are:

- **Business owners available?** Are the stakeholders who truly understand the business requirements *available* to participate as *business owners* in the process?
- **Fixed time, staff and/or budget?** Is there a *fixed timeframe, staff allocation* and/or *budget allocation* for this work?
- **Teams of four to eight staff?** Is the organization in a position to allocate *four to eight staff members* to work on the delivery team?

If the answer to each of the above questions is *yes*, then you are positioned to implement the full ACTION plan described in *Chapter 5: Responsive Planning* for this business activity.

If stakeholders are *not* available to participate as business owners in the process, then much of the value of the ACTION plan will not be able to be leveraged by the organization, particularly responsive planning, business-value-driven prioritization and direct stakeholder engagement. This means that you are restricted to using the

Agile approaches that the delivery team can use independently, such as tangible outcomes (to provide immediately usable outputs for the organization) and lean techniques (to make the process as efficient as possible). The lack of stakeholder involvement significantly reduces the power of Agile approaches, but delivery teams can at least endeavor to produce some business value without their participation.

In the unusual circumstance that stakeholders are available to participate as business owners in the process, but the work is *not* being driven by any time, staffing or budget constraints, then the impact of using the ACTION plan is somewhat reduced. Business owners and delivery team members can still use the ACTION plan to ensure that work progresses and that ongoing work continues to meet the needs of the organization. However, even a successful initiative that uses this approach may not get the same impact in influencing the organization as an equivalent activity that was able to achieve results within measurable constraints.

If stakeholders are available to participate as business owners in the process, and the work is being driven by time, staffing and/or budget constraints, but you are only able to commit *a small number of people* to do the work (i.e. to be on the delivery team), then you can use a *scaled-down* version of the ACTION plan. In this situation, you would still hold iteration planning and outcomes review sessions, but some of the techniques that are used to increase the productivity of the delivery team (e.g. pairing) may be more limited. With a small team, there is also a greater risk to the delivery timeline if even one of the team members is unavailable to do the work (particularly in a delivery team that has only two people). The benefits of the ACTION plan can be achieved in this situation; the additional risk factor of having such a small delivery team just needs to be considered in the equation.

Using Agile approaches for current activities

If you are interested in using Agile approaches on an activity that your organization is *currently* doing, then the key question to ask yourself is whether the intended activity is *adding to* or *refining* the current work.

If you are looking to *refine* the work that your organization is currently doing (i.e. make business processes more efficient), but this refinement is not likely to require the addition of new capabilities, processes or outputs, then you are best positioned to use the lean techniques described in *Chapter 13: Waste Management* for this business activity.

If you are looking to *add new capabilities, processes or outputs* to work that your organization is currently doing, then this activity may require a *hybrid* of Agile approaches:

- **future activity** work to address the unknown element of the additions that you are planning
- **refinement** work to consider using the addition of new capabilities, processes or outputs to make the current process more efficient.

In the Agile approaches selection tool, the path for including lean techniques when adding to current business activities is marked with a dotted line, indicating that this is an optional activity that may not always suit the needs of the organization (or that may not be achievable with the level of work required to implement the proposed additions).

The selection tool also has a number of other dotted lines on the right-hand side that connect the Agile approaches identified in the blue boxes to other approaches. These dotted lines indicate the potential for the organization to incorporate a hybrid of Agile approaches, depending on the nature of the business activity. For example, it is possible for organizations to use lean techniques to refine current business activities, and then to implement these refinements using the ACTION plan (as was the case for the manufacturing and warehouse activity refinement in the pharmaceutical company case study). Equally, an organization that is undertaking work for a future business activity (or adding to a current one) can use lean techniques to ensure that the processes and outputs that they are creating are as efficient as possible from the very start.

One final note: the Agile approaches selection tool is a guideline to help you determine which Agile approaches can deliver the greatest real productivity gains for your organization, but the final decision of which Agile approaches will (and will not) work within the dynamic and constraints of your workplace is left to each organization. Identifying that lean techniques could bring your organization more efficient business processes is one thing; asking the organization to consider replacing their current equipment (or their extensively documented procedures) is something else entirely.

The information in *Chapter 18: Introducing Agile Within Your Organization* provides guidance on the best way to overcome common hurdles in the adoption of Agile approaches, such as cultural resistance.

CHAPTER 18: INTRODUCING AGILE WITHIN YOUR ORGANIZATION

Although the prospect of introducing Agile approaches within your organization may seem a bit daunting at first, it *can* be done. Agile approaches have been used successfully by numerous organizations worldwide over the past three decades, including Yahoo!, Microsoft, Google, , Bankwest, SunCorp and Wells Fargo. These approaches have been equally successful in commercial, government and not-for-profit organizations of all sizes,[60] particularly throughout the United States and Europe. Making Agile approaches work in your organization *is* an achievable task – it may just require some creative introduction in order to get the attention of key decision makers and the interest from staff.

Dip your toes or dive right in?

There is no one formula for introducing Agile approaches within an organization. Historically, some organizations have preferred to start by trialing Agile approaches on a small set of projects, in order to see how effective they are – and then expanding their use of Agile as staff became more comfortable with approaches, such as responsive planning. Other organizations, including the forward-thinking senior executive of BT,[61] have jump-started the adoption process by instituting a top-down mandate for

[60] See list of these organizations in the *Agile in a Nutshell* chapter.

[61] *Agile Coaching in British Telecom,* Meadows L & Hanly S (2006): *www.agilejournal.com/articles/columns/column-articles/144-agile-coaching-in-british-telecom*.

using Agile approaches across the organization, with the directive for all staff to deliver high business-value outcomes every 90 days.

Unless you work for an exceptionally forward-thinking organization, however, you are likely to find that acceptance of Agile approaches requires a few "runs on the board" before executives will be willing to try these approaches on a larger scale. So, if you want to be in a position to apply these approaches within your organization, you need to be prepared to apply them on a few small projects, publicize the outcomes, and use their success to motivate other areas of the organization to do the same. The following section, *Choosing the right kick-off point*, provides some guidelines for you to use in determining the best projects to use as your starting point.

If the prospect of convincing your organization to trial Agile approaches on even a few small projects still seems out of reach, it may be easier for the organization to start off by trialing selected Agile techniques, instead of endeavoring to adopt an entire Agile approach in the first instance.

For example, your organization could begin to more directly involve internal and external stakeholders in the delivery process. This does not require formal iteration planning and outcomes review sessions; just encouraging internal and external audiences to provide more regular feedback while work is being undertaken. Applying this one technique alone could significantly improve the quality of the outputs that are being delivered, as well as provide the stakeholders with realistic expectations on what they will be receiving.

Once you have successfully enlisted the involvement of internal and external stakeholders in the delivery process (and people have begun to see the value in this technique), you can consider introducing another Agile technique, such as breaking down large deliverables in a project into *smaller, achievable milestones* that can be adjusted as the work is delivered to meet the ongoing requirements of the organization. This is similar in concept to iterative delivery approaches that people in the organization may already be familiar with, but the key difference is the project team's ability (and authorization) to *adapt* the work that they are doing as the requirements mature, instead of blindly adhering to the originally documented upfront objectives simply because they were signed off.

Adding one Agile technique at a time can progressively move the organization into the ACTION plan without having to make a large initial commitment. In fact, for some organizations, these techniques become so embedded in the corporate culture that there is no need to give the work that they are doing a formal name. That is, of course, unless you want to officially take credit for the successful work that people are doing!

Choosing the right kick-off point

Although you can introduce Agile approaches by trickling in Agile techniques one by one, the ideal situation for more rapid adoption is for your organization to select one or two initiatives that are important enough for their success to be meaningful, but not so important that executives will not be willing to consider taking innovative approaches to fulfill the requirements. These initiatives can be anything from formal time-boxed projects (e.g. product launches, corporate events) to value-added outputs required by the organization (such as corporate reports or service improvements). In order to make their success as meaningful as possible, however, the following two criteria should be met:

- The initiative must involve work that has a level of *unknown outcomes* which are dependent on the feedback provided by the internal and external stakeholders who will benefit from this work. For example, using Agile approaches to deliver a new customer satisfaction survey that determines the optimal degree of contact that the organization's support teams should provide – *versus* using Agile approaches to make small, contained changes to an existing customer satisfaction survey, such as measuring the effects of changing the survey layout or the order of the questions.
- The initiative must have a commitment from key internal and external customers (i.e. business owners) that they are willing to be involved in the delivery process for at least eight hours every four weeks. This is a pre-requisite for Agile approaches to be successful at any scale, but it is especially critical if the initiative is going to be used as a platform for demonstrating tangible outputs and business-value generation. *See Chapter 8: Real-time Customer Feedback* for an indication of how much time is likely to be required from each participating business owner, depending on their degree of involvement.

The intention is that the outcome of using Agile approaches to deliver these initiatives will be able to be used as the launching pad for convincing other areas of the organization to consider using these approaches in their work, which also feeds into the strategies recommended in

Chapter 20: Expanding the Use of Agile in Your Organization.

Work that is too predictable (i.e. too "safe") will not have the same level of impact in selling Agile approaches to the organization, even if it is successful. Work that is undertaken without the direct involvement of the business owners will inevitably vary from their true requirements (which is why the ACTION plan requires business owners to be actively involved in the process). Work that does not bring a significant enough benefit to the organization will not have the same impact in influencing executives, even when the results of the initiative are highly successful.

Even if you are in a position to influence the adoption of Agile approaches across an entire area of the organization, you may still want to begin with a few selected initiatives, so that employees can get used to the structure and dynamic of Agile approaches – and be motivated by their effectiveness – before these approaches are more broadly applied.

Agile-by-stealth

One of the five fundamental questions asked in *Chapter 17: Selecting Agile Approaches That Best Meet Your Needs* was the extent to which you are in a position to influence the decision to use Agile approaches in your organization. If you are in a formal leadership position, you are likely to have the discretion to make the decision within the area that you manage; however, if you are not in a formal leadership position, you may need to use an approach known as "Agile-by-stealth" to get the process going.

Agile-by-stealth is a subtle way of introducing Agile approaches to an organization from the ground up. Agile approaches in the IT industry have traditionally been promoted through "bottom-up" channels, i.e. software developers who introduced these approaches to their team leaders, who then presented them to management. Generally this involves using Agile techniques through informal channels, such as:

- Deciding as a team that you are going to use Agile techniques within the work that you do, including:
    - doing your work in self-imposed time-boxed iterations to ensure that you are producing outcomes for the organization every two to four weeks
    - monitoring and measuring the progress of your work through velocity tracking tools such as burndown charts
    - applying lean techniques in the work that you do to ensure that you are continually focusing on the core value stream
    - establishing high-communication channels within the team, such as face-to-face meetings (instead of numerous back-and-forth e-mails) and daily stand-up meetings to check in with each other where possible
    - pairing with your co-workers on the work that you are doing, so that you can each review and critique the other's work while it is progressing.
- Making arrangements with one or more representatives from the business area to work with you on a deliverable as an "unofficial" business owner. This person can assist you in prioritizing the work that is needed, advise you on the work as it is progressing, and do a hands-on review of the work that you have done before it is presented to other people in their business area.

Even if the successful outcomes of your work are not sufficient to convince management to consider Agile approaches more formally, you will have at least delivered higher quality outcomes than if you had been using traditional approaches to do this work.

Of course, there is always the danger that adopting selected Agile techniques without the underlying principles being agreed with management could make them more difficult to use. For example, your manager may not understand why two people need to work on something that was originally assigned to one person (i.e. pairing). Or, they might not see the need for the team to get together each morning to review the work that they have completed, the work that they are planning to do, and the issues that they have encountered (i.e. the daily stand-up meeting). In an ideal world, you can point them toward the resources listed in *More Information on Agile* to explain the value and worldwide use of Agile approaches. Or perhaps, consider moving to an organization that encourages employees to continuously improve the work that they do.

A shared understanding of Agile

The only way for Agile to be successful in your organization is for the people who participate in the process to be aware of both the *intent* and the *mechanisms* of using Agile approaches. This will significantly reduce the potential for the misapplication of Agile approaches that could eliminate the possibility of wider organizational support altogether.

Before you begin using Agile in your organization, you should consider how the basics of these approaches are going to be disseminated to the people who will be involved in the process.

For some organizations, the best way to educate participants is to empower them to learn about these processes themselves, through online resources and books, such as those listed in *More Information on Agile.* Your corporate intranet can include an Agile resources page that provides links to relevant sites, and allows the people in the organization to exchange their questions, concerns and ideas about the use of these approaches before work begins

For other organizations, sharing of information may be best achieved by creating an easy-to-use guide that explains the basics of Agile approaches (such as the "Agile Cookbook" that was created by BT), and then supplementing these guides with internal training sessions to walk through and demonstrate these approaches.

Alternatively, you may want to educate a small group of staff members in using Agile approaches for one initiative, and then document the outcomes of their work as a case study to bring to larger groups in the organization.

Whichever way you decide to share this information, it is critical that participants understand both the approaches and their respective roles (e.g. business owner, delivery team member, Agile facilitator). It is equally important that they appreciate the returns that they are likely to receive from their participation – including higher business-value outcomes, empowered delivery teams and less "fire-fighting" to meet their deadlines – so that they are motivated to get started.

CHAPTER 19: USING AGILE TOOLS

Once you have selected the Agile approaches that are best suited to your business activities – and the participants have committed to using (or trialing) these approaches – you are ready to begin.

This section provides additional information on the tools that you can use to implement the ACTION plan steps described in *Chapter 5: Responsive Planning.*

Responsive budgeting

The *Using the customer to manage your budget* section of *Chapter 8: Real-time Customer Feedback* identified the value that Agile approaches can bring in allowing the organization to better manage budget expenditures. In particular, this section focused on the use of *responsive budgeting* to adjust expenditures as Agile work progresses, based on the business value of the work remaining.

Most Agile initiatives will be constrained by a budget allocation that is identified at the start of the process. Whether or not the budget is realistic, this is the amount available for the Agile team to use. So, it is critical that the team members endeavor to maximize the business value that can be delivered within this constraint.

The calculation for determining how much work can be undertaken within the available budget is straightforward:

- Determine the *per iteration* cost of the resources on the delivery team using the standard full-time equivalent

(FTE) calculations in your organization for the two- to four-week period: this is the *delivery team cost.*

- Add in the *per iteration* costs for the part-time work of the business owners (the *business owner cost*):
  - o for internal stakeholders, this is usually estimated as eight hours of work for each business owner per iteration
  - o for external stakeholders (e.g. customers), add in any overhead costs associated with their participation in each iteration.
- Combined, these two amounts represent the cost per iteration of the resources involved. This combined figure is the *Agile team cost.*
- Identify any additional overhead costs that are known upfront, such as equipment that needs to be purchased or facilities that need to be acquired. This is the *known overhead costs.*

Then use the formula in Figure 20 to determine how much work can be achieved within the allocated budget for that initiative:

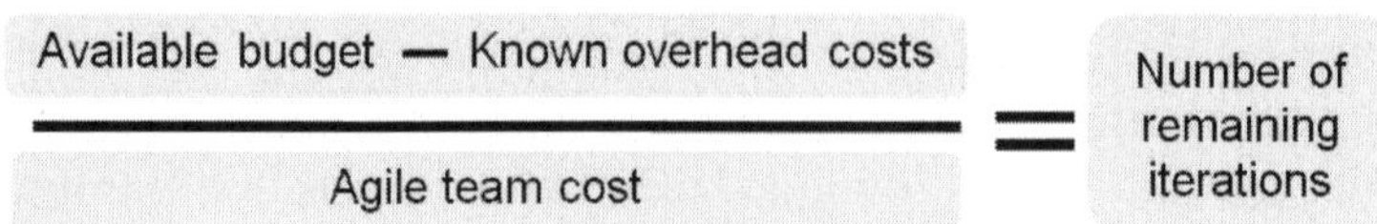

Figure 20: Budgeting formula

The *number of remaining iterations* identifies the duration of work that the Agile team can commit to within the initially allocated available budget.

At each iteration planning session, the business owners need to revisit this calculation based on the information available at that time, specifically:

- the remaining available budget
- any additional known overhead costs (e.g. equipment that is now needed based on a newly-identified requirement)
- any changes to resourcing levels in the Agile team.

Running this same calculation at each iteration planning session will allow the Agile team to know how many more iterations are remaining within the available budget – and, most importantly, it will enable the business owners to calculate the business value of the remaining work against this figure. This will help business owners determine whether the value of proposed work aligns with the cost of subsequent iterations, which can help the organization to determine whether or not the initiative should continue.

Responsive budgeting is another tool available to convince decision makers about the value of Agile approaches. It provides ongoing confirmation for the organization that further expenditure is (or is not) justified, based on the projected business-value return. This empowers the organization to regularly determine whether there is greater business value in continuing the work in the Agile initiative, or in reallocating resources to other high-priority activities.

Expected business-value calculation

The *Measuring cost/benefit* section of *Chapter 6: Business-value-driven Work* provided a formula that business owners can use to assign an expected business value to each actionable goal as part of their iteration planning.

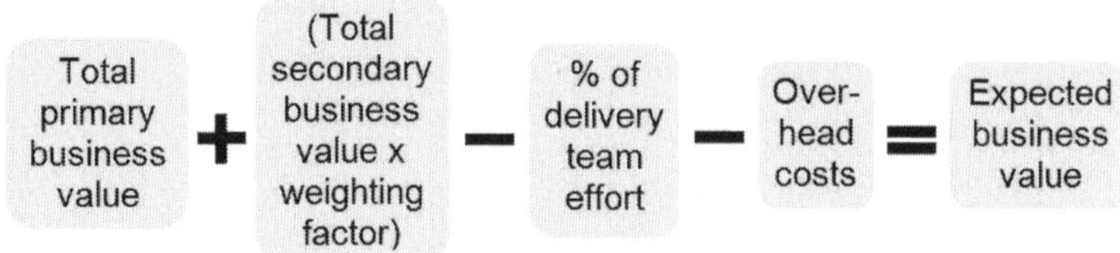

Figure 21: Expected business-value formula

In order to use this formula to assess the expected business value of each proposed actionable goal, you need to determine the following:

- The *total primary business value* of the actionable goal, based on the expected revenues, profits or overhead reductions that it will generate for the organization.
- The *total secondary business value* of the actionable goal, based on its ability to increase customer service, employee satisfaction, etc. as listed in *Secondary business-value outcomes,* and how that equates to a quantifiable value based on your organization's KPIs.
- A *weighting factor* for the secondary business-value outcomes (if appropriate) to reflect the fact that these outcomes do not directly result in revenue, profits or overhead reductions. If the secondary business-value outcomes are considered equally important within your organization, then the weighing factor should be set to 1.0.
- A *% of delivery team effort* value using the delivery team cost described in *Responsive budgeting* multiplied by the percentage of effort that would need to be

allocated by the delivery team in the forthcoming iteration, in order to deliver the actionable goal.

- An *overhead costs* value (if appropriate) to reflect any additional equipment or facilities that would be needed to deliver the actionable goal.

The end result of this calculation is the expected business value that is assigned to the actionable goal (and written on the user story card for that goal), so that the actionable goal can be given a relative priority when determining the work that will be done by the delivery team in the forthcoming iteration.

The requirements backlog

Chapter 12: Immediate Status Tracking described the value of the *requirements backlog* as a reporting tool that enables both business owners and delivery teams to monitor the progress of work against the agreed business requirements in each iteration. This section gives you more detail on the information provided in the requirements backlog, as shown in the following diagram:[62]

---

[62] Adapted from simple product backlog example courtesy of *http://agilesoftwaredevelopment.com*.

Charity golf day requirements backlog

ID	Value (x$100)	Description	1	2	3	4	5	6
		Iteration # / **Effort needed for minimum event requirements**	107	48	28	0	0	0
1	50	Get an agreed event date	5	0	0	0	0	0
2	50	Reserve a venue	12	0	0	0	0	0
3	20	Organize response tracking with Customer Service	2	0	0	0	0	0
4	30	Design and print invitations	12	0	0	0	0	0
5	20	Organize catering	4	0	0	0	0	0
Iteration 1		*Goal: Set up event venue and invitations*						
6	80	Invite customers and partners	16	6	2	0	0	0
16	10	Set event agenda	2	1	0	0	0	0
17	10	Organize an alternative date for the event if it is raining	-	2	0	0	0	0
7	50	Notify media of event	16	3	1	0	0	0
8	20	Order trophies	2	2	0	0	0	0
9	50	Organize for all executives to attend the event	4	3	3	0	0	0
Iteration 2		*Goal: Send invitations and organize event logistics*						
10	80	Track invitation responses	16	15	6	0	0	0
11	40	Match customers with sales team members	8	8	8	0	0	0
12	20	Fill empty spots with additional employees	4	4	4	0	0	0
13	50	Arrange venue and caterer pre-payments	4	4	4	0	0	0
Iteration 3		*Goal: Track invitations and finalize logistics*						
Milestone: Minimum requirements for event								
14	5	Order golf balls with custom logos	8	8	8	8	8	8
15	3	Order golf shirts for employees	4	4	4	4	4	4
18	2	Organize a golf cart for each foursome	4	4	4	4	4	4
Iteration 4		*Goal: Add more services and promotional items*						
Milestone: Enhanced event options								
		Effort in the whole backlog	123	64	44	16	16	16

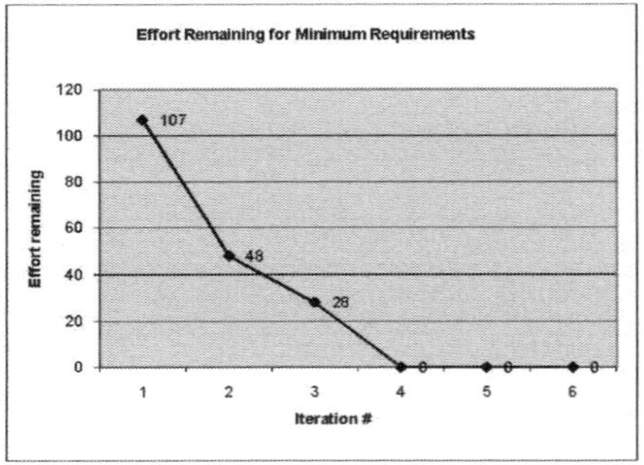

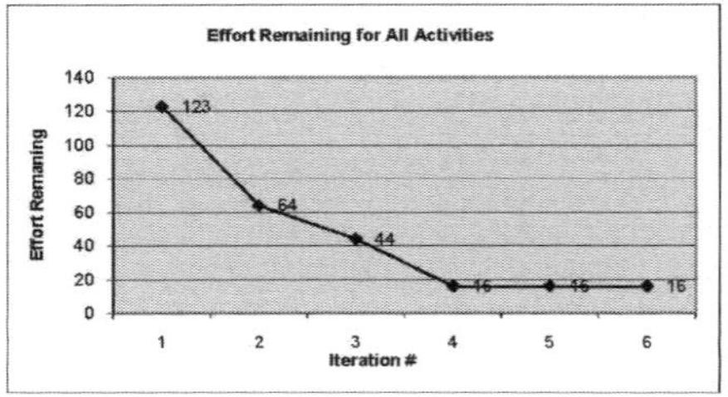

Effort Remaining for Minimum Requirements

Effort Remaining for All Activities

http://agilesoftwaredevelopment.com/scrum/simple-product-backlog

Figure 22: Requirements backlog

In this example, the delivery team is tasked with undertaking activities related to the planning of the organization's charity golf day. The event is scheduled to occur three months (12 weeks) from now, so the Agile team has broken down the work required into six iterations (with two weeks allocated for each).

The tasks listed are in top-down priority order representing the business owners' assessment of the most critical work that needs to be completed for this event to be successful. Each task is grouped into one of the six iterations; with the work allocated for the first iteration being a combination of both the highest-priority tasks *and* the tasks that require the most lead time (e.g. "reserve a venue"). The tasks at the bottom of the list (beneath the third iteration) are lower-priority activities (e.g. "order golf balls with custom logos") that will only be included in the event planning if time and resources allow.[63]

Each iteration has a shaded line beneath it that represents the *primary goal* for that iteration, as defined by the Agile team. This enables the delivery team to have a bigger picture context of what the organization is endeavoring to achieve with the activities listed for that iteration.

---

[63] It should be noted that some Agile teams opt to only include in the requirements backlog tool those activities that the delivery team committed to work on in a scheduled iteration (i.e. only the highest-priority requirements). Any requirements that are not in a scheduled iteration (i.e. lower-priority requirements) remain on a separate list which can be revisited by the Agile team at the next iteration planning session and scheduled into a future iteration where required. Others argue that these lower-priority tasks should remain on the requirements backlog, so that they can be used as "backfill" for the delivery team, if they are able to complete their committed scope of work before the end of an iteration. It is left to each Agile team to determine which approach they would prefer to use in managing their requirements backlogs, depending on the nature of the work required.

Beneath two of the iteration goal lines are *milestones* that represent significant achievements and decision points that the business owners want to draw attention to. In the example provided, the business owners have defined a milestone of the *minimum requirements* for the event to go forward, with all work beneath that milestone considered optional. These milestones are not just a visual tool to group activities; they are core measurements in the team's progress, as explained in *The burndown chart* section that follows.

The column directly to the left of the list of tasks represents the *expected business value* of each task, as determined using the calculations provided in the *Measuring cost/benefit* section of *Chapter 6: Business-value-driven Work*.

To the right of the task list are a series of columns that represent the delivery team's estimation of the *remaining effort* required to complete each task in each iteration. The numbers in these columns represent *units of effort*, a measurement that can be adapted to suit each organization's preferred method for reporting on resource utilization.

In most organizations, units of effort would be measured in *person days* or *person hours*. However, other organizations may choose to use longer durations depending on the nature of the required work (e.g. *person weeks*), or they may prefer to use measurements that track resource time by other factors that impact duration (e.g. the *complexity* of each task). For the purposes of this example, *remaining effort* represents the number of *person hours* required to complete each task.

This requirements backlog diagram shows the Agile team's progress (and work remaining) at the start of the third iteration as described in the following:

- The values in the *Iteration* # columns reflect the amount of work (effort) that is remaining at the end of the second iteration, in order for each activity to be completed.
- Where the value in the Iteration #3 column for an activity is a *lower number* than in Iteration #1 and #2 (e.g. "notify media of event"), this usually indicates that progress has been made on that activity in the past two iterations.
- Where the value in the Iteration #3 column for an activity is a *higher number* than in Iteration #1 and #2 (e.g. "organize for all executives to attend the event"), this usually indicates that the original effort allocation for the activity was underestimated, and the delivery team has determined that more work may be required to complete that activity.
- Where the value in the Iteration #3 column for an activity is *zero* (e.g. "reserve a venue"), this indicates that the activity has most likely been completed in the first two iterations (or that the Agile team has jointly determined in the outcomes review session that sufficient work has been done on this activity and no further work is needed).
- Where an activity has a *dash* in the Iteration # column (e.g. "organize an alternative date for the event if it is raining") this indicates that a *new requirement* has arisen since the initial planning for this event. In this case, "organize an alternative date for the event if it is raining" is a new requirement that only arose when the business

owners spoke with other organizations which had scheduled similar events.

This requirements backlog diagram represents a "snapshot in time" for the delivery team's work. The list (and priority order) of the requirements is reviewed at each iteration planning session, and may change based on the outcomes of that session. The effort remaining details in the Iteration # columns are always changing based upon the information that the delivery team maintains in their delivery backlog.

At the very right of the requirements backlog diagram are two *burndown charts* that are described in the following section.

The burndown chart

The *burndown chart* is a graphical display that is used in a number of Agile tracking tools to visually depict the remaining work required for a milestone to be achieved.

In the requirements backlog diagram, there are two burndown charts displayed:

- The top burndown chart shows the amount of effort remaining for the delivery team to achieve the first milestone (minimum requirements for event). The left-hand axis shows the effort remaining for this work to be completed (i.e. person hours); the bottom axis shows which iteration that work has been (or is scheduled to be) undertaken. In this example, the top burndown chart shows that, as at the start of the third iteration, there are 28 more person hours of effort remaining, in order for the minimum requirements for the event to be met.

- The bottom burndown chart shows the amount of effort remaining for the delivery team to achieve *everything* listed in the requirements backlog, including the activities that are listed as enhanced event options after the third iteration. In this example, the bottom burndown chart shows that, as at the start of the third iteration, there are 44 more person hours of effort remaining in order for all of the listed requirements for the event to be met.

The burndown charts provided in the requirements backlog are visually similar to the burndown charts provided in other Agile tracking tools, such as the delivery backlog and the executive dashboard. However, each of these tools uses burndown charts to track information specific to the needs of the audience, as explained in the following two sections.

The delivery backlog

The delivery backlog is similar in function to the requirements backlog, except it tracks the effort remaining for the *detailed tasks* that are being done by the delivery team *within each iteration.* This section gives you more detail on the information provided in the delivery backlog, as shown in the following diagram:[64]

[64] Adapted from simple sprint backlog example courtesy of *http://agilesoftwaredevelopment.com*.

Charity golf day delivery backlog

Iteration 3 goal: Track invitations and finalize logistics

ID	Task	Day in iteration / effort remaining													
		1	2	3	4	5	6	7	8	9	10	11	12	13	14
		32	32	31	28	26	22	22	21	18	16	16	16	16	16
10	**Track invitation responses**														
	Get daily reports from Customer Service	8	8	7	6	6	5	5	5	4	3	3	3	3	3
	Keep VP of Sales appraised of key customers who respond	4	4	3	3	3	3	3	3	3	3	3	3	3	3
	Keep venue updated if numbers look much smaller or larger than expected	1	1	1	1	1	1	1	1	1	1	1	1	1	1
	Check with the mailroom for any returned invitations	3	3	3	2	2	2	2	2	1	1	1	1	1	1
11	**Match customers with sales team members**														
	Confirm strategic matches with VP of Sales and CEO	2	2	4	4	4	4	4	4	4	4	4	4	4	4
	Confirm which sales team members are attending the event	2	2	2	2	1	1	1	1	1	0	0	0	0	0
	Get more current copy of sales team client list	1	1	0	0	0	0	0	0	0	0	0	0	0	0
	Match customers from invitation responses	3	3	3	3	2	2	2	2	1	1	1	1	1	1
12	**Fill empty spots with additional employees**														
	Identify employees who are best positioned to meet with customers	3	3	3	2	2	2	2	1	1	1	1	1	1	1
	Confirm preferred employee list with VP of Sales	1	1	2	2	2	2	2	2	2	2	2	2	2	2
13	**Arrange venue and caterer pre-payments**														
	Confirm purchase order approval with Finance	1	1	0	0	0	0	0	0	0	0	0	0	0	0
	Hand-deliver certified checks from Finance	3	3	3	3	3	0	0	0	0	0	0	0	0	0

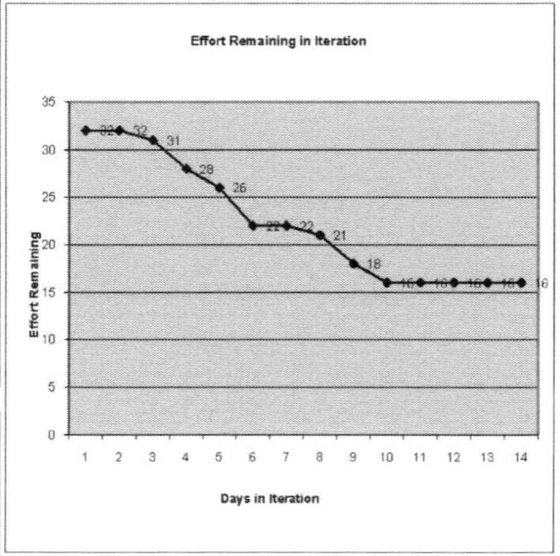

http://agilesoftwaredevelopment.com/scrum/simple-sprint-backlog

Figure 23: Delivery backlog

In this example, the delivery team is tasked with undertaking activities related to Iteration 3: Track invitations and finalize logistics for the organization's charity golf day. Each of the activities listed in the requirements backlog for Iteration 3 (e.g. "track invitation responses") has been carried over to the delivery backlog for this iteration, but each activity has been further broken down into the individual tasks that the delivery team must undertake in order to complete this activity (e.g. "get daily reports from customer service").

The columns on the right-hand side represent the *amount of effort* that is remaining for each task on each day of the iteration. As this is a two-week long iteration, each column represents one of the 14 days in that iteration. (Some organizations prefer to only track *business days* in the detail of the delivery backlog, in which case, only 10 columns would be displayed.)

The delivery backlog shown in the diagram represents the progress of the delivery team at *Day 9* of Iteration 3. Effort remaining is tracked in a similar way to the requirements backlog with:

- *reducing* left-to-right values for each task generally indicating that progress has been made
- *unchanging* left-to-right values for each task generally indicating that there has been no progress
- *increasing* left-to-right values for each task generally indicating that the task is more complex or time-consuming than originally estimated.

The critical thing to notice in the delivery backlog is the ID number assigned to each task in the leftmost column. This number corresponds to the equivalent Activity ID in the requirements backlog, allowing the effort remaining details in the delivery backlog to be *automatically* carried over into the requirements backlog for real-time status reporting. This means that all the delivery team needs to do during the course of each iteration is to maintain the daily "effort remaining" values for the individual tasks within each of the activities scheduled. Consequently, no other formal status reporting should be needed.

Further information on each of these tools is available from the list of resources in *More Information on Agile*.

CHAPTER 20: EXPANDING THE USE OF AGILE IN YOUR ORGANIZATION

Once you have a few successful "runs on the board" with Agile initiatives within your organization, the next step is to establish a strategy for *broadening the awareness* of the value of Agile approaches across the organization – and *encouraging other areas* of the organization to trial these approaches.

This strategy should include four key elements:

- educating the organization on the business value of Agile approaches
- encouraging specific people in the organization to trial these approaches in their area
- helping interested areas of the organization in selecting the Agile approaches that are best suited to their activities
- providing assistance (and, where appropriate, experienced staff members) to help each area in their initial application of these approaches.

Educating the organization about Agile approaches and *encouraging selected people to trial Agile approaches* can both be achieved through a number of channels, including: networking through the business owners who have seen the power – and success – of these approaches firsthand; holding internal "roadshow" events to show people the tangible outcomes from your Agile work; and identifying an internal champion within senior management with sufficient influence to encourage its use.

Helping interested areas in selecting Agile approaches can be done using *The Agile approaches selection tool*, along with the resources listed in the *Bibliography* for any additional information that may be required.

The flexibility of Agile approaches allows each area of your organization to apply the most appropriate Agile practices and techniques (and combinations thereof) to suit their specific business activities – and to adopt Agile approaches at their own pace. When an area of your organization is ready to trial Agile approaches, *providing assistance* for each area's initial Agile work is an important element in ensuring that their first exposure to these approaches is as positive and productive as possible.

Every time employees apply Agile approaches, they grow more confident in their use. The initial gut reaction to resist empowering the delivery team is replaced by the proven knowledge that this is an extremely effective way to achieve successful outcomes. The inclination to want everything delivered at once is replaced by an appreciation for prioritizing outputs by the business value that they can bring to the organization.

As new areas in the organization trial Agile approaches, they can benefit greatly from involving one or two people on the Agile team who have been through the process before. These experienced Agile resources can act as advisers and facilitators in the process, ensuring the approaches are followed correctly and allaying any concerns that staff might have as they move away from their traditional ways of working. Furthermore, once these areas have been through a couple of Agile initiatives, they can take on the adviser role for others in the organization. This not only creates a larger (and stronger) network of

Agile practitioners within the organization, it decentralizes the responsibility for any one area to be involved in each Agile initiative.

The bottom line is that your organization *can* achieve real productivity gains using Agile practices and techniques. The challenge is to implement Agile approaches in a way that best meets the specific needs, constraints and dynamics of your organization.

MORE INFORMATION ON AGILE

The following are general, methodology-specific and practice-specific Agile sources that you can refer to for further information:

General information on Agile

Agile Alliance: *www.agilealliance.com*

Agile: An Executive Guide – Real results from IT budgets, Jamie Lynn Cooke, IT Governance Publishing (2011): *www.itgovernanceusa.com/shop/p-351-agile-an-executive-guide.aspx#.UwnXNcHFKSo*

AgileCanberra forum: *https://au.groups.yahoo.com/neo/groups/agilecanberra/info*

Agile Connection: *www.agileconnection.com*

AgileKiwi – Practical Agile Software Development: *www.agilekiwi.com*

Agile Manifesto: *www.agilemanifesto.org*

AgileSoftwareDevelopment.com: *www.agilesoftwaredevelopment.com*

Alistair Cockburn: *http://alistair.cockburn.us/*

Everything you want to know about Agile – How to get Agile results in a less-than-agile organization, Jamie Lynn Cooke, IT Governance Publishing (2012): *http://www.itgovernanceusa.com/shop/p-549-everything-you-want-to-know-about-agile.aspx#.UwnTgc4xgqZ*

Fundamentals of Agile Project Management: An Overview (Technical Manager's Survival Guides), Gonçalves M, Heda R, ASME Press (2010): *www.amazon.com/Fundamentals-Agile-Project-Management-Technical/dp/0791802965/ref=sr_1_117?s=books&ie=UTF8&qid=1297939406&sr=1-117*

The New Methodology

www.thoughtworks.com/articles/new-methodology

The Power of the Agile Business Analyst, Jamie Lynn Cooke, IT Governance Publishing (2012): *http://www.itgovernanceusa.com/shop/p-1379-the-power-of-the-agile-business-analyst.aspx#.Uwpw2s4xgqY*

Start with Trust, Start with a Retrospective, Stevens P, Agile Software Development (2008): *http://agilesoftwaredevelopment.com/blog/peterstev/start-trust-start-retrospective*

User Story Discussion:

http://c2.com/cgi/wiki?UserStoryDiscussion

Specific Agile methodologies

Overview

A Practical Guide to Seven Agile Methodologies, Coffin R, Lane D: Part one: *www.devx.com/architect/Article/32761; Part two: www.devx.com/architect/Article/32836*

Scrum

Scrum Alliance: *www.scrumalliance.org*

Glossary of Scrum Terms, Szalvay V, Scrum Alliance, Inc. (2007): *www.scrumalliance.org/articles/39-glossary-of-scrum-terms*

Scrum and Agile Presentations by Mike Cohn of Mountain Goat Software (various dates): *www.mountaingoatsoftware.com/presentations*

DSDM

What is DSDM? Clifton M, Dunlap J (2003): *www.codeproject.com/KB/architecture/dsdm.aspx*

DSDM Explained, Davies R, JAOO (2004): *www.agilexp.com/presentations/DSDMexplained.pdf*

FDD™

An Overview of FDD™ – Web Development Methodology: *www.influxive.com/fdd-overview.html*

Feature-Driven Development™ (FDD™) and Agile Modeling, Ambler S W: *www.agilemodeling.com/essays/fdd.htm*

Lean

Common Questions Organizations Ask About Lean Manufacturing, Keberdle CF, Lean Solutions Group, LLC (2008): *www.leansolutionsgroup.com/images/Common_Questions_About_Lean_Mfg.pdf*

Lean Principles, Kilpatrick J, Utah Manufacturing Extension Partnership (2003): *http://mhc-net.com/whitepapers_presentations/LeanPrinciples.pdf*

Lean Primer, Larman C & Vodde B (2009):

www.leanprimer.com/downloads/lean_primer.pdf

Leading Lean Software Development: Results Are Not the Point, Poppendieck.LLC (2009): *www.poppendieck.com/pdfs/LLSD_intro.pdf*

Running Agile: A Practitioner's View to Lean and Agile: *http://runningagile.com/*

XP

eXtreme Programming™: a gentle introduction: www.extremeprogramming.org

Kanban

Kanban (overview): *www.crisp.se/kanban*

Kanban and Scrum – making the most of both, Kniberg H and Skarin M (2010): *www.infoq.com/minibooks/kanban-scrum-minibook*

RUP®

IBM Rational Unified Process® (RUP®): *www-01.ibm.com/software/awdtools/rup*

Agile Modeling and the Rational Unified Process® (RUP®):

www.agilemodeling.com/essays/agileModelingRUP.htm

EssUP

Essential Practices:

www.ivarjacobson.com/uploadedFiles/Pages/Knowledge_Centre/Resources/Collateral/Resources/EssentialPractices2_Brochure.pdf

AUP

The Agile Unified Process (AUP):

www.ambysoft.com/unifiedprocess/agileUP.html

Crystal

Crystal methodologies:

http://alistair.cockburn.us/Crystal+methodologies

Industry research on Agile

6th Annual State of Agile Development Survey 2011, VersionOne: *http://www.versionone.com/pdf/2011_State_of_Agile_Development_Survey_Results.pdf*

The state of application development in enterprises and SMBs: business data services North America and Europe, Stone J, Database and Network Journal (April 1st 2007): *www.thefreelibrary.com/The+state+of+application+development+in+enterprises+and+SMBs:...-a0162832944*

Selected Agile case studies

Agile Coaching in British Telecom, Meadows L and Hanly S (2006): *www.agilejournal.com/articles/columns/column-articles/144-agile-coaching-in-british-telecom*

Rolling out Agile in a Large Enterprise, Benefield G, Proceedings of the 41st Annual Hawaii International Conference on System Sciences (HICSS) (2008): *www.computer.org/csdl/proceedings/hicss/2008/3075/00/30750461-abs.html*

Information on TQM and KAIZEN

Total Quality Management (TQM) – An Integrated Approach to Quality and Continuous Improvement, Kotelnikov V (last updated January 27th 2011) *www.1000ventures.com/business_guide/im_tqm_main.html*

KAIZEN – The Japanese Strategy for Continuous Improvement, Kotelnikov V (last updated November 9th 2010): *www.1000ventures.com/business_guide/mgmt_kaizen_main.html*

Cost/benefit calculation resources

Activity-Based Costing (ABC), SiliconFarEast.com (2005): *www.siliconfareast.com/abc.htm*

Cost Reduction Potential, Tyner Blain (2006):

http://tynerblain.com/blog/2006/09/25/cost-reduction-potential/

Other industry resources

BPMN Information:
www.bpmn.org/

BPMS Watch: Ten Tips for Effective Process Modeling, Silver B, BPMInstitute.org (2008):
www.bpminstitute.org/articles/article/article/bpms-watch-ten-tips-for-effective-process-modeling.html

AUTHOR'S NOTE ON AGILE RESOURCES

The majority of the resources listed in *More Information on Agile* are primarily focused on the application of Agile approaches in the IT and manufacturing sectors (as these industries have been the predominant users of these approaches to date). There is currently very little published information on the use of Agile approaches across all industry sectors.

For this reason, I have established a dedicated public website for these topics (*www.RealProductivityGains.com*), to provide a foundation for communities of thought around Agile business concepts; a launching pad for discussion forums and blogs on business optimization; a place to download general business Agile tools; and a platform for business people to exchange and critique ideas on the successful application of efficiencies, including Agile approaches, in every industry.

ITG RESOURCES

IT Governance Ltd sources, creates and delivers products and services to meet the real-world, evolving IT governance needs of today's organisations, directors, managers and practitioners.

The ITG website (*www.itgovernance.co.uk*) is the international one-stop-shop for corporate and IT governance information, advice, guidance, books, tools, training and consultancy. On the website you will find the following page related to project governance and the subject matter of this book:

www.itgovernance.co.uk/project_governance.aspx.

Publishing Services

IT Governance Publishing (ITGP) is the world's leading IT-GRC publishing imprint that is wholly owned by IT Governance Ltd.

With books and tools covering all IT governance, risk and compliance frameworks, we are the publisher of choice for authors and distributors alike, producing unique and practical publications of the highest quality, in the latest formats available, which readers will find invaluable.

www.itgovernancepublishing.co.uk is the website dedicated to ITGP. Other titles published by ITGP that may be of interest include:

- The Power of the Agile Business Analyst

  www.itgovernance.co.uk/shop/p-1457.aspx

- Everything you want to know about Agile

  www.itgovernance.co.uk/shop/p-549.aspx

- Directing the Agile Organisation

  www.itgovernance.co.uk/shop/p-1369.aspx

We also offer a range of off-the-shelf toolkits that give comprehensive, customisable documents to help users create the specific documentation they need to properly implement a management system or standard. Written by experienced practitioners and based on the latest best practice, ITGP toolkits can save months of work for organisations working towards compliance with a given standard.

Toolkits that may be of interest include:

- ITSM, ITIL® & ISO/IEC 20000 Implementation Toolkit

  www.itgovernance.co.uk/shop/p-872.aspx

- IT Governance Control Framework Implementation Toolkit

  www.itgovernance.co.uk/shop/p-1305.aspx

Books and tools published by IT Governance Publishing (ITGP) are available from all business booksellers and the following websites:

www.itgovernance.eu *www.itgovernanceusa.com*

www.itgovernance.in *www.itgovernancesa.co.za*

www.itgovernance.asia.

Training Services

IT Governance offers an extensive portfolio of training courses designed to educate information security, IT governance, risk management and compliance professionals. Our classroom and online training programmes will help you develop the skills required to deliver best practice and compliance to your organisation. They will also enhance your career by providing you with industry standard certifications and increased peer recognition. Our range of courses offer a structured learning path from Foundation to Advanced level in the key topics of information security, IT governance, business continuity and service management.

Our *Implementing IT Governance: Foundation and Principles* training course delivers introductory training to raise awareness, build knowledge and develop a complete understanding of IT governance and its implementation. It has been specifically designed to show delegates how to create a single integrated management framework that ensures that IT truly supports and delivers on all organisational strategies and objectives.

Full details of all IT Governance training courses can be found at *www.itgovernance.co.uk/training.aspx*.

Professional Services and Consultancy

The IT Governance Professional Services team can show you how to apply Agile concepts to the most complex development projects. Our expert consultants can guide and inspire you in the use of Agile, providing you with the practical techniques to improve delivery efficiencies, control your implementation costs, and meet your sales targets by building customer loyalty.

We will show you the Agile methods that create flexibility and ensure adaptability to changing circumstances, accepting that nothing changes more than your Customer's needs. You will learn how to change from a traditional hierarchy towards self-empowered individuals and teams. In this way, you will develop engaged employees with the responsibility, accountability and authority to deliver to the Customer's Requirements, shaping and directing outcomes, while regularly delivering partial, though functional, products.

For more information about IT Governance: Consultancy and Training Services see:

www.itgovernance.co.uk/consulting.aspx.

Newsletter

IT governance is one of the hottest topics in business today, not least because it is also the fastest moving.

You can stay up to date with the latest developments across the whole spectrum of IT governance subject matter, including; risk management, information security, ITIL and IT service management, project governance, compliance and so much more, by subscribing to ITG's core publications and topic alert emails.

Simply visit our subscription centre and select your preferences: *www.itgovernance.co.uk/newsletter.aspx*.